Of the thousands of decompression dives that Gary Gentile has made, 200 of them were on the Grand Dame of the Sea: the *Andrea Doria*. In the early 1990's, he was instrumental in merging mixed-gas diving technology with wreck-diving. In 1994, he participated in a mixed-gas diving expedition to the *Lusitania*, which lies at a depth of 300 feet.

Gary has specialized in wreck-diving and shipwreck research, concentrating his efforts on wrecks along the eastern seaboard, from Newfoundland to Key West, and in the Great Lakes. He has compiled an extensive library of books, photographs, drawings, plans, and original source materials on ships and shipwrecks.

Gary has written scores of magazine articles, and has published thousands of photographs in books, periodicals, newspapers, brochures, advertisements, corporate reports, museum displays, postcards, film, and television. He lectures extensively on wilderness and underwater topics, and conducts seminars on advanced wreck-diving techniques, high-tech diving equipment, and wreck photography. He is the author of more than five dozen books: primarily science fiction novels and non-fiction works on diving and on nautical and shipwreck history. The Popular Dive Guide Series will eventually cover every major shipwreck along the east coast of the United States.

In 1989, after a five-year battle with the National Oceanic and Atmospheric Administration, Gary won a suit which forced the hostile government agency to issue him a permit to dive the USS *Monitor*, a protected National Marine Sanctuary. Media attention that was focused on Gary's triumphant victory resulted in nationwide coverage of his 1990 photographic expedition to the Civil War ironclad. Gary continues to fight for the right of access to all shipwreck sites.

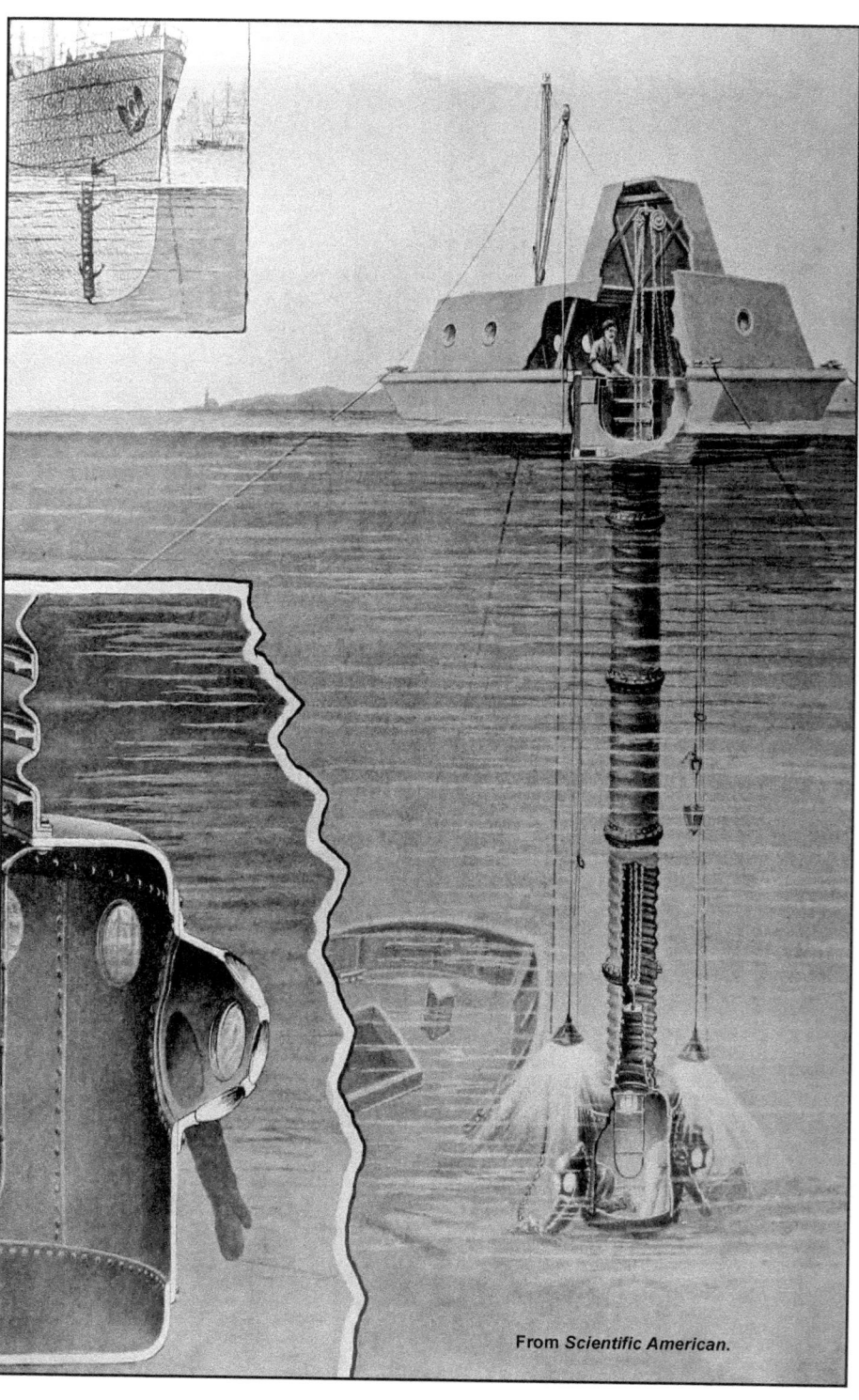

From *Scientific American*.

Shipwrecks of Maine and New Hampshire

by Gary Gentile

Gary Gentile Productions

Copyright 2015 by Gary Gentile

All rights reserved. Except for the use of brief quotations embodied in critical articles and reviews, this book may not be reproduced in part or in whole, in any manner (including mechanical, electronic, photographic, and photocopy means), transmitted in any form, or recorded by any data storage and/or retrieval device, without express written permission from the author. Address all queries to:

Gary Gentile Productions
3 Lehigh Gorge Drive
Jim Thorpe, PA 18229

Additional copies of this book may be purchased from the same address by sending a check or money order in the amount of $20 U.S. for each copy (plus $4 postage per order, not per book, in the U.S. Inquire for shipping cost to foreign countries). Alternatively, copies may be ordered from the author's website and paid by credit card:

http://www.ggentile.com

Picture Credits

All uncredited photographs were taken by the author. The photo on the front cover is the *Howard W. Middleton*. The back cover photos are from the author's collection. Top: A painting of the *Anne C. Maguire* as the *Golden State*. Middle left: Commemmorative coin of the State of Maine. Bottom: An artistic rendering of a China clipper. The author's photo on page one was taken by Cheryl Novak. Every attempt has been made to contact the photographers or artists whose work appears in this book, if known, and to ascertain their names if unknown; in some cases, copies of pictures have been in public circulation for so long that the name of the photographer or artist has been lost, or the present whereabouts are impossible to trace. Any information in this regard forwarded to the author will be appreciated. Apologies are made to those whose work must under such circumstances go unrecognized.

International Standard Book Numbers (ISBN)
1-883056-52-7
978-1-883056-52-0

First Edition

Printed in U.S.A.

CONTENTS

INTRODUCTION 7

SHIPWRECKS OF MAINE
    Alice E. Clark 9
    Amaretto 12
    Anne C. Maguire 14
    Annie L. Henderson 17
    Bay State 19
    Bohemian 22
    Cambridge 24
    City of Portland 26
    Cora F. Cressy 29
    Cornwallis 36
    D. T. Sheridan 41
    Eagle 56 44
    Edna M. McKnight 51
    Edward J. Lawrence 53
    Empire Knight 56
    F. C. Pendleton 66
    Gardiner G. Deering 67
    Georgetown 72
    Georgia 76
    Hartwelson 80
    Helen B. Crosby 83
    Hesper / Luther Little 84
    Howard W. Middleton 88
    Irvington 90
    Jessica Ann 93
    Joseph S. Zeman 97
    Mary F. Barrett 98
    North America 102
    Nottingham 103
    Oakey L. Alexander 109
    Polias 113
    Royal Tar 116
    S-21 119
    Sagamore 124
    Susan P. Thurlow 126
    Wandby 128
    Washington B. Thomas 132
    W.G. Butman 135

SHIPWRECKS OF NEW HAMPSHIRE
- *Camilla May Page* — 137
- *Mary A. Brown* — 140
- *New England* — 142
- *Number 3666* — 146
- *O-9* — 149
- *Pythian* — 154
- *Samuel J. Goucher* — 155
- *Wild Cat* — 158

SHIPWRECKS OFFSHORE
- *Cherokee* — 160
- *Gulf Stream* — 164
- *Marine Merchant* — 167
- *Novadoc* — 171
- *Port Nicholson* — 172
- *Robert & Richard* — 196
- *Dornfontein* — 199
- *William H. Machen* — 201

SUGGESTED READING — 203
GPS CAVEATS — 204
GPS and LORAN NUMBERS — 206
BOOKS by the AUTHOR — 218

A postcard picture of Somes Sound during its heyday as a shipping channel for the transportation of granite from Hall Quarry. The schooner in view is representative of the kind of vessels that transported granite to distant ports.

INTRODUCTION

Many fairy tales start with the sentence, "It was a dark and stormy night." Many Maine shipwreck stories start, "It was a dark and foggy night . . . or day," whatever the case may be. The indicative word here is "foggy." Many vessels wrecked on or off the coast of Maine by dint of persistent fog. Many vessels stayed on or off the coast of Maine by dint of the rocky shore. In other coastal States, with gently sloping sandy beaches, stranded vessels were often pulled off the bar by salvage tugs at high tide. Not so in Maine. Or at least not so many. Most vessels that ran aground, stayed aground. Or went to pieces before they could be ungrounded.

The most numerous victims in this regard were the windjammers of yesteryear. They lacked the manmade motive power to back off a bar before the wooden hull started to disintegrate. They often went to pieces within days; sometimes within hours, before the crew could be rescued or abandon ship safely in the middle of a storm. The rocky coast of Maine is littered with islands, reefs, ledges, and barely submerged rocks, all of which combined to spell disaster for the unwary mariner.

I started my Maine shipwreck survey work in 1990. Or I should say, I tried to. I visited every dive shop along the coast and asked the proprietor what he knew about nearby shipwrecks. The answer was invariably, "Nothing." Nor could they point me to any dive boats that could take me to any shipwrecks. Not only did they know nothing about shipwrecks, but they did not even care about them. All their customers dived from shore for the sole purpose of observing marine life.

I refrained from saying, "How boring." I liked observing marine life. But I found it more fulfilling to observe it while exploring shipwrecks. My trip was not totally wasted. I visited maritime museums and conducted historical research. But afterward, I decided to concentrate my efforts to produce the books in my Popular Dive Guide Series about shipwrecks off States in which wreck-diving was an accepted activity.

It took twenty-five years to complete *Shipwrecks of Maine and New Hampshire*.

I wish I could have explored many of the wrecks that are covered in this volume, but infrequent returns met with the same attitude: wreck-diving was not big business, and charter boats were not docked in every marina. The few local wreck-divers who engaged in the activity dived from private boats that were either unknown or unavailable to me. Perhaps some day . . .

The Somes Sound Wreck

I feel compelled to inform the few local divers who are interested in shipwrecks that there are literally hundreds of wreck sites that have yet to be discovered. I want to encourage them to search for these remnants of the past.

The particular problem that is associated with locating wrecks off the coasts of Maine and New Hampshire is the rocky bottom. The seabed off most other States consists of sand: an underwater desert on which shipwrecks provide almost the only spot of relief. A depth-sounder or sonar unit can easily spot a wreck on an unobstructed plain. But an uneven surface disguises wrecks and associated low-lying debris.

The submerged bottom off Maine and New Hampshire can be extrapolated by the adjacent geological features: tall mountains, steep slopes, rocky rises, and so on. A covering of seawater does not alter the terrain.

Despite the fact that the seabed is littered with wreckage, most of it is not discoverable by electronic means. A magnetometer can find metal wrecks, or wooden wrecks that have a sufficient quantity of metal in their construction or cargo. But the standard methods of discovering wrecks seldom apply.

I had one near success which I would like to pass on to the next generation of underwater explorers. I call it the Somes Sound Wreck. I first learned about this wreck from Mike de Camp. He learned about it from residents during summer vacations. According to local lore, a sailing vessel of unspecified rig was transporting granite from Hall Quarry when it sank in the sound for causes that went unrecorded. This shipwreck has achieved almost mythic proportions among area inhabitants, usually by word of mouth, but sometimes by writers who related oral history.

I have never been able to confirm the wreck's existence. I went looking for it anyway. De Camp told me to contact the John Williams Boat Company, which now occupies the site of the old quarry, because he was friends with the owner. I did, and was given permission to launch a boat from the company's ramp. I then convinced Harry Dutton to tow his boat *Shania* from Massachusetts to Maine in order to search for the wreck.

We marked two targets in Somes Sound, but before I had time to don my dive gear, the tide ebbed and Harry was afraid that if we did not proceed straightaway for the ramp, the water would be too low to get the boat out of the water until the next flood, way after dark. We barely made it. Harry had work commitments that put an end to our search trip. And so I was left with unfulfilled wonder about whether one of those targets was indeed the Somes Sound Wreck.

I have included the coordinates in the GPS/Loran list at the back of this book. I have only one request: if you dive on an actual shipwreck, let me know what you found and the condition of the wreck. Likely it has never been dived on before. Good luck!

Appreciations

I do not remember when or how Dave Clancy and I started corresponding. I think it was sometime in the mid-2000's. He was a Maine resident who relocated to Florida. Yet he still retained his interest in New England shipwrecks. He created and still maintains a website called Hunting New England Shipwrecks. The Internet address is http://wreckhunter.net/startpage-wreckhunter.htm (or wreckhunter.net for short). The website lists hundreds of shipwrecks from half a dozen States, and provides statistical information about their loss and location.

We learned that he had ship pictures and information that I did not have, while I had ship pictures and information that he did not have. We arranged to meet at a convenient hotel during my next excursion to the Sunshine State. I brought my copy stand, photographic collection, and shipwreck folders; he brought his photographic collection and shipwreck folders. Then we photographed the pictures that the other did not have, and shared information about them. In that way we both fleshed out our collections. Some of the pictures on the following pages are credited to his collection.

I met Joe Cushing at his home in New Hampshire. He suggested the names of wrecks in his neck of the woods (or ocean): wrecks that I should cover because of their local interest. Without his help, I would not have known about some of these wrecks.

ALICE E. CLARK

Built: 1898
Previous names: None
Gross tonnage: 1,622
Type of vessel: Wooden-hulled four-masted schooner
Builder: Percy & Small, Bath, Maine
Owner: J.S. Winslow & Company, Bath, Maine
Port of registry: Portland, Maine
Cause of sinking: Ran aground
Location: Long Island Ledge, off Isleboro in Penobscot Bay

Sunk: July 1, 1909
Depth: 60 feet
Dimensions: 227' x 43' x 20'
Power: sail

GPS: 44-21.022 / 68-51.299

The *Alice E. Clark* was involved in several maritime incidents to her fame, shame, and maim.

In her first year of operation she chanced upon the Clyde Line freighter *Croatan* off the capes of Virginia. The *Croatan* was on a passage from New York City to Wilmington, North Carolina when fire was discovered in one of the cargo holds. Within ten minutes the fire spread from stem to stern. Captain E.M. Hale, master, order abandon ship – and not a moment too soon, for there was an explosion in the hold followed closely by a second one.

There was time to lower only one lifeboat before the deck was engulfed by the conflagration. The passengers – who had taken accommodation in the freighter's six staterooms – and those crewmembers who remained onboard were forced to jump overboard in order to escape the flames. They were all wearing life preservers. The lifeboat rowed around the burning vessel and picked up the swimmers. Five people perished from drowning.

The *Alice E. Clark* in the grand days of sail. (From the collection of Paul Sherman.)

The flames attracted the attention of Captain Leslie Clark, master of the *Alice E. Clark*, which was on a passage from Norfolk, Virginia to Portland, Maine. At the moment, the schooner lay becalmed some six miles from the catastrophe. Nonetheless, Captain Clark dispatched a boat that was rowed by a handful of able-bodied seamen. They were able to pluck a dozen people from the sea: people who had been adrift for more than an hour in the cold November water.

The schooner also took aboard the *Croatan's* lifeboat with the other survivors. All twenty-two souls were cared for by Captain Clark's wife and members of the crew. They were furnished with food, clothing, and enough money to send them home from Vineyard Haven, Massachusetts, where they disembarked from the savior schooner.

On January 21, 1906, the *Alice E. Clark* was proceeding through fog on a starboard tack when she heard the signal of an unseen vessel that was making a port tack. The two vessels collided. The majority of the damage was sustained by the *Alice E. Clark* when the schooner *Mary F. Barrett* struck her port side "about 3 feet abaft main rigging, damaging same, carrying away mainmast, and other damage. Damage estimated at $5,000. No one injured; no loss of life."

Government investigators "found that schooner *Mary F. Barrett*, the vessel required to keep out of the way by the international rules for preventing collisions, owing to the direction of the wind did not clearly hear the fog signal of the other vessel, until such time as collision was inevitable, when every endeavor was made to avoid same."

The ultimate loss of the *Alice E. Clark* was quick, but follow-up salvage operations stretched out for five months.

The schooner was transporting $8,000 worth of coal from Norfolk, Virginia to Bangor, Maine when she struck Frank's Ledge in a full-blown gale. The incoming tide filled the holds with seawater to a depth of six feet. Captain MacDonald and the crew abandoned ship in a lifeboat and made it safely to shore.

Salvors at work. (From the collection of Bill Carter.)

At high tide, the main deck lay under 8 feet of water. The vessel that had cost $64,000 to build eleven years earlier was still worth $50,000; the cargo was fully insured but the hull was only partially insured.

Captain MacDonald entertained hopes of raising the schooner in one piece. He wrote to the owners, "The vessel has hardly twisted any and preserves her shear perfectly. She lies fair on bottom for whole length." He speculated that the hull lay on smooth rock.

Salvage work commenced on July 13 by jettisoning the coal during times of low tide. It took but a week to remove nearly half the coal. Work progressed well for the next two weeks as much of the 2,400 tons of coal was loaded onto lighters. Then came the job of sealing the hatches and pumping out the water. That was when the clockwork salvage operation ended. The hull had barely been pumped out when the schooner rolled over onto her starboard side, and remained on her beam ends. That was the end of total hull salvage. The decision was made to strip the vessel of everything of value.

On August 3, it was reported that "after unsuccessful efforts had been made to float her," she was sold to Fields Pendleton, of New York, for $1,260. His outfit continued the job of removing coal at the rate of 40 tons per day. He also unstepped the topmasts and salvaged the rigging. By the end of September, Pendleton had reduced the schooner's weight to the point at which he thought he could right and raise the hull.

Not until October 29 was he ready to float the vessel. Good weather worked in his favor, but although most of the cargo had been removed, the hull stubbornly refused to be pumped fully dry. The final notice about the salvage attempt appeared on November 17: "It is believed her bottom has been pierced by sharp rocks and it is doubtful if she can ever be floated. Some cargo remains in her."

This prognostication proved prescient. The *Alice E. Clark* remained where she struck. And continues to remain.

The sad shipwreck. (From the collection of Dave Clancy.)

AMARETTO

Built: 1918
Previous names: *Muriel*
Gross tonnage: 31
Type of vessel: Wooden-hulled sardine carrier
Builder: Goudy & Stevens, Boothbay, Maine
Owner: Spencer C. Fuller, Vinalhaven, Maine
Port of registry: Rockland, Maine
Cause of sinking: Scuttled by pirates
Location: 2 miles east of Owl's Head

Sunk: July 21, 1985
Depth: Unknown
Dimensions: 62' x 14' x 7'
Power: diesel engine

Lat/lon: 44-05-35 N / 68-59-55 W

Piracy? In today's world? In Maine? Hard to believe, but true.

In its broadest sense, piracy is defined as robbery at sea: theft of either a vessel's cargo or of the vessel itself.

Piracy goes back a long way – all the way back to the beginning of shipping. For the United States, piracy started in the early 1800's, shortly after the thirteen colonial States separated from England and formed a federated union. Aside from the Revolutionary War, the fledging U.S. Navy's earliest actions were against the Barbary states that were situated in northern Africa, along the south coast of the Mediterranean Sea: the so-called "shores of Tripoli" that is part of the Marine Corps anthem.

Piracy runs rampant today, largely conducted by terrorists or by the citizens of third world nations. Many a tanker and freighter have been pirated for their multi-million dollar cargoes. In peacetime, merchant vessels do not carry an armed guard to repel

Amaretto in dock. (John Upton photo.)

boarders; this makes it easy for heavily-armed pirates to match speed and board vessels in waters that lack a naval presence. However, piracy in American waters is almost unheard of.

Why anyone would steal a 67-year-old fishing vessel is difficult to understand. The potential reward hardly seems to justify the risk. And certainly a boatload of sardines would not add much incentive. Could this have been a case of maritime joyriding? No one knows because the culprits were never apprehended.

All that is known about the theft with any degree of certainty is that a person or persons unknown absconded with the *Amaretto* right from her dock, then scuttled her several miles away. How the pirates reached a position of safety after scuttling the sardine carrier is anyone's guess.

In fact, previous owner Joe Upton did guess – or perhaps speculate is a better word. He figured that a competitor stole and scuttled the boat so he would "have more market for himself." Upton imagined a man with an outboard skiff tying up to the *Amaretto* in the black of night, throwing off the dock lines, starting the engine, and scooting into the western bay. The thief – or pirate, if you will – then started the fish pump, lowered the hose into the water, and arranged the discharge so that it flooded the fish holds and engine room. The man then escaped on his skiff while the boat was sinking.

The Coast Guard searched for the wreck with side-scan sonar, with negative results. The putative location and depth was purely guesswork. Furthermore, according to NOAA, "Possibility that vessel is shifting due to remaining buoyancy." And, "Position of wreck using approx. range and bearing from Owls Head falls in 272 ft." This despite the fact that the same NOAA record put the depth at 120 feet.

Although the Coast Guard did not locate the wreck site, it was not considered to be a hazard to navigation.

For what it is worth, note that *Merchant Vessels of the United States* named Spencer C. Fuller as sole owner at the time of the *Amaretto's* loss, whereas NOAA records assigned dual ownership to Spencer and Dayle Fuller. MVUS also lists the length as 62 feet, not 71 feet as given in NOAA records.

By the way, sardines and herring are synonymous. When a herring is put into a can and sealed for consumption, it becomes a sardine.

Postcard picture of a typical sardine carrier, with herring boats and dories in the background. The dory in the foreground is closing a seine filled with herring to be loaded into the sardine carrier.

ANNE C. MAGUIRE

Built: 1852
Previous names: *Golden State*
Gross tonnage: 917
Type of vessel: Wooden-hulled bark
Builder: Jacob Westervelt, New York, NY
Owner: D. &. J. Maguire, Quebec, Canada
Port of registry: Buenos Ayres, Argentina
Cause of sinking: Ran aground
Location: Portland light

Sunk: December 25, 1886
Depth: on the rocks
Dimensions: 186' x 40' x 21'
Power: Sail

The bark that ended her long career on the rocks in front of the Portland light began her career as the clipper ship *Golden State*. A clipper ship was full-rigged with an immense spread of quadrilateral sails that captured heaven's breath more than any other sailing vessel then in existence. Clippers became famous in the China tea trade in the middle of the nineteenth century. They were known for their speed and fine lines.

For some reason, the *Golden State* is not well established in the modern public consciousness. Yet in her heyday she was every bit as fast and respected as other clippers whose names are always on the lips of nautical historians who wish to name-drop as a way to inform the media of their arcane knowledge, by mentioning such clippers as *Cutty Sark*, *Thermopylae*, and *Sovereign of the Seas*. There are no whiskeys or plastic model kits or cruise ships that carry her name, thus the *Golden State* has become unintentionally slighted.

The *Anne C. Maguire* rigged as a bark. (From the collection of Bill Carter.) Here she is seen in Russell's Floating Dock, which was located on the St. Lawrence River in Levis, Quebec, Canada. See the back cover for a painting of her as a China clipper under full sail.

A postcard picture of he *Anne C. Maguire* on the rocks in front of Portland light.

The *Golden State* sailed around the Horn under a number of skippers and for different outfits, New York to San Francisco being one of her popular routes. Each passage took at least three months to complete, without ever touching land along the way; but there were no Indians to fight. She frequently sailed to China – hence the nickname China clipper – Hong Kong, Shanghai, and Japan on a regular basis. In 1867 she sailed from China to New York with a cargo of tea that sold for a million dollars.

Contemporary artist Fitz Henry Lane painted a portrait of the *Golden State* entering New York harbor. Not only is the painting lackluster in both color and detail, but some of the sails are reefed, so that the impression of a clipper ship under full sail in a raging wind is not represented.

A much better painting was done by Charles Robert Patterson in 1935. Although he did not have the opportunity to see the *Golden State* in person, he captured the wind and the glory of a clipper ship sailing the way it should be represented.

The *Golden State* was one of the most long-lived clipper ships to carry on the trade. She served in that capacity for more than thirty years.

In 1883, the *Golden State* was sold to the Maguire brothers. They rerigged the ship as a bark, and renamed her *Anne C. Maguire*. Most modern writers misspell the given name as Annie, with an i. Perhaps that is because some wag painted her name incorrectly on the rocks at Portland light, where she later came to grief, and subsequent writers did not bother to look up her listing in the *Record* of the American Bureau of Ships or in other primary sources. The rock art also errs in claiming that the *Anne C. Maguire* ran aground on Christmas Eve, whereas she struck the ledge in front of the lighthouse on Christmas Day.

Witness this account that was published in the *New York Maritime Register*, the official organ of the New York Maritime Exchange, on December 29: "*Anne C. Maguire* (Arg bk), O'Neil, from Buenos Ayres for Portland, Me, in ballast, ran ashore night of Dec 25 on the rocks near Portland Light. The crew all got ashore safely. The captain mistook the direction of the light and the distance from the shore. The bark lies in a bad position and was condemned. Men were engaged in stripping her on the 27th."

Succinct but accurate.

The *New York Times* added a bit of background to put the aging vessel in perspective: "Portland, Me., Dec. 27.—A survey has been held on the bark *Anne C. Maguire*, ashore at Cape Elizabeth, and she has been condemned. Her bottom is badly stove and she will go to pieces in the first storm. The *Maguire* was formerly the well known clipper ship *Golden State*, hailing from New-York, which made many excellent passages between New-York and San Francisco in the early days of California trade."

There were no fatalities or injuries. Captain Daniel O'Neil, his wife, and the crew scrambled overboard and climbed up the rock face, where they met Joshua Strout, keeper of the lighthouse, who was going to their assistance. Strout led the survivors to the lighthouse, where he and his family cared for them.

On December 28, the battered hulk was sold for the princely sum of $157. "She held together until morning of Jan 1st when she commenced to break up."

It was reported on January 19 that "the U.S. Marshal's sale of wreckage from bark *Anne C. Maguire* . . . will foot up a total of about $1,600."

And so the stately and almost anonymous clipper ship-turned-bark faded into history after an ignominious end.

The rocks off Portland light.

ANNIE L. HENDERSON

Built: 1880
Previous names: None
Gross tonnage: 428
Type of vessel: Wooden-hulled three-masted tern
Builder and owner: H.M. Bean, Camden, Maine
Port of registry: Boston, Massachusetts
Cause of sinking: Burned

Sunk: September 1, 1906
Depth: Unknown
Dimensions: 141' x 32' or 35' x 12'
Power: sail

Location: Penobscot River, Bangor Harbor

The *Annie L. Henderson* suffered two major indignities during a long and useful career in the maritime business of hauling freight. She was rigged as a tern, which was a local Maine way of saying a three-masted schooner.

The first indignity occurred on September 10, 1882, when the staunch fore-and-after was only two years old. Under the command of Captain Isaac Fountain, she was on a passage from Apalachicola, Florida to Boston, Massachusetts with a cargo of yellow pine flooring when she ran aground on Rose and Crown shoal, off Nantucket Sound in Massachusetts. She was stuck fast.

The captain decided to lighten the load by jettisoning some of the wood. His plan worked and the vessel floated free, but her hull had been strained during the time the vessel was stranded, by rolling from side to side in the surf. The schooner flooded until the hull was filled with water, at which point she slipped back onto the seabed. A storm was on the horizon. In order to save the lives of his crew, Captain Fountain ordered abandon ship. The men rowed the lifeboat to the nearby town of Wauwinet.

Under most circumstances, that would have been the end of the *Annie L. Henderson*: she should have been either battered to pieces or pounded off the shoal and sunk in deep water. Instead, she drifted off the shoal during the following night's storm, partially supported by the buoyancy of her cargo. Had she been transporting coal she undoubtedly would have gone straight to the bottom.

The now-floating schooner was spotted from the top of a tower in Wauwinet. At that time she was adrift some fifteen miles to the south. Captain Fountain wasted no time in mustering his crew, securing the fishing smack *Osprey*, and going after his command. They sailed past the *South Shoal* lightship. The *Osprey* was still twelve miles away from the schooner when the wind suddenly died. Nothing daunted, the captain, his crew, and three of the men from the *Osprey* launched a boat and rowed hard after the distant schooner.

In the meantime, a collier came across the *Annie L. Henderson*, found her abandoned and low in the water, so her crew decided to strip the vessel of everything of value before torching her as a hazard to navigation. The finders had not yet started their work when Captain Fountain et al arrived.

"A bargain was struck whereby they gave her up to the new-comers, who made sail on her, and with the assistance of the smack worked her in to New London [Connecticut], which they reached on the night of the 20th."

Twenty-two years passed before she suffered her second and final indignity. She was idling at a wharf in Bangor, Maine, while a gang of longshoremen were busily engaged in shoveling a cargo of coal out of her holds, when a nearby building caught fire. Fueled by windborne coal dust, the blaze rapidly spread through wooden structures that lined the waterfront. The dockworkers and the seven crewmembers of the *Annie L. Henderson* abandoned ship and ran from the conflagration as the masts and crosstrees caught fire. Soon the running rigging was burning like candle wicks.

Airborne embers flew like lightning bugs over the ship. Sparks and glowing ashes descended through the open hatchways into the holds, where they ignited the remaining coal. Crewmembers unleashed the dock lines in an effort to shove off the schooner, but an outboard barge prevented a quick escape. By the time a tugboat was able to move the barge, the *Annie L. Henderson* was burning from stem to stern like a huge floating bonfire. Throngs of people stood helpless on land, watching the fiery pageant as if it were a fireworks display. "While she was ablaze aloft and on deck, the wind set her directly across to Brewer, where she poked her blazing jib boom into a shed used for storing sand at the rear of the Hathorne Mfg. Co.'s works, setting the building on fire."

Another tug arrived on the scene. Nothing could be done to save the schooner, so the tug towed her away from the Brewer wharf in order to prevent her from igniting other buildings and creating more devastation. The tug grounded the schooner on a midstream shoal, "where she burned all day and night," a spectacle to behold amid dense black smoke and the bright red scintillation of wildly glowing embers.

Firefighters and horse-drawn engines eventually managed to extinguish the flames and save most of the surrounding buildings. When all was said and done, the damage was great but no lives were lost. As for the *Annie L. Henderson*, she was little more than a smoldering hulk that lay stranded on a sandbar. And there she remained . . .

. . . for the next three years. In 1908, the Army Corps of Engineers was charged with broadening and deepening the channel. According to COE reports, the *Annie L. Henderson*, "when nearly discharged of a cargo of coal at Bangor, Me., the vessel caught fire and finally sank in about 15 feet of water at mean low tide and burned to the water's edge. Being an obstruction to navigation, an allotment of $1,500 for removal of the wreck was made August 7, 1908. A contract has been made for removal of the wreck, and the work is expected to be done during July 1909."

Other wrecks and obstructions were scheduled for removal while the COE concentrated its efforts on dredging operations. Work on the schooner in question did not go according to plan, but the saving grace was a reduction in cost. COE: "The removal of the wreck of the schooner *Annie L. Henderson*, Bangor Harbor, Penobscot River, Maine, was completed November 20, 1909. The total cost was $1,030.06."

How much of the wreck was removed went unstated. Perhaps part of the lower hull still resides on a lonely bar in the middle of Bangor Harbor.

Postcard picture.

BAY STATE

Built: 1895
Previous names: None
Gross tonnage: 2,211
Type of vessel: Side-wheel passenger vessel
Builder: New England Company, Bath, Maine
Owner: Eastern Steamship Corporation, Boston, Massachusetts
Port of registry: Boston, Massachusetts
Cause of sinking: Ran aground
Location: Holycomb Reef or McKenney Point, Cape Elizabeth

Sunk: September 23, 1916
Depth: on the rocks
Dimensions: 281' x 42' x 15'
Power: coal-fired steam

Lat/lon: 43-34-28 N / 70-11-53 W

It is ironic that a shipwreck with such a dramatic photographic history has so little of a story to tell. By "little" I mean that hundreds of passengers and crewmembers survived with no injuries or fatalities, although I suspect that the people who abandoned ship under dire circumstances did not think much of having such an adventure, and certainly would not have wanted to repeat it.

A dense fog enshrouded Cape Elizabeth when the *Bay State* rounded the headland on September 23, 1916. On board were anywhere from 150 to 200 souls – account differ greatly – who had departed Boston, Massachusetts the evening before, with the expectation of arriving safely in Portland, Maine the following morning. The midpoint of the cruise was interrupted when the side-wheeler ground to an abrupt halt on an outthrust rock ledge that was known as Holycomb Reef or McKenney Point.

The *Bay State* was equipped with wireless radio. When the Marconi operator, A.R Gardner, tapped his key to transmit an SOS, he found that the apparatus had been damaged by the sudden stop. In those days, wireless sets were simple, most of the components were exposed, and operators were trained to make on-the-spot repairs. Gardner replaced the broken condenser with a new one from the spare parts box. Within minutes he was able to send a call in Morse code for help.

The distress signal was intercepted by the Cape Elizabeth Naval Station and the Coast Guard cutter *Ossipee*. The Naval Station dispatched the tugs *Portland* and *Cumberland* to the scene of the stranding. The *Ossipee* was at sea but not nearby.

Captain Levi Foran, master of the *Bay State*, sounded the steam whistle. The loud toots alerted personnel at the Cape Elizabeth Coast Guard Station. Captain Sumner Dyer, the station keeper, and some of his men put to sea in a surfboat, while the rest of the crew went overland with the breeches buoy.

A patrolman spotted the stranded steamer through a rift in the fog. He ignited a Coston's flare as a signal. Either the captain did not spot the light before the *Bay State* struck the rocks, or the vessel was already ashore when it was sighted.

In very short order a massive rescue operation was underway. First to arrive on the scene was the Coast Guard surfboat. Despite heaving seas, the surfboat managed to reach the *Bay State*, and offered to offload the passengers. However, Captain Foran decided to wait and see if a rescue tug could pull the vessel off the ledge.

Next to arrive was the *Portland*. By this time the *Bay State* had been driven broadside to shore, and was rolling with the waves. A towing hawser was secured between

Above: this postcard picture taken shortly after grounding shows the state of the sea as the tide recedes. Below: a postcard picture taken at low tide, after much of the wreck had been dismantled.

Below: this picture was taken much later in the dismantling process, during extreme low tide. High seas have torn apart the superstructure and deposited some of it on land. Note the people in the left foreground. (From the collection of Bill Carter.)

the *Portland* and the *Bay State*, but it parted under the strain of attempting to pull the stranded vessel off the ledge against an incoming tide. Later, as the hull grated on the jagged rocks during the ebbing tide, the bottom was torn open so that the lower compartments soon flooded. This spelled the end for saving the *Bay State*. There might have been a boiler explosion as the sea invaded the fire room, but the engineers had anticipated this event by blowing off excess boiler steam, and extinguishing the fire.

Getting the passengers off the *Bay State* became the next priority: one that proved to be a delicate operation in worsening seas. Boats from the *Portland* and *Cumberland* assisted. Rope ladders were lowered over the side at the gangways. Passengers had to climb down the ladders and jump into boats that rose on the crests and fell into the troughs. The boats then transported the occupants offshore to the *Portland*, which later transferred them to the *Ossipee* after that vessel's arrival.

"Captain Dyer and the men in the coastguard boat narrowly escaped being drowned, as their craft was standing alongside when the *Bay State* rolled down upon them. The motor boat was caught under the garboards and the stern of the small craft was forced under water. The lifesavers jumped into neighboring dories, but one man stuck to his post so that when the *Bay State* rolled back the lifeboat was extricated from her predicament."

What took only a few paragraphs to describe took all day to accomplish. Fourteen crewmembers remained onboard the *Bay State*. After nightfall, they signaled for the lifesaving crew to take them off the vessel. It took a couple of hours for the lifesavers to get the Lyle gun in position, fire a messenger line to the stranded steamer – which stood a distance of three football fields from the closest point of land – and rig the breeches buoy. It was after ten o'clock before the *Bay State* was totally abandoned.

The hull was valued at anywhere from $200,000 to $400,000 (estimates differ), and the cargo was worth $80,000.

The Steamboat Inspection Service blamed Captain Foran for the accident, and suspended his master's license for three months. Captain Foran complained that the Lighthouse Service had taken the *Portland* lightship off station for repairs, and that the temporary expedient of a gas and whistle buoy was inadequate for navigating in fog. When he heard the buoy's whistle, he mistook it for the one at Old Anthony's rock. The SIS countered with the statement that the buoys "are the best money can buy and are of the type used at all important and dangerous places along the coast. Foran's employer, the Eastern Steamship Corporation, sided with their captain.

Even though there is no outward resemblance between them, the *Bay State* was a sister ship of the *Portland*, which was lost with all hands on November 27, 1898. (For details, see *Shipwrecks of Massachusetts: North*.)

The reason their appearance is so dissimilar is that, when the Eastern Steamship Corporation purchased the *Bay State* in 1910, the superstructure was completely rebuilt: "She was swept clean at the main deck and everything above that was new. Her beam was widened, new feathering paddle wheels replaced the old radial kind, and at the same time the paddle shaft was lowered. Twenty-eight new staterooms were also added."

The wreck on the rocks was sold to salvors who slowly dismantled the superstructure and hull, and even removed the propulsion machinery, until nearly nothing remained of the once stately passenger vessel.

BOHEMIAN

Built: 1859
Previous names: None
Gross tonnage: 2,190
Type of vessel: Wooden-hulled screw steamer
Builder: W. Denny & Brothers, Dumbarton, Scotland
Owner: Montreal Ocean Steamship Company (Allan Line), Montreal, Canada
Port of registry: Probably Montreal, but possibly Liverpool or Glasgow
Cause of sinking: Ran aground
Location: Staples Cove, off Cape Elizabeth

Sunk: February 4, 1864
Depth: 25 feet
Dimensions: 298' x 38' x 17'
Power: coal-fired steam

The *Bohemian* was a 13-knot transatlantic steamer that transported passengers and freight between various ports in the British Isles and various ports in Maine and Quebec. She operated unhampered during the American Civil War despite Union blockaders and Confederate raiders and blockade runners.

On her final voyage she departed from Liverpool on February 4, 1864, bound for Portland, Maine. On board were nineteen cabin passengers, 199 steerage passengers, and approximately one hundred crewmembers. Her cargo was estimated to be worth a million dollars.

The *Bohemian* was long overdue as she approached the coast of Maine on an evening when a thin haze had settled over the water. Captain Robert Borland cautiously reduced speed to two and a half knots. Thus the vessel was barely maintaining steerageway. Rockets were fired as a way to signal for a pilot to guide the vessel across the harbor. The haze had the effect of reducing the illumination of lights on the shore of Cape Elizabeth. The dimness caused Captain Borland to misjudge the distance from land, making him think that his vessel stood farther offshore than it was actually located.

The hull scraped over Alden's Rock, a jagged ledge that tore a hole in the bottom. Five crossthwart bulkheads divided the vessel into six watertight compartments. Nevertheless, seawater poured into the engine room and boiler room at an alarming rate. Captain Borland raced for the nearby shore in an attempt to beach the vessel before she sank. The *Bohemian* reached a depth of four fathoms when she settled to the bottom.

Although the seas were fairly calm, a heavy ground swell was running. Captain Borland ordered abandon ship. Four of the five lifeboats were launched safely. Lifeboat number two swamped and its occupants, Irish immigrants, drowned.

According to contemporary accounts, lifeboat number 1 made two trips to shore, saving some 150 people in all. Lifeboat number 3 landed ninety-four people in Broad Cove. Lifeboat number 4 put twenty-five people on the beach. Lifeboat number 5 carried twenty-five people into Portland Harbor. These numbers are all approximate.

The officers remained on board overnight. They managed to save most of the mail bags.

Twenty-seven bodies were recovered and examined by the coroner, James Gould. Fifteen were identified. The remainder were described in the hope that friends or rela-

tives could identify them. Some of the descriptions read thus: "Young Woman Aged about 22 Light Compl." and "Boy 2 years old" and "Girl 5 years old dark B Hair plaid dress White tunic" and "Man Supposed Fireman by dress." Fireman referred to a boiler room crewmember.

Also found were "A part of a human body female" and "A child with the head gone" and "Unknown Boy about ten years old" and "Unknown Girl 7 or 8 years old." Some bodies were so mutilated and their clothing so torn that it was impossible to recognize them by their features or dress. "Generally they had no clothing on their persons."

It was later reported: "The greater portion of the hurricane-deck and officers' quarters have broken up, but the main-deck and hull remain firm. As the baggage was stowed on the upper-deck and under the bridge, it was all washed overboard, and will undoubtedly be a total loss. The sea has swept every thing clear from that quarter."

Although Captain Borland was found guilty of an "error in judgment," government officials realized that the navigation channel was poorly marked. The emplacement of bell buoys helped to avoid a similar catastrophe.

Also as a result of the loss of the *Bohemian*, the height of the Portland Head lighthouse was increased by twenty feet, by means of building a brick extension on the top. In addition, the fourth-order Fresnel lens was replaced by a brighter, second-order Fresnel lens.

Today, the wreckage of the *Bohemian* is a popular dive site, where numerous buttons from an eclectic cargo lie scattered along the shallow seabed.

CAMBRIDGE

Built: 1867
Previous names: None
Gross tonnage: 1,337
Type of vessel: Wooden-hulled side-wheel steamer
Builder: John English & Sons, New York, NY
Owner: Sandford Steamship Company (Boston and Bangor Line), Boston, Mass.
Port of registry: Boston, Massachusetts
Cause of sinking: Ran aground
Location: Old Man Ledge, off George's Island

Sunk: February 10, 1886
Depth: 20 feet
Dimensions: 248' x 37' x 13'
Power: coal-fired steam

GPS: 43-50.683 / 69-18.934

    The *Cambridge* was a long-time standby for passenger and freight service along the New England coast. For nearly two decades she provided fast and reliable transportation under a variety of named shipping lines as the mother company went through several corporate changes.

    In the year preceding her loss, she was overhauled to the tune of $36,000. The overhaul included replacement of her worn-out boilers. "She had 63 staterooms and accommodations for 450 passengers. The saloon occupied about the entire length of the boat, with windows on each side and end, affording outlooks upon the scenery along her route. The section forward of the engine was the dining room. The interior furnishings were attractive, and the boat was a favorite with passengers going east. She carried nine lifeboats, a life raft, and several hundred life preservers. The company valued her at about $100,000, and she was insured for $50,000 in the Boston Marine and other offices in Boston and New York."

From the collection of Dave Clancy.

On the morning of February 10, 1886, the *Cambridge* was "on her trip down" from Bangor to Boston when she got off course and struck Old Man Ledge. She listed to starboard and commenced to flood through rents in her wooden hull. Captain Ingraham ordered abandon ship. The lifeboats were swung out on their davits and lowered to the water in an orderly and timely manner. There was no panic among the passengers, who numbered between twenty and eighty.

"The passengers and crew took to the boats, and landed on George's Island, five miles distant. The best of order prevailed, and no accidents occurred in transferring the passengers."

The wreck lay pinned to the rock by the weight of her heavy freight, some of which washed out of the hull "and scattered along shore, and was being picked up by fishermen."

On February 17, it was reported that the hull broke so that "only the two boilers and the steam-pipe remain in view. . . . Quantities of freight have been found scattered up and down the coast in the possession of fishermen and others, portions of which were surrendered to the owners. The pilot house of the stranded steamer was fallen in with by Capt Griffin, of tug *L A Belknap*, who took off the boards with the steamer's name on them."

By the 24th, the heavy freight was entirely gone. "The larger part of the machinery remained, but it was very much broken up by the heavy sea."

According to the last mention in the maritime news: "A party from the Portland Wrecking Company, who went to the Old Man Ledge on Mch 19 to examine the wreck of stmr *Cambridge*, found very little of the vessel left, except some of the machinery. The boilers could not be found, and have probably washed into deep water. What remained of the *Cambridge* was sold by auction on the 28th (at Boston) to H S Kaler, of Portland, for $1,000."

Drawn by Samuel Ward Stanton.

CITY OF PORTLAND

Built: 1873
Previous names: None
Gross tonnage: 1,026
Type of vessel: Wooden-hulled side-wheel steamer
Builder: Portland, Maine
Owner: International Steamship Company, Boston, Massachusetts
Port of registry: Eastport, Maine
Cause of sinking: Ran aground
Location: Northwest Ledge, Penobscot Bay

Sunk: May 8, 1884
Depth: 20 feet
Dimensions: 240' x 32' x 14'
Power: coal-fired steam

GPS: 44-02.932 / 69-02.998

The biggest hazard on Maine and nearby Canadian waters was the sheer number of submerged rocky reefs that snagged passing vessels which were slightly off course or lost in ever-present fog. The biggest complaint among nineteenth-century mariners was the dearth of lighthouses and offshore aids to navigation, such as bell buoys.

One of the most outspoken proponents of the implementation of navigational aids was Captain Pike, master of the *City of Portland*. Thus it was with great relief that "the captain and pilots of the Steamer *City of Portland* are pleased to testify to the great improvements in the lights upon the coast of New Brunswick, between Cape Spencer and East Quoddy. They are now visible from fifteen to twenty miles – double the distance they could be seen before the change. A bell at East Quoddy would add greatly to the safety of vessels and steamers approaching the coast."

Captain Pike's comments fall into the category of prescience. According to the 1884 schedule of the International Steamship Company, "Steamers *City of Portland*, *Falmouth*, and *State of Maine* leave Railroad Wharf, Portland, at 6 o'clock P. M., Mondays and Thursdays during the winter and spring season, and from early in May till December every Monday, Wednesday and Friday, at the same hour. During the summer season five trips per week will be made from Boston, viz. : every Monday, Tuesday, Wednesday, Friday, and Saturday, leaving at 8.30 A. M. (on the Tuesday and Saturday trips steamer does not touch Portland."

The fare ranged from $1.25 to $3.50, depending upon destination: Boston, Eastport, Calais, or St. John. Ah, those pre-inflation days . . . Today's rate for a cab ride in New York City will take you about a block for the same amount of money (although the shouting and gesticulations are free of charge).

On her final voyage, the master of the *City of Portland* was Captain D. Larcom. His two pilots were captains F.A. Bibber (First Pilot) and J.A. Wheeler (Second Pilot). All three testified about events leading to the catastrophe. The *City of Portland* was on route from Portland, Maine to Saint John, New Brunswick. She was carrying 130 passengers and crew, plus a large general cargo.

According to Second Pilot Wheeler, "I went on watch at 1 o'clock [in the morning], relieving the first pilot. The steamer was two miles westward of Monhegan inside. I had directions to call the first pilot when we reached White Head, which I did. In four minutes we reached the light. Captain Bibber took his position at one window of the pilot house and I was at the other. Made Ash Point bell where we always swing to go

From the collection of Dave Clancy.

out through Sheep Island Channel on our course east-north-east. I gave the order [to the helmsman] to put the wheel to port and gave her course east-north-east; ran half a minute and sighted the striped buoy on the northern Grindstone Ledge, one point [11-1/4 degrees] on the port bow, which I reported to the first pilot, who said 'All right.' We then were one minute from the buoy. I said, 'Hadn't we better port, so as not to go too close to the buoy?' and Captain Bibber said 'Yes,' and I gave the orders to port. In ten seconds we struck, then going 12 knots an hour. There was 12 feet of water forward of the pilot house and three fathoms at the stern as the steamer lay.

"A fisherman told us the buoy was out of position. I don't think the steamer swung as quickly as usual when abreast of Ash Point, thus throwing us a little off the usual channel. If she had slid off the ledge after striking, she would have sunk in deep water."

First Pilot Bibber had a slightly different perspective: "I was called at White Head. We made Ash Point bell all right and swung north-east, and made Sheep Island striped buoy two points on the port bow; put the wheel hard aport to clear it and struck in two minutes. Have been a pilot on this coast 25 years. The only explanation I have on the accident is that the buoy had drifted out of place. Had the steamer gone its width to the south'ard she would have cleared all right."

Captain Larcom had this to say: "I turned into my bunk at midnight. The steamer then was on the course outside of Monhegan and first pilot Bibber was in charge. I knew nothing more till awakened at 3.30 o'clock by the shock of the striking. I then ran hastily out and gave the necessary orders. I saw at once that the steamer was hard aground and there was no danger. The officers and crew worked finely. The boats were cleared away immediately, and all means of safety were taken. I sent the mate ashore to get help from Rockland; we were about two miles from the mainland, and the water was comparatively calm, being about dead low tide.

"In less than half an hour after striking Capt. Wallace of Owl's Head came up with a sloop and took about half of our passengers. The steamer *Rockland*, arrived at 6.30 o'clock and took the balance of the passengers. I am satisfied that the accident would not have been more serious had the steamer slid off the ledge for the pumps would have kept her afloat till she reached Rockland, but as she settled on the ledge the water reached the furnaces, the steam was blown off, the tide began making and the wind freshened from the westward. The after part of the steamer began warping to pieces, when I left at 10 o'clock, being the last man to leave and the after part was gone. There won't be a stick above water by morning.

"I have been 16 years steamboating, and this is the first disaster of any nature. The only cause I can ascribe is the strong tide increased by the force of an easterly wind setting us directly on the ledge. The pilot had run that channel a hundred times. It was always my custom to be on deck when running among the islands. When her course was changed I should have been called though I don't know as I could have done any more than the two pilots on the deck. I have seen the steamer go through that channel scores of times all right."

A local correspondent appended details of the aftermath and abandonment: "While the passengers were being transferred, a horse, the only one on board, jumped over board and swam around the steamer, and then coming back, put his fore feet up on the guard and looked up in a pleading manner. Two men in a dory rowed up towards him, and one of them seized his halter, while the other pulled away. In this manner the horse was pulled to the shore, nearly two miles distant.

"As it was quite cold on the steamer, one of the young ladies among the passengers was asked to take a blanket to keep her warm; but she said, 'No, if I am going to drown I want to look decent.'

"While some of the ladies were getting into a boat from the steamer, a man jumped into it from on board, and nearly capsized it. . . . The light house vessel is particular about the buoys in this channel and within a week had been through here. Officials are reticent as to the cause of the accident, but opinion inclines somewhat to a drifting of the buoy as the true reason."

"Twenty feet to starboard would have carried the vessel clear, and under the stern of the steamer as she lies in 21 feet of water at low tide."

The White Head Lifesaving Station had closed for the summer just a few days prior to the accident. Nonetheless, when the lighthouse keeper spotted the stranded steamer at dawn, he hoisted the assembly signal in order to gather the far-flung crew who manned the station. He then informed the station keeper, a man named Shea. Shea went to the mainland where he gathered three of the lifesavers who were still in the vicinity.

According to United State Lifesaving Service records, "The surfboat was launched, and shortly afterward they fell in with two other members of the crew, who were hurrying to the station in obedience to the assembly signal. They then started for the scene of the disaster, having a strong head wind and current to contend with; but after a hard pull of three hours and forty minutes reached the wreck, which they found was partly under water. The passengers and crew had been safely taken off by the steamer *City of Rockland* and carried to Rockland, a few miles distant. The life-saving crew therefore turned their attention to saving all the property possible, which was put on board of a small schooner chartered by the captain. After loading the schooner with all she could carry, a lot of baggage and other articles of value was put into the surf-boat and landed at the station. A few days later (May 12) the crew of the station set out in their boat and searched the shores of the adjacent islands and the mainland, and succeeded in finding a large quantity of the cargo and baggage belonging to the wrecked steamer, which would otherwise have been lost. Everything they saved was dried and put in as good order as possible, and then turned over to the proper owners."

CORA F. CRESSY

Built: 1902
Previous names: None
Gross tonnage: 2,499
Type of vessel: Wooden-hulled five-masted schooner
Builder: Percy & Small, Bath, Maine
Owner: Keene Narrows Lobster Company, Bremen, Maine
Port of registry: Unregistered
Cause of sinking: Scuttled
Location: Keene Narrows Lobster Company wharf, at Keene Narrows

Sunk: 1938
Depth: Visibly exposed
Dimensions: 273' x 45' x 27'
Power: sail

GPS: 43-59.066 / 69-24.862

The *Cora F. Cressy* had – and continues to have – a varied and flavorful career.

She has been touted as the largest five-masted schooner ever built. This statement is true as far as it goes, but the restrictive criterion is somewhat misleading and implies more than it states. There were six- and seven-masted schooners that were larger than the *Cora F. Cressy*.

Majestic as she appeared under full sail, the *Cora F. Cressy* was built for the freight trade: a utilitarian vessel like hundreds or thousands of similar windjammers that plied the seven seas under sail. She transported cargoes over water the way eighteen-wheelers transport freight over land. Yet she was destined for much more than the purpose for which she was built . . . and much less.

Like many twentieth-century sailing vessels, the *Cora F. Cressy* was outfitted with a donkey boiler to provide steam for a windlass. This made raising the anchor less onerous for the crew. Without a windlass, anchors had to be raised manually by pushing against capstan bars and walking around in a circle. The machinery was also used to raise the gaffs in order to unfurl the sails. Thus the size of the crew that was needed to man the schooner could be significantly reduced; half a dozen able-bodied seamen could do the work that required a crew of four times as many on a square-rigged vessel.

Postcard picture.

As a freighter her most common cargo was coal. Her first notice that was out of the ordinary occurred in 1904, when she was two years old. The schooner's master paid off the second mate in Norfolk, Virginia, for reasons that were not explained in court documents. As a result, some of the seamen refused to work "and were put in irons until they were ready to obey orders."

The court noted, "The imprisonment was justified, unless the refusal to work was justified."

The seamen justified their refusal to work by citing a statute which stipulated that a domestic vessel was not allowed to put to sea without a second mate. Seamen in those days were largely uneducated, and many were illiterate. Seamen were not the kind of people who engaged in seagoing employment by first attending college and memorizing all the legal tracts that pertained to their trade. I seriously doubt that their refusal to work had anything to do with the legality of the situation. It seems more likely that the seamen were in league with the second mate, or that they refused to work in protest at his dismissal, and that their lawyer discovered the appropriate statute that fortuitously pertained to their case.

In any event, the court found that "the master's violation of law does not excuse the crew's total refusal to work the vessel, either at Norfolk or after leaving port. Hence the libelants have failed to prove any false imprisonment."

The *Cora F. Cressy* case was adjudicated on June 20, 1904, and has been cited in several subsequent cases and books on maritime law . . . but it has always been taken out on context.

The opinion reads, "That the master of a vessel failed to replace a second mate who had been paid off at an intermediate port, as required by Rev. St. paragraph 4516 [U. S. Comp. St. 1901, p. 3071], was no excuse for the total refusal of members of the crew to work the vessel, and was therefore no defense to the master's right to punish them for their disobedience." (Brackets were included in the original text.)

What ruling citers failed to mention was the second paragraph of the court's decision: a left-handed judgment for the master which read, "It follows that the master was justified in docking the crew's wages during their confinement, but, as he failed to comply with the provisions of Rev. St., paragraph 4597 [U. S. Comp. St. 1901, p. 3115], I am disposed to mark my disapproval of this irregularity by disallowing the deduction. Decree for balance of wages, without costs." (Brackets were in the original text.)

In other words, the court found that the master had the right to imprison seamen who refused to work, but in this particular case, because he did not replace the second mate before the vessel's departure, as required by law, he had to pay the seamen's wages for the time they spent in irons. Both master and seamen were guilty of violating a law, somewhat in the vein of contributory negligence in automobile crashes.

The *Cora F. Cressy* found herself in another legal wrangle in 1907. On March 16 of that year, she arrived at Sabine Pass, Texas to take on a load of sulfur in bulk. March 17 was a Sunday, a nonworking day, so on Monday morning the master notified the charterer's agent that he was ready to receive cargo. The schooner was ready but the Union Sulfur Company was not. There was only one loading berth; it was already occupied, and several other vessels were swinging at their anchorage waiting to be loaded in their turn. The *Cora F. Cressy* was at the end of the line.

And there she swung . . . for three weeks. Everyone understands that time is money. For those three wasted weeks the *Cora F. Cressy* was not earning any money, plus she still had wages to pay to her crew. Loading sulfur did not commence until April 8; by April 11, she was fully loaded with 3,000 tons of sulfur. But what of the lost time? The master made a claim for demurrage. The company agreed, and the agent endorsed the bill of lading thus:

"The schooner *Cora F. Cressy* was ready for cargo at 9:00 a. m. on March 18, 1907. Finished loading at noon, April 11, 1907. Assuming that her cargo consists of 3,000 tons, her lay days expired on April 11, 1907, at 9:00 a. m., as per charter party, dated January 11, 1907; hence demurrage is due this vessel for 13 days and 3 hours."

The reason for the disparity in demurrage days was that the company was obligated to load only 300 tons per day. At that rate it would have taken ten days to load 3,000 tons. The difference between obligated loading time and actual loading time accounted for the disparity in demurrage days.

The problem arose later when the Union Sulfur Company reneged at paying demurrage. Samuel Percy, owner of the schooner, sued. With a signed document in evidence, the court had no difficulty in finding for the plaintiff. But it took two years for the case to be tried.

Another case took even longer. Percy employed the Lee Towing Company to tow the *Cora F. Percy* along the East River in New York City. "The larger tug (*Maren Lee*) took position ahead with the usual towing line, the *Herman Lee* made fast on the starboard quarter of the schooner, and the flotilla started, entering the East River through Buttermilk Channel. There was a strong flood tide in the river, and the tugs attained considerable speed, it is said as much as seven miles an hour. At the same time the tug *Cumberland*, with two light barges in tow on short hawsers, was coming down the river on a voyage from Boston to Baltimore. Congestion of shipping compelled the *Cumberland* to get over on the Brooklyn side of the East River" at the time the converging tugs passed each other in opposite directions.

"The master of the *Herman Lee* left his tug on the schooner's starboard quarter and took position on the latter vessel's forecastle head. The schooner's master was not aboard." The *Herman Lee* was not secured to the schooner; it was merely in position to push against her starboard quarter.

At that moment the schooner sheered "with such violence that the *Maren Lee* was unable to check the sheer before the schooner came in contact with one of the *Cumberland's* barges, injuring both vessels."

The court found that the captain of the *Herman Lee* was "untrustworthy, not only in his report to the local inspectors, which is extremely uncandid, but also in his conflicting stories of the orders given to his tug." Either he gave the wrong order to the helmsman of the schooner, or his hand signals were insufficiently clear to be interpreted properly. In either case, he was found at fault because he was a licensed pilot who was solely in charge of the navigation of the *Cora F. Cressy* at the time of the collision.

Appeals continued until 1922, by which time Percy no longer owned the *Cora F. Cressy*. He had sold her in 1917 to the France & Canada Steamship Company. Nonetheless, he was partially liable for damages because the cost of repairs to the barge, which was owned by the Consolidated Coastwise Company, exceeded the value of the *Herman Lee*, and so Percy was ordered to make up for the deficit. I wonder why the value of the *Maren Lee* was not used to pay for damages.

In 1920, wireless apparatus was added to the *Cora F. Cressy*. In the days before voice communication via radio, Morse code was used to transmit messages. Rather than identify a vessel by spelling out the name, each vessel that was equipped with wireless was assigned a four-letter signal code. The code letters for the *Cora F. Cressy* were KRPC. Radio operators on vessels that intercepted a wireless transmission would identify the transmitting vessel by looking up the call letters in a code book.

On March 11, 1924, the *Cora F. Cressy* was weathering out a storm at anchor in Nantucket Sound. The ferocity of the storm grew to such proportions that her master decided that the shallow waters of the sound were worse than the deep waters of the open sea. He weighed anchor and headed for the ocean. In retrospect the choice was a wise one, for the six-masted schooner *Wyoming* remained in the sound and was lost with all hands. (For details, see *Shipwrecks of Massachusetts: South*.)

The use of schooners as low-cost providers was gradually yielding to steamers. Because sailing vessels had to rely on the vagaries of the wind for propulsion, they required more time to transport a cargo than a steam freighter, which could make deliveries faster and more reliably. Sailing vessels were going out of vogue. Many – perhaps most – ended their days as schooner barges: aging schooners that were dismasted and converted to barges that were towed in strings at the end of a hawser. The days of sail were winding down because competition from propeller driven vessels was too keen.

In 1925, the *Cora F. Cressy* was sold for $3,610 to the Boston Ship Brokerage Company. Her new owner fixed her up and sent her back to sea, where she managed to earn her way for three more years. During this time she suffered a bizarre accident: her master, Captain Frank Perkins, was killed when he fell into a hold through an open hatchway. There was no one else on the vessel who knew navigation. The beleaguered seamen did not know where they were located, or what direction to take in order to reach their destination, or for that matter any safe harbor. The unusual situation called for transmitting an SOS on the wireless set. Eventually a Coast Guard cutter located the idly drifting schooner and towed her to the nearest wharf.

She struggled in the coal trade for three lean years before finally furling her sails. Then she was laid up and almost put to rest. I say "almost" because she was one of the few fore-and-afters that was lucky enough to be reanimated at the insistence of impresario Frederick Kauffman. Her new job was housing a floating restaurant in Boston, Massachusetts. She commenced this new phase of her career in 1929.

Some secondary sources claim that she was employed as a speakeasy. This is absurd. Speakeasies, Prohibition, and flappers flourished in the Roaring '20's, when the 1919 Volstead Act (the Eighteenth Amendment to the Constitution) prohibited the drinking of alcohol for the purpose of recreation. Establishments that sold illegal liquor to the imbibing public had to be hidden where Revenuers could not find them: in concealed basements or behind hidden panels or secret doors. The era of bootlegging ended in 1933, when the Twenty-First Amendment repealed the Eighteenth.

The *Cora F. Cressy* was prominently tied to a wharf at the city docks, where "sticking out like a sore thumb" is an old-time cliché that comes readily to mind. Her 100-foot-tall masts – or sticks, as they are called in the trade – stuck up literally and more visibly than the proverbial sore thumb.

In her new guise she was known as *Levaggi's Show Boat*. Most of the weather deck was covered by a long deckhouse that stretched almost from stem to stern. It served as a lounge and dance floor, the latter boasting 3,000 square feet for doing the fox trot and Charleston. Excellent cuisine was served to patrons who were surrounded by vivid nautical paintings amid colorful décor. The show boat catered to the rich and

MAINE

From the collection of Bill Quinn.

well-to-do. It was anything but a lowlife honkytonk.

The tall still-stepped masts protruded more than a hundred feet through the roof (or the overhead) like a row of planted trees that could be seen from many blocks away. Temperance fanatics would have discovered the existence of intoxicating beverages even if the Untouchables had overlooked it. The Noble Experiment of the 1920's was a precursor to today's war on drugs, in which a vocal and politically connected minority desired to control the habits of the vast majority.

The showboat schooner did not stay put. She visited other Massachusetts locations sporadically, most notably Nantasket and Pemberton beaches, where the lack of dockage required boats to transport patrons to and fro. The entertainment and exclusivity made it worth the time, trouble, and money that it cost to get aboard. She also did a short stint in Providence, Rhode Island.

The *Cora F. Cressy* served in this legitimate capacity for nearly ten years, until manager Jack Levaggi moved inland, in 1938. He was a bona fide restauranteur who by then ran a fancy dining hall, ballroom, and tap and grill at the corner of Massachusetts Avenue and Norway Street. His famous Flamingo Room featured such performers and entertainers as bandleaders Guy Lombardo and Tommy Dorsey, Chick Webb's orchestra, jazz singer Ella Fitzgerald, and so on.

According to the National Park Service, "In 1938, after lying idle for sometime [sic], she was towed to East Boston where the masts were removed. Learning that *Cressey* [sic] was available for the asking, Bernard T. 'Bunny' Zahn of Bremen, Maine, hired a tugboat and had her towed to his lobster pound, where she served as pound office and breakwater. Lack of help during World War II shut down Zahn's operation temporarily."

From the collection of Bill Quinn.

The NPS also noted that the bilges were filled with sand, and that "a hole was cut into her starboard side to allow shoreside access to her 'tweendecks, then in use as a lobster pond." This statement does not make sense because the schooner's port side faces land.

In 1990, the aged schooner was nominated for inclusion on the National Register of Historic Places, under the misspelled name *Cora F. Cressey*.

The NRHP nomination form notes, "In spring of 1988, approximately 40 feet of her stern fell into the cove at the cut. The bowsprit has fallen; her main deck has largely collapsed, yet her remaining hull largely retains its shape. Though her steam hoisting engine was removed before she left for Maine, some machinery such as the after capstan and a windlass, survive. Some traces of the wooden rail remain aboard. Other sections of it were removed to the Maine Maritime Museum in Bath, Maine, together with other items of her equipment. These include the steering gear, including the tiller and worm; an assortment of cabin paneling, mouldings [sic] and combings from the deckhouse; a window slide from the afterhouse, the rack for capstan bars; and at least one turnbuckle and chainplate."

Despite this description of gross breakdown, the visual evidence to support it, and an additional twenty-five years of accelerated degradation, today the archaeology program of the National Park Service claims that the deteriorating hulk is "nationally significant" and "intact." The NPS must have a different definition of "intact" than the rest of the world. And one must wonder why, if the hulk was nationally significant, no efforts were made to preserve it.

Today, the crumbling hulk is barely recognizable as a vessel. Both the bow and stern have collapsed below the surface. Only the rotting sides of the midship area maintain the shape of the hull. Timbers that have fallen outboard fore and aft have created a submerged hazard that only local mariners know how to avoid. The one-time splendid sailing vessel and showboat is nowadays used as a breakwater for lobster boats: an eyesore whose eventual removal – like that of the *Hesper* and *Luther Little* (which see) – will be a costly enterprise.

From the collection of Paul Sherman.

Shipwrecks cannot be preserved by means of bureaucratic fiat. This truism is clearly demonstrated by comparing the historic picture above with the current picture below. (Note that the smokestack in the picture above belongs to the tug on the starboard stern of the *Cora F. Cressy*.)

To see the disintegrating remains, from Route 1 take Route 32 south to Bremen, turn left onto Keene Neck Road. Follow that for a mile and a quarter and turn left onto Keene Narrows Road; this is a dirt road but the surface is compacted. After one block turn right onto Cora Cressey Road, whose surface also consists of compacted dirt. The road curves left after a quarter mile. From this vantage point you can see the wreckage over the roofs of the lobster shanties, far enough from shore to create a protected channel for lobster boats that dock there.

CORNWALLIS

Built: 1921
Previous names: *Canadian Transporter*
Gross tonnage: 5,458
Type of vessel: Freighter
Builder: J. Coughlan & Sons, Vancouver, British Columbia
Owner: Canadian National Steamship Company, Quebec, Canada
Port of registry: Montreal, Quebec
Cause of sinking: Torpedoed by *U-1230* (Kapitanleutnant Hans Hilbig)
Lat/lon (attack position): 43° 59' North / 68° 20' West

Sunk: December 3, 1944
Depth: Unknown
Dimensions: 400' x 52' x 28'
Power: Oil-fired steam

On the night of November 29-30, 1944, the *U-1230* arrived not *off* the coast of Maine, but *on* it. The U-boat's primary objective was to disembark two espionage agents onto a deserted New England shore. This was not the first time that spies had been delivered to the American coast by German U-boats. The U.S. Army maintained a constant if somewhat sporadic vigil on those parts of the eastern seaboard that were uninhabited, for just such an occurrence as the *U-1230* intended. The Federal Bureau of Investigation followed leads in order to capture spies that managed to sneak through the coastal patrol net.

The two enemy agents who landed by inflatable raft were William Colepaugh and Erich Gimpel. According to the official interrogation report, after crossing the Atlantic Ocean and arriving off the coast of Maine, the *U-1230* "began her passage into Frenchman Bay. She proceeded submerged on Schnorchel until 1900. At 1600, Great Duck Island and Baker Island were sighted and a fix was taken. At 1900, the boat collided with a whistling buoy. After this event, the Schnorchel mast was lowered and the boat proceeded at periscope depth on electric motors. She ran with the tide and the current proved stronger than was anticipated, resulting in the completion of the mission some hours earlier than had been anticipated.

"The U-boat, once inside the Bay, did not follow the normal channel but proceeded between Porcupine Island and Iron Pound Island. At about 2230, she was half mile off shore. A white house on Crabtree Point was sighted and the U-boat surfaced with her decks awash and only her conning tower above water.

"The U-boat circled around to within a few hundred yards of the shore. A rubber boat was brought up from below and was inflated by a special line which ran through the conning tower hatch and connected with the electric compressor. Colepaugh stated that the inflation was absolutely soundless. Two unarmed members of the ship's company rowed the two agents ashore and then returned to the U-boat."

The agents proceeded on foot along a rural road through an inch and a half of snow that was still falling. They were spotted almost immediately by teenager Harvard Hodgkins, who was returning home from a dance. A few minutes later, they were spotted by Mary Forni, who was driving home from a card party after midnight. Forni took particular notice of the men because they were dressed in clothing that was unusual for the weather and the locality – shoes instead of boots, odd-looking overcoats and hats – plus they were carrying luggage.

From the author's collection.

Forni: "They just weren't like normal Mainers in November. You just never saw anybody walking without boots when it was snowy like that."

The next morning, Forni reported the incident to her next door neighbor, the wife of Deputy Sheriff Dana Hodgkins and coincidentally the mother of Harvard. The elder Hodgkins was away on a hunting trip, so the sightings received no official recognition until he returned home the following day. These sightings of a suspicious pair of pedestrians instigated an FBI manhunt which, in the event, led to a dead end.

Armed with handguns and $60,000 in United States currency, the spies managed to escape further notice and to blend in with American crowds as they made their way to New York City by means of public transportation: first by cab, then by train. But their freedom on American soil was short-lived. They separated in the core of the Big Apple when they had a falling out over their mission and the money.

Colepaugh was an American citizen who had defected to Germany where he received training in explosives and as a spy. Gimpel was a German national whose command of the English language was limited and whose accent was thick. Although Gimpel was the leader of the team, Colepaugh knew his way around the States. They needed each other in order to work effectively, both in sending information to Germany and in disrupting American production by destroying key installations, primarily hydroelectric dams and a heavy-water production facility.

Colepaugh spent most of his time drinking and womanizing. He got cold feet after a few weeks. On December 26, 1944, he turned himself in to the FBI. He then informed on Gimpel, and told FBI agents where they were likely to find him. Agents who were now armed with Gimpel's description stationed themselves at several locations that the German spy frequented. They arrested Gimpel on December 30.

After both spies were in custody, FBI director J. Edgar Hoover told the press that the FBI had apprehended the spies by following leads that originated from Hodgkins and Forni: a complete fabrication that was intended to make the FBI look good by taking credit for their capture – a policy of making false claims that continues to the present day.

Gimpel was reticent under interrogation, but Colepaugh was talkative, perhaps in the hope that he would not be executed, as other spies had been, if he provided worthwhile information. He described U-boat designs, construction, armament, bases, operations, and capabilities. He also gave a history – as much as he knew – of the U-boat that transported him and Gimpel across the Atlantic Ocean.

Neither Gimpel's silence nor Colepaugh's loquacity did them any good. A military tribunal found them both guilty as charged, and sentenced them to hang by the neck until they were dead. Two fortuitous events saved their lives. Three days prior to their planned execution President Roosevelt died. Vice President Truman ordered a thirty-day stay of execution for all prisoners in the country as a way of mourning Roosevelt. After Truman took office and the mourning period ended, he commuted their sentences to life imprisonment.

Gimpel was paroled in 1955. He fled the country and lived out his life in South America. He died in Brazil in 2010.

Colepaugh was paroled in 1960. He continued to live anonymously in the United States until his death in 2005.

In 2003, the supposed landing site was nominated for inclusion on the National Register of Historic Places.

While the above stated drama was occurring on land, dire events were occurring at sea. On December 3, 1944, Hilbig spotted the Canadian freighter *Cornwallis*, which was traveling independently from the Caribbean island of Barbados to Saint John, New Brunswick, with a cargo of sugar in bags and molasses in barrels. As she followed the coastal shipping route, her "port and starboard running lights, and dim white light on foremast were burning."

At about ten o'clock that night, "there was an explosion on the starboard side near #1 hold. Hatch cover of #1 hold was blown off. No fire broke out, but survivors smelled smoke which resembled that coming from a shell case which has just been fired. Vessel sank rapidly by the head in less than 10 minutes. Survivors did not know whether a distress signal had been sent but an SSSS message from 'off Desert Rock' was intercepted by the Yarmouth, Nova Scotia Radio at 1005 from an entirely unidentified source. All confidential codes are presumed to have gone down with the ship.

"All of the five survivors were in the crew quarters aft at the time of the explosion. The standby man on watch called all hands. The survivors rushed on deck and attempted to lower the starboard lifeboat located amidships. The vessel was sinking rapidly with a starboard list, and the davit caught and smashed the lifeboat before it could be cast free. The survivors then jumped or were washed overboard as the vessel sank under them. They swam to rafts, were sighted later in the morning by planes, and were picked up by a fishing boat and Navy rescue vessels at 1800. Survivors were landed at Rockland, Maine. Total ship's complement 48; 5 survivors, 5 known dead and 38 missing presumed dead."

At 11:34 in the morning, the fishing vessel *Iva M* reported sighting bodies and barrels. At 13:40, the fishing boat *Notre Dame* picked up either two or all five survivors. (The records are unclear.) Three survivors may have been rescued by either a "crash boat," a Navy destroyer, or a Coast Guard cutter.

In the interests of corroborating history, I would like to mention that after I published an account of the loss of the *Cornwallis* in *Track of the Gray Wolf* (1989), I received a letter from Margaret Kirlis in which she sought to offer some insights and corrections to the official version of the tragedy. Mrs. Kirlis was a cousin of the vessel's master. She wrote, "Captain's name was Emerson Horace 'Bob' Robinson and not, Robertson, as indicated."

She noted that the "Chief Radio Officer was John Walsh of Halifax, lost, and I assume, the one who sent out the distress call." She also noted that the *Cornwallis's* ultimate destination was Halifax, Nova Scotia.

Furthermore, she knew the names of the five survivors: Elmar 'Blackie' Cossman, John Buffitt, Jimmy Bonnar, Steve Lesage, and John Christiansen. One of the eight naval gunners was Able Seaman Hoffe.

She thought that the "*Cornwallis* went down at 43°9'N 68°20'W, which puts her closer to Mt. Desert Island than Mt. Desert, Maine close by Casco Bay."

Finally, "Please note, the *Cornwallis* had been previously torpedoed on 11 September 1942, at 13°05'N 59°36'W while under the command of Captain Duncan MacLeod by U-boat 514, possibly commanded by Auffermann. Captain MacLeod was given the O.B.E. for saving his crew and managing to sail the crippled *Cornwallis* to either Norfolk, Virginia or Charleston, North Carolina (unidentified as yet)." (Readers should note that Charleston is located in South Carolina.)

When I revised the out-of-print *Track of the Gray Wolf* in 2006 as *The Fuhrer's U-boats in American Waters*, I incorporated relevant information as Kirlis suggested.

German records confirm that Kapitanleutnant Hans-Jurgen Auffermann was in command of the *U-514*, and that he was credited with torpedoing the *Cornwallis* in the harbor at Barbados on September 11, 1942. In this regard, it should also be mentioned that five other crewmembers were awarded decorations as a result of this incident. According to official records, after Captain MacLeod ordered abandon ship, he and five volunteers remained onboard in order to save the vessel from sinking. Because the propulsion machinery had been knocked out of commission by the torpedo, the *Cornwallis* was towed in sinking condition to Mobile, Alabama for permanent repairs.

The *U-514* survived the war. It was scuttled in the North Sea as part of Operation Deadlight.

As an interesting sidelight, the fishing vessel *Candy B II* was dragging the seabed about eight to ten miles southwest of Monhegan Island when skipper Norman Brackett and deck hand Richard Sykes hauled in the net and found among the catch of fish a binnacle that was still attached to a section of wooden decking. After doing some research, Brackett determined that the binnacle had come from the *Cornwallis*.

The actual location of the *Cornwallis* is unknown; or if the wreckage is known, it is unidentified. Contemporary official records suggest that the vessel sank where the water was 50 fathoms deep.

In March of 2013, the National Oceanic and Atmospheric Administration wasted a bundle of the taxpayers' money by compiling a 43-page Screening Level Risk Assessment Package on the *Cornwallis*. The avowed purpose of the Package was to assess the environmental risk if the vessel were to release vast quantities of oil that "could pose a substantial pollution threat."

The stupidity of this Package was three-fold. In the first place, the *Cornwallis* was not a tanker that was loaded with a huge quantity of bunker oil, but a freighter that was transporting sugar and molasses: commodities that hardly constitute a menace to the environment. Besides, after 69 years of submergence, the sweet-tasting carbohydrates must long since have dissolved in seawater.

Second, in 1967, the U.S. Coast Guard conducted the Sunken Tanker Project in which it was determined that no wrecks that sank during World War Two contained *any* substantial quantity of their petroleum cargoes, because the oil had long since leaked out a drop at a time through rust holes as the tank compartments slowly disintegrated. It was senseless to repeat a study that was conducted 46 years earlier, with negative results.

Third, NOAA admitted in the Package that it did not know the location of the *Cornwallis*. So even if NOAA had deduced that a substantial risk existed – a deduction that could have been based only on conjecture, and not on any factual findings – it could have done nothing about it. The Package was written and assembled without doing any fieldwork. NOAA relied solely on guesswork.

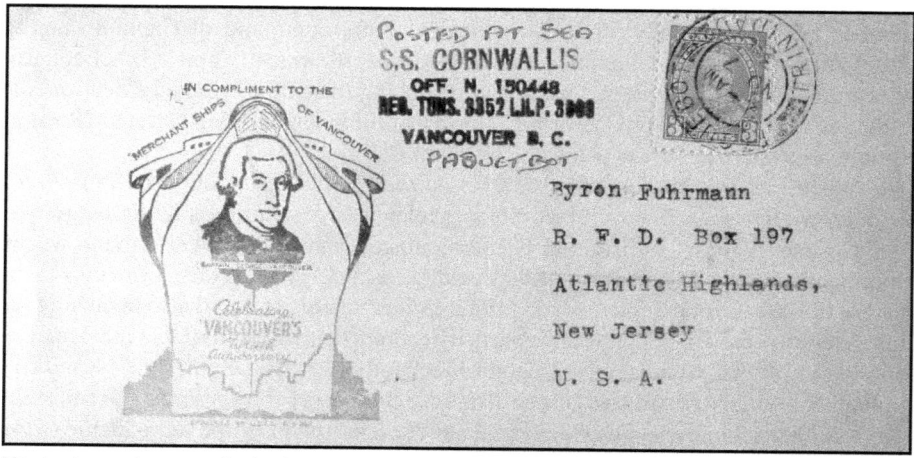

Merchant vessels were authorized to operate as post offices so that seaman could mail letters and packages and receive same. This envelope was posted at sea, then franked and mailed at the next port of call, in this case Trinidad. The word "PAQUEBOT" on the left side of the cancellation is French for "mailboat."

D.T. Sheridan. (From the collection of Dave Clancy.)

D. T. SHERIDAN

Built: 1939
Previous names: None
Gross tonnage: 267
Type of vessel: Tug
Builder: Ira S. Bushey & Sons, Brooklyn, New York
Owner: Sheridan Towing Company, Philadelphia, Pennsylvania
Port of registry: Philadelphia, Pennsylvania
Cause of sinking: Ran aground
Location: Lobster Cove, at the southwest corner of Monhegan Island

Sunk: November 6, 1948
Depth: Visibly exposed on land
Dimensions: 110' x 26' x 13'
Power: diesel engine

GPS: 43-45.369 / 69-19.308

From the collection of Dave Clancy.

What should have been an ordinary tow job turned into disaster when the tugboat *D. T. Sheridan* encountered dense fog as she was hauling a pair of coal-laden barges – the *Blanche Sheridan* and the *Rockhaven* – from Boston to Bangor. Winds in excess of thirty knots did not help matters.

The fog was so thick that the crew of the tugboat could not see the first barge in the string. And the crews of the barges could not see either of the other vessels. Each crew was isolated in a spooky white miasma like a character in a fantasy movie.

Dawn did not alleviate the situation. According to Arthur Fournier, a deck hand on the *Blanche Sheridan*, "All of a sudden, the D.T. is blowing the danger signal: *blat blat blat blat blat*. The captain says to me, 'Go forward and let go the anchor,' and the *Rockhaven* let his anchor go the same time. And there's the D.T. broached sideways on the beach. We ran headfirst onto the beach but didn't turn sideways – our bow was on the beach and our stern in 75 feet of water, and the *Rockhaven* was in 140 feet. His anchor down kept us from swinging sideways."

Quick thinking and prompt action kept the barges from suffering the same fate as the tug. "They [on the *Rockhaven*] put their dory overboard and got the guys from the tug and brought them back to the *Blanche*, and the lighthouse keeper on Monhegan notified the Coast Guard."

The standard profile view favored by artists and photographers. Cheryl Novak poses for scale.

The surf soon rolled the *D.T. Sheridan* onto her port side. Later, another tug towed the barges to their destination, but the *D.T. Sheridan* soon broke up from being pounded against the rocky coast. Monstrous waves from succeeding storms lifted the hull onto land above the normal high tide mark, where it became the subject of a number of artists and photographers.

The wreck is still there and still visible on the rocky spit. The distinct shape of the starboard hull arcs into the air. The rudder and propeller shaft lie on the rocks below, where they are exposed at low tide. Other parts lay scattered about: the fantail abaft the hull, the funnels, deck house, and bridge smashed to pieces farther inland. These rusty steel plates and other components comprise a dire warning to those who go down to the sea in ships.

Monhegan Island is reachable only by boat. Ferries depart daily from Boothbay Harbor, New Harbor, and Port Clyde. These are people ferries only. No vehicles are allowed on the island except for those that are owned by year-round residents, who number around seventy-five. The island measures about a mile in length and half a mile in width, so that hiking some of the extremely rugged trails can be accomplished in a day. Expensive accommodations are available on the island for those who wish to stay overnight.

Day-trippers can cross on a morning ferry, explore the island, and return on an afternoon ferry. Such short-term visitors should note that Monhegan Island is not tourist friendly to daytime visitors. There are no public restrooms anywhere on the island. One small restaurant is located next to the wharf. I saw one mobile vendor – read hotdog stand – that furnished food and drink, but it was closed. Wild apple trees were dropping fruit from their branches, so after consuming the picnic lunch that I brought with me, I lived off the land on these local delicacies. Trees served admirably as latrines.

This oblique angle provides more information than the picture above. Cheryl Novak posing again.

While waiting for the return ferry I witnessed the "reserve" with which single-day guests were treated. The temperature was in the forties, the wind was blowing twenty to twenty-five knots, and rain was falling heavily. Yet, although the ferry was tied to the wharf, ticket-holders were not allow to board. One woman in her seventies, who had no raingear or warm-weather apparel, sought the comfort of the unheated cabin. As she shuffled across the gangplank, a crewmember shouted at her, "Get back!" He told her that boarding time was fifteen minutes before departure.

The wharf has no shelter: no shade from the hot summer sun nor protection from autumn wind and rain. There isn't even a bench for trail-weary legs. A couple dozen wet and shivering people had to stand for half an hour, hunched over and exposed to the elements until the appointed time, under the watchful eyes of the captain and crew who lounged in the dry warmth of the wheelhouse.

There is no doubt about the name of the wreck. It is possible to crawl through holes in the hull to explore the interior. Load marks were placed on the stem the same way as the name: raised beads from a welding torch.

There are no paved roads on the island. Purchase a map when you buy your roundtrip ticket on the mainland. Trails are shown and both named and numbered on the map. There are road signs at the trailheads and intersections. Note that the names and numbers on the map do not always correspond with the names and numbers on the signs. If you are not skilled at orienteering, a compass might be helpful on an overcast day. At least it will point you to the west side of the island.

To reach the wreck site, walk up the hill and turn right at the T onto Monhegan Boulevard (which is unsigned). After a while this single-lane "boulevard" becomes Lobster Cove Road. Continue in a southerly direction. After the road becomes a trail that weaves through a bit of forest, you'll find yourself on a sort of bluff that overlooks the coastline. From here you can see the wreck in the distance, slightly left of straight ahead. Work your way down the rocky path as it winds its way to the wreckage. Do not wear flip-flops unless you have plenty of splints with you. The distance from wharf to wreck is a mile.

EAGLE 56

Built: 1919
Previous names: None
Displacement tonnage: 615
Type of vessel: Patrol boat
Builder: Ford Motor Company, Detroit, Michigan
Owner: U.S. Navy
Sunk: April 23, 1945
Depth: 132 to 150 feet, or 180 to 300 feet
Dimensions: 200' x 25' x 7'
Power: coal-fired steam turbine
Official designation: PE-56
Cause of sinking: Torpedoed by *U-853* (Oberleutnant zur See Helmut Fromsdorf)
Location: Off Portland, Maine
Lat/lon: 43° 29'.2N / 70° 05.6W (typed that way in the Administration Report)
Lat/lon: 43°-30!0 N / 70°-06!9 W (typed that way in USS *Selfridge's* Action Report
Lat/lon: 43°-29.5 N / 70°-07 W (typed that way in the USS *Woolsey's* War Diary
Lat/lon: 43 30 00 N / 70°-06 00 W (typed in "Non-Submarine Contacts" (1968)

World War One created a desperate need for warships of all types. One type that the U.S. Navy needed in quantity was a patrol craft that was intermediate in size and range between wooden-hulled submarine chasers and steel-hulled destroyers. Thus was born the Eagle Boat: a steel-hulled design that measured two hundred feet in length, that could cruise at eighteen knots, and that was armed with a pair of 4-inch deck guns, one 3-inch deck gun, and two .50-caliber machine guns.

At the onset of war, all the usual shipyards were working overtime on the construction of large warships and merchant vessels. This induced the Navy Bureau of Construction and Repair to design a vessel that could be mass-produced at plants that did not engage in shipbuilding. When President Woodrow Wilson thought of mass-production, he naturally thought of the originator of automobile mass-production, Henry Ford. Wilson invited Ford to be a member of the United States Shipping Board, a position that Ford accepted.

Ford had valuable advice to offer with respect to the Eagle Boat design. First, he suggested that the hull be fabricated from flat steel plates instead of rolled steel plates. This would save time not only in the production of the plates, but in fastening the plates to the frame. This accounts for the Eagle Boat's blocky appearance. Second, he proposed the installation of steam turbine engines instead of gasoline engines. The steam turbine was more reliable than the gasoline engine, and was more economical to operate. The Navy accepted his advices.

Ford then built a new assembly plant outside Detroit, Michigan for the construction of the Eagle Boat fleet. Sixty Eagle Boats were constructed and sent down the St. Lawrence River to the open ocean. The end of the war – on November 11, 1918 – halted further production. None of the Eagle Boats engaged the enemy. The peacetime Navy had little use for them. Of the few that were retained, few saw service in World War Two. Some were transferred to the U.S. Coast Guard in 1919. Most were sold to private buyers in the 1930's.

At the outbreak of war, *Eagle 56* was put into action primarily on anti-submarine patrol, sometimes as a convoy escort. In these capacities she roamed along the eastern seaboard, either looking for trouble or protecting merchant vessels. Her first engage-

Generic Eagle Boat. Courtesy of the National Archives.

ment with enemy activity occurred on February 5, 1942, when the *China Arrow* was torpedoed and sunk by the *U-103*. The Eagle Boat was dispatched to search for survivors. Rescue vessels searched for two days before the Coast Guard cutter *Nike* picked up a group of bedraggled men in three lifeboats. During the search, *Eagle 56* reported a U-boat some thirty-five miles east of Five Fathom Bank and dropped depth charges.

Her next engagement occurred on the morning of February 29, 1942, after intercepting a radio transmission from an army patrol plane which had spotted a cluster of life rafts amid a large field of flotsam. *Eagle 56* was in the vicinity, so she rushed to the transmitted location, where she rescued twelve survivors from the U.S. destroyer *Jacob Jones*. One of the survivors died on the way to port.

The *Jacob Jones* had been torpedoed the previous night by the *U-578*. The loss of life was terrible: 134 officers and men. (For details, see *Shipwrecks of Delaware and Maryland*.)

On April 4, 1942, *Eagle 56* picked up a dead body from the *David H. Atwater*.

Eagle 56 was again called to rescue when the *Gypsum Prince* sank after colliding with the *Voco* at the mouth of the Delaware Bay. (For details, see *Shipwrecks of Delaware and Maryland*.) The date was May 3, 1942. The Eagle Boat recovered one body. When she later returned to the wreck site to place a navigational buoy over the sunken freighter, she struck the submerged hull and lost her propeller. The *Allegheny* towed her to the Philadelphia Navy Yard for repairs and a replacement propeller.

The next two years were relatively uneventful for the Eagle Boat. In 1944 she was assigned to the Naval Air Station in Brunswick, Maine. One of her duties was to tow a target so that Navy pilots could practice bombing runs before they were shipped overseas. The day of reckoning for *Eagle 56* was April 23, 1945. She was proceeding from one practice area to another when a tremendous detonation occurred amidships and tore the hull in two.

Lieutenant (j.g.) John Scagnelli was asleep in his bunk when "I was awakened by a terrific explosion. Concussion pulled me right up out of my sack and threw me against the bulkhead and the skin of the ship on the port side. Immediately afterward, the ship started to list to starboard. I went out into the passageway as fast as I could. The passageway was filled with steam. It seemed to me that it was low pressure steam from the pipes leading forward from the boiler to the anchor winch. It was not live, hot steam.

It seems to me that while in the passageway I smelled a sharp odor which reminded me of powder smell but I can be mistaken on this. The ship was headed seaward at the time, but I do not know the course. Ahead of me in the passageway was RM LYNDON. He was bleeding very badly. Blood seemed to be gushing from his head. He may have been in the radio shack at the time. He got into the water ahead of me and I remember calling to him, but he just floated away. When I got on deck immediately aft of the bridge I was on the Port side. I crossed over toward the Starboard. The ship was apparently broken in two just forward of the pressure bulkhead which is the after bulkhead of the boiler room. I noticed that the stack was gone. That is to say, all of the stack was gone except jagged remains which took approximately two (2) feet above deck. In going from my room up to the deck and passageway out, I went up over a ladder which is placed directly above the magazine. The ladder was intact and the passageways through which I passed were filled with steam but did not impress me as being particularly damaged although there was considerable debris in them. Some of the deck plates near the base of the stack seemed to be buckled out and upward. Yet, generally speaking, the deck seemed to be intact, except for the jagged edge where the ship was broken in two. When I got across to the starboard side, the water was about chest deep so that I just swam away from the ship. I had no opportunity to see whether there was any damage visible on the starboard side because it was so well under water as I swam away. I saw the stern float separately from the bow while I was swimming, but I did not see any other object of any kind. My guess would be that when I shoved off from the forward part of the ship that the stern was over 50 yards away, but probably less than 100 yards. The stern sank first and the bow was the last to go under. None of the decks were hot and I have no impression of any discomforting amount of heat at any time while abandoning ship. I saw no vapors or gases coming out of the remains of the stack as I crossed the deck to shove off. The bridge was under water by the time I swam away. My guess is that I was in the water about 20 minutes before the Destroyer picked me up. I have no idea as to the cause of this explosion, except to say that it is inconceivable to me that the boiler explosion could have caused such damage. . . . It is inconceivable to me that there could have been any explosion in the magazine because of the fact that the ladder up which I escaped was, as stated before, intact and I used the same without any difficulty. I am quite sure that there was not more than one explosion but that the entire damage was caused by one terrific concussion. . . . The doctor on the way in did not wash me or clean me up. When I was first interviewed I had not been bathed so you can judge yourself how much oil I swam through. In my judgment oil in the fuel lines and around the boiler and engine rooms would account for all the oil in the water. I do not believe that the fuel tanks were ruptured."

Enlisted survivor Edward Lockhardt was on the watch below, on the starboard side of the after engineers sleeping compartment, when "the explosion threw me inboard. The explosion was not terrific and there wasn't much concussion where I was. I do not think it was a torpedo. I've seen quite a few ships torpedoed and there didn't seem to be enough smoke. The bow was separated from the stern by quite a distance, but I can't say how far. The stern went down first and then in a little while the bow went down. I didn't smell any smoke or other odor. Other than the bow and stern, I did not see any other large objects in the water. I did see quite a lot of dead fish, however, and that is the reason why I have been thinking that it may have been a mine which caused the explosion.

Another enlisted survivor, John Lutrell, was stretched out on the top sack in the after compartment when "there was lots of concussion and blast. The sacks fell down and men were knocked around. I could see the frames breaking and water rushing in the After Escape Hatch. There seemed to be some smoke in the Compartment but it was very light. I guess there were about 15 men in the compartment. I got topside and saw men all over the deck. The ship was in two pieces, the stern at a 45 degree angle. I climbed up on the bulkhead, dove into the water and swam away. I grabbed some driftwood, hung on, and was later picked up by the Destroyer. I think I smelled gas smoke on the idea of carbon dioxide in the Compartment. The bow of the ship was about 200 feet from the stern and I saw both parts go down."

Yet another enlisted survivor, John Wisniewski, was thrown out of his sack. "As soon as I got on the deck, I tried to go amidships to get some life jackets which were stored in the forward part of the after deck house. However, the ship was well under water as I went forward and so I turned around and came aft and went up the ladder to the top of the after deck house as I thought there were life jackets there also. From the top of the after deck house I could look forward and clearly see that the ship was down amidships. . . . At this same time, while I was on the after deck house, I saw a black object about 500 yards away on the starboard bow. It looked exactly like a submarine with a conning tower. . . . I know one of the men who was nearby, perhaps EDWARDS, said 'Dam that sub.' I grabbed an empty 5 gallon can as I could find no life jackets and about that time went under. My dungarees got hooked on a bolt and I remember that I had to tear them to get free. I remember that it took me a long time to come to the surface and when I finally did, I shot out of the water 4 or 5 feet. I remember that I came

Bow view of *Eagle 58* and stern view of *Eagle 33*. (Both courtesy of the National Archives.) Note the narrow hull and crowded conditions on deck.

up on a swell and could see land on my right. I remember that the bow of the Eagle Boat was then on my left and I would judge that the submarine was bearing about 0445 degrees relative to the bow of the Eagle, although I did not see it from the water."

When other vessels in the area observed the explosion, they immediately turned to the scene of the disaster. First to arrive was the USS *Selfridge* (DD-357) sixteen minutes after the explosion. She steamed into the middle of the oil slick and launched a whaleboat. Ten minutes later the Portland Examination vessel (*Nantucket*, LV-112) reached the scene and launched three boats. Rescuers wasted no time in plucking sailors out of the near-freezing water. (Later, the Navy decided that the Portland Examination vessel arrived first, "the destroyer shortly thereafter.")

The *Selfridge* was loitering while boats from the Portland Examination vessel continued to scour the area, "when a sound contact was made. . . . The [whale]boat was cast off, speed increased to fifteen (15) knots and a depth charge attack was made at 1253 with negative results. . . . After the attack the contact was not picked up again. In the meantime the USS *Woolsey* had arrived on the scene and was close aboard when the attack was made. After searching for a few minutes, the *Selfridge* proceeded to the vicinity of the examination vessel to receive three (3) survivors from that ship. When all survivors were on board, *Selfridge* proceeded to Portland, Maine and transferred the survivors to the U.S. Naval Dispensary, Grand Trunk Pier, Portland, Maine." (Note that the *Selfridge* dropped eleven depth charges.)

Reports differed about the explosion, sinking, and aftermath of the *Eagle 56*. According to the *Selfridge's* initial report of April 24, "There was a white column of smoke or vapor about one hundred (100) feet high. It appeared larger than that from a depth charge, persisted for at least twenty seconds, and had the appearance of an external, rather than an internal, underwater explosion."

Also from the *Selfridge*: "The explosion was very heavy; the ship broke in two immediately. The stern section sank in about two minutes; the bow section sank vertically at 1228 [about fourteen minutes after the explosion]. The sound contact was sharp with well defined trace; it was plotted practically stationary. It was about 1000 yards outside the slick of the explosion." (Later, the Navy adopted sinking times as seven minutes and seventeen minutes respectively.)

In the *Selfridge's* Antisubmarine Action Report, of April 25, the sonar target was described slightly differently: "The echo was sharp and narrow, indicating the presence of some metallic subject, rather than bottom reverberations. The contact may have been on the stern section of the PE56, which had sunk some thirty minutes earlier."

The initial death toll was given as fifty-four. Later, this number was reduced to forty-nine because some men were found to be on leave or AWOL, and were not onboard at the time of the catastrophe. Only two bodies were recovered from the water.

In retrospect, it is fortunate that anyone survived the sinking of the Eagle Boat. The water temperature was 42°, and "no survivors were wearing life jackets or warm clothing." It should also be noted that "several officers of the *Selfridge* went over the side to assist in rescue."

I first wrote about the *Eagle 56* in 1989, in *Track of the Gray Wolf*: a comprehensive look at U-boat warfare in the Eastern Sea Frontier (from Maine to Florida). I had no preconceived notions about how the *Eagle 56* was lost. I simply accepted the information in primary historical records from both American and German archival sources.

The *U-853* was operating off the coast of Maine at the time the Eagle Boat blew up and sank. German sources credited the *U-853* with the "kill," and I had no reason to doubt the conclusions of the Allied Assessment Committee, which worked hand-in-hand with German naval historians after Germany's capitulation, in order to ascribe "kills" to specific U-boats that were known to have been operating in the area at the time of a particular action.

Although the Assessment Committee did not have access to Ultra decrypts of intercepted German naval transmissions, it did have access to German records that survived Allied bombing missions. As a result, missing information introduced a bias in the way the Committee ascribed "kills."

Germany published the accumulated U-boat information in 1968. An English edition – updated and revised – was published in 1983: *Axis Submarine Successes 1939-1945*. In the preface, Jurgen Rohwer wrote, "The gradual though still incomplete release of British and American Ultra signal descriptions that began in 1975 has enabled us to fill quite a few war-related gaps in Axis and, particularly, German U-boat command records."

Much to England's chagrin, the U.S. declassified World War Two documents after thirty years. The British withheld its classified documents from the public for fifty years. Thus the secret of Ultra was trumped by a more lenient American declassification protocol.

The *U-853* did not return from its patrol. It was depth-charged to destruction on May 6, 1945: one day after torpedoing and sinking the *Black Point*, and one day before Germany's unconditional surrender. There were no survivors. (For details of both sinkings, see *Shipwrecks of Rhode Island and Connecticut*.) It was credited with sinking the *Eagle 56*.

However, two other U-boats were operating off the coast of Maine during the final month of the war: *U-857* and *U-879*. Neither one of those U-boats survived either. Thus there is no way to establish with certainty which U-boat sank the *Eagle 56*. I explained this situation when I revised and expanded *Track of the Gray Wolf* and retitled it *The Fuhrer's U-boats in American Waters*, in 2006.

Little matter: the historical record still indicated that *Eagle 56* must have been torpedoed by a U-boat. The only doubt was which one of the three fired the fateful and fatal torpedo. The Tenth Fleet was unable to determine or predict their precise locations because none of them made radio broadcasts whose locations could be triangulated, and whose messages could be intercepted and decrypted. Thus when American Ultra intelligence was declassified and examined in detail, it did not clarify the situation.

It was not until Paul Lawson contacted me in the late 1990's that I learned that the U.S. Navy disagreed with the Assessment Committee's later evaluation, which was confirmed by German naval records, and determined instead that the Eagle Boat "probably" sank due to a boiler explosion. Worse yet, the Navy did not revise its conclusion even after the Committee found otherwise. This meant that the Eagle Boat's crewmembers were denied certain honors and medals that they should have received as a result of enemy action.

The majority of surviving witnesses testified that they spotted a submarine at a distance of approximately five hundred yards, or between one-quarter and one-half mile. They also testified that the concussion rose upward and from the starboard side, tossing sailors against bulkheads as if they were tenpins.

Observers on nearby vessels saw the ship rise several feet into the air as a result of the explosion. A plume of water shot from one hundred to three hundred feet into the sky. The water column endured for as long as fifteen seconds.

On the other hand, two Navy boiler experts testified that they thought it might be possible for a boiler explosion to damage the hull badly enough for it to crack, and that wave-generated twisting motions could complete the rupture of the hull. However, none of the survivors noted the presence of superheated steam, and all testified that the seas that day were mild.

On June 1, 1945 – after the Court of Inquiry completed its investigation into the probable cause of the loss of *Eagle 56* – the Navy officially adopted the "boiler explosion" opinion, but with reservations that were annotated by Rear Admiral Felix Gygax: "The Convening Authority has determined by separate investigation that as far as is known there were no friendly mines, torpedoes, depth charges or other explosive mechanisms that were unaccounted for and that could have caused the explosion that resulted in the loss of the U.S.S. EAGLE (PE 56). With respect to that part of the opinion of the court of inquiry giving the cause of the accident as that of a boiler explosion, the Convening Authority considers that the evidence does not support this unqualified conclusion and believes that there is at least equal evidence to support the conclusion that the explosion was that of a device outside the ship, the exact nature of which is undetermined. It might have been an enemy mine or an enemy torpedo. It would seem that the boiler explosion, if it occurred, and in any case, the disrupted steam connections, could have been incident to, and could have augmented the effect of, a water column produced by an explosion outside the vessel."

Despite the allowable concession – or equivocation, if you prefer – the officially accepted cause left the crewmembers high and dry with regard to awards such as the Purple Heart.

This was where Lawson took the bull by the horns, or the stem by the hawser. Single-handedly he led a campaign to convince the modern Navy to reverse the opinion, and to recognize that the Eagle Boat's men either died or survived at the hands of enemy aggression. He worked on this project prodigiously for years. Not only did he accumulate a mountain of historical documents, but he located some surviving crewmembers. Nor did his energies cease there. He also organized search trips that were dedicated to locating the two sections of the hull on the bottom of Casco Bay.

In this latter goal he was unsuccessful. Garry Kozak, one of the foremost side-scan sonar experts in the world, used the latest model Klein side-scan unit to examine the rocky seabed where the *Eagle 56* was supposed to have sunk. In the statistical sidebar I have listed four extrapolated positions, all of which stand in close agreement. Lawson found others that confirmed them. Yet no wreckage was found anywhere in the vicinity.

The failure to locate the wreck did not lie with the equipment or the operator: both of which (or whom) are beyond reproach. The failure must lie in contemporary positional data. Or perhaps the destruction was so severe that the hull has collapsed over the intervening years, and was buried by accumulating sediments.

More important than the failure to locate the wrecked sections of the *Eagle 56* was Lawson's resounding success in convincing the Navy to reverse its original opinion – "Not enemy action – Explosion" – and to give the Eagle Boat's crewmembers the recognition that they so justly deserved.

Hail! Hail!

EDNA M. McKNIGHT

Built: 1918
Previous names: None
Gross tonnage: 1,326
Type of vessel: Wooden-hulled four-masted schooner
Builder: R. L. Bean, Camden, Maine
Owner: Boston Maritime Corporation, Boston, Massachusetts
Port of registry: Boston, Massachusetts (at time of abandonment)
Cause of sinking: Abandoned
Location: Mill Cove, Boothbay Harbor

Sunk: 1928
Depth: Visibly exposed
Dimensions: 209' x 41' x 20'
Power: sail

Lat/lon: 43-51-07 N / 69-38-06 W

Not every vessel on the high seas had an exciting career. The *Edna M. McKnight* is one whose career might best be described as lackluster. She had the misfortune to be built at a time when the age of sail had long since passed. She was somewhat of a dinosaur in the land of mammals. In this case the mammals were equivalent to steamships that could proceed fast and reliably, and did not have to depend upon the moods of the heaven's breath for propulsion.

She worked in the coal and lumber trades for nearly a decade before she vanished from the registries. Her last appearance in the *Record* of the American Bureau of Ships was 1927. She did not actually sink. She was abandoned on the mud flats in Mill Cove, where a handful of other outdated sailing vessels kept her company. At low tide she could be high and dry. At high tide only the lower part of her hull was submerged.

According to the reminiscences of A.F. Willis, who sailed into Boothbay Harbor

A postcard picture of laid-up schooners in Boothbay Harbor. The *Edna M. McKnight* appears to be third from the right, already dismasted. Perhaps images like this are why Maine is known as the schooner graveyard State.

The worse for wear. (From the collection of Dave Clancy.)

in 1937 as a cabin boy aboard the two-masted auxiliary schooner *Annie and Reuben*, at that time seven hulks shared the schooner graveyard at Mill Cove: *Courtney C. Houck, Edna M. McKnight, Freeman, Harry G. Deering, Helen Barnet Gring, Maude M. Morey*, and *Zebedee E. Cliff*.

Information about the final dispositions of these vessels is sketchy. Local lore has it that the *Edna M. McKnight* was set afire some time during her residence, perhaps in celebration of the end of World War Two. Today that scenario is difficult to confirm. The wreck has broken down so much throughout the decades that hardly any of the hull protrudes above the surface of the water. Now the once-majestic schooner is little more than a faded memory and some scattered ribs and planks.

Nearby but no longer visibly exposed lie the *Courtney C. Houck* and the *Elizabeth Cook*. The other schooners that Willis mentioned were towed away.

Today the hull is almost out of sight but contiguous under water.

EDWARD J. LAWRENCE

Built: 1908
Previous names: None
Gross tonnage: 3,350
Type of vessel: Wooden-hulled six-masted schooner
Builder: Percy & Small, Bath, Maine
Owner: Chase, Leavitt & Company, Portland, Maine
Port of registry: None (registration suspended)
Cause of sinking: Fire
Location: A few hundred feet north-northeast of Fort Gorges, on the west side of the Little Diamond Island, near the entrance to Portland Harbor

Sunk: December 27, 1925
Depth: 40 feet
Dimensions: 320' x 50' x 23'
Power: sail

GPS: 43-40.132 / 70-13.134

The *Edward J. Lawrence* led a valuable if undistinguished career as a work-a-day collier that largely transported coal from Norfolk, Virginia to various ports in Maine. Many a business manager and homeowner owe the warmth in their shops and houses to cargoes of black diamonds that were delivered to local docks for burning in their furnaces. Think of wooden-hulled sailing vessels as the oil and propane delivery trucks of the early 1900's.

The *Edward J. Lawrence* might have been completely forgotten by modern day historians had it not been for Thomas O'Connor, who wrote a detailed account of the schooner's death throes. According to him, fire erupted from the forward hold when the schooner was anchored off Fish Point, in Portland Harbor, two days after Christmas of 1927, shortly after noon. A passing motorist – Clinton T. Swett – spotted tendrils of smoke wafting into the air from the moored schooner. He called the fire department which set subsequent events in motion.

Responding to the call were the Portland fire boat, the Coast Guard cutter *Ossipee*, and the Customs boat *Chicopee*. They started battling the blaze by first tying up to the bow of the schooner's hull: the *Ossipee* on the port side, the *Chicopee* on the starboard

The *Edward J. Lawrence* in her glory days. (From the collection of Bill Carter.)

Sister ship *Eleanor A. Percy* receiving coal from the same dock from which the *Edward J. Lawrence* received coal, in Norfolk, Virginia. (From the author's collection.)

side. The *Ossipee* ran fire hoses to the smoking hatchway while the *Chicopee* ran same into the boiler room.

The *Edward J. Lawrence* was equipped with a donkey boiler to furnish steam for the capstan and the hoisting machinery. By not having to weigh anchor and hoist the sails by hand, as in the old days of sailing vessels, it was possible to man the schooner with a handful of sailors instead of dozens.

By the time the firefighters commenced operations, fierce flames had burned through the bulkhead that separated the boiler room from the forward hold. Thus the reason for attacking the blaze from two directions and working toward the middle.

Firefighting was quickly hampered by extremely low temperatures. Portland recorded 4 degrees Fahrenheit. It was presumed to be below zero on the waterfront. Water from the fire hoses froze on contact with wood, turning the deck into a skating rink. Variable winds fanned the flames and blew black coal smoke in all directions. Without crampons on their rubber boots, firefighters slid across the slippery deck, often falling to their knees and buttocks, or landing horizontal on the ice-covered deck. Some of them were knocked backward by the force of the water that blasted from the nozzles. What must have looked like a slapstick comedy would have been funny to onlookers had the situation not been so dire.

Extinguishing the fire proved to be futile as flames erupted through the hatchways, preventing firefighters from pouring water on the base of the conflagration. Nonetheless, firefighters stayed on the job all afternoon. Then the worst case scenario occurred: the wind aligned itself with the collier's length so that it fanned the flames aft until fire and smoke vented from the after hold. The whole interior of the schooner was afire.

By this time firefighters had poured so much freezing water into the holds that the schooner assumed a starboard list. If she sank in place she might block the channel. Firefighters severed one of the anchor chains. The *Ossipee* and the tugboat *Cumberland* commenced to shove the burning collier toward shoal water in hopes of grounding her in an out-of-the-way place. They succeeded just in time, for the *Edward J. Lawrence* settled gently to the bottom while her upperworks continued to blaze until the hulk became little more than a burned-out hulk.

And there she stayed.

The fire-blackened remains have been a popular dive site for many years. The hull below the waterline is partially intact, with ribs rising more than 20 feet off the bottom. Finding the wreck used to be easy: look for the tips of exposed ribs that protruded above the surface of the sea. Nowadays, ongoing collapse has reduced the wreck's vertical profile, but the remaining hull is still visually stunning.

The wreck can be a hazard to navigation, particularly at low tide. On June 4, 2011, the tourist schooner *Wendameen* ran onto the wreckage and stuck there like a bug that was mounted on a pin. As the tide ebbed, the schooner started to list as the side that was not impaled fell away with the falling water level.

"The wreck [of the *Wendameen*] occurred at 1740 a few hundred feet north-northeast of Fort Gorges on the west side of Little Diamond Island, near the entrance to Portland Harbor. Winds and seas were calm when the grounding occurred. The tide was ebbing but still two hours before low tide."

Although the wreck of the *Edward J. Lawrence* is marked on the chart, there was no warning buoy to alert mariners about the dangerous obstruction.

A Falmouth police boat rescued the *Wendameen's* passengers and crew. There were no injuries, just inconvenience.

Rather than attempt to yank the schooner off the wreckage, and possibly puncture the hull, salvors waited until the next high tide gently lifted the vessel off the obstruction. "*Wendameen* was not damaged in the incident and was back in service the following day."

This is the kind of wreck that I like to write about: one in which no injuries or fatalities occurred, and in which the vessel survived the incident without harm or destruction. And one in which the attending sightseers and vacationers will have an exciting experience to talk about for the rest of their lives.

As for the *Edward J. Lawrence*, she still sits silently on the seabed, waiting for divers who wish to explore her burnt and collapsing remains.

Hot time in cold weather. Note the boat's fire hose spraying water. (From the collection of Bill Carter.)

EMPIRE KNIGHT

Built: 1942
Previous names: None
Gross tonnage: 7,244
Type of vessel: Freighter
Builder: William Doxford & Sons, Sunderland, England
Owner: Ministry of War Transport (Buries Markes, managers)
Port of registry: Sunderland, England
Cause of sinking: Ran aground (on Boon Island Ledge)
GPS: (bow) 43-07.601 / 70-24.898

Sunk: February 11, 1944
Depth: 20 to 120 feet (bow); 250 feet (stern)
Dimensions: 428' x 56' x 35'
Power: twin diesel engines

(stern) 43-06.200 / 70-27.100

By 1944, the U-boat war off the eastern seaboard was just about finished. That year, only five vessels were attacked in the Eastern Sea Frontier, which stretched from the Canadian border to northern Florida. Of these, only two sank. Compare this to the first six months of 1942, when Nazi U-boats sank more than one hundred vessels.

The east coast was so safe that many coastwise vessels traveled independently: not in convoy and without escort. But natural marine obstacles were still a hazard.

According to a special report in the War Diary of the ESF, "The British Steamship *Empire Knight* enroute to New York from St. John, New Brunswick, ran aground on Boone Island Ledge about 1423 11 February 1944. At this time, the wind was approximately Force 7 from the Northeast with a rough sea. Storm warnings of snow and zero visibility had been forecast and broadcast for this area at 0600 the same day...

"It will be noted from enclosure (1) that immediate steps were taken to send the nearest available seagoing Naval and Coast Guard tugs to the scene. Any assistance rendered to the *Empire Knight* to get her off the ledge would have to be given at the earliest practicable moment owing to the rough sea and force of wind from the northeast. The wind was expected to increase to Force 10. The nearest Naval port to the scene was Portsmouth, New Hampshire, and the next nearest was Casco Bay. One of these, the *Abnaki* was scheduled to depart for the Cape Cod Canal and to points south about one-half hour after receipt of distress signal and would, therefore, pass near Boone Island Ledge. Efforts to divert this tug were unsuccessful. Another seagoing tug, the *Kalmia*, at Casco was required for services at Casco. The third one, *Arikara*, was not yet ready for active service at sea. The tug, *Falcon* at Portsmouth was made available at once, but this vessel required time to get up steam. The Coast Guard tug *Kaw* was at the Cape Cod Canal and would probably require twenty hours to reach the scene due to the heavy seas. The *Wandank* was at Newport assigned to important tests of the Bureau of Ordnance by verbal orders from the Office of the Chief of Naval Operations.

"The Coast Guard Buoy Tender *Cactus* was at Rockland and the Coast Guard Buoy Tender *Ilex* was at Portland. The AM-98 (USS *Firm*) was on patrol about 25 miles away from the scene. The Net Tender *Gumtree* was in Portland. All the available vessels that could be of assistance were ordered to proceed to the scene as quickly as possible.

"In view of the reported condition of the *Empire Knight* as well as the state of the sea, it was apparent that the ship would not be able to last long on this ledge and that

Official U.S. Coast Guard photo.

it was necessary to rescue the personnel aboard as soon as practicable. The location of the *Empire Knight* under sea, wind and visibility conditions existing made it problematic just how much these vessels could do in the matter of rescue. This was especially true if the ship broke up during the night. A late weather forecast indicated a wind shift to the northwest in the morning which should assist in the rescue of survivors by providing better visibility and by possibly beating down the sea. The master of the *Empire Knight* was given this forecast and he decided to hold off abandoning ship until daybreak.

"The AM-98 (USS *Firm*) arrived at the scene about 1800 but was unable to get closer than about 1000 yards. This vessel, however, remained nearby in contact with the *Empire Knight* during the night and stood by to be of immediate assistance should the vessel begin to break up.

"During the night of 11 and 12 February, the following vessels arrived at the scene: AM-98 USS *Firm*, USS *Falcon*, USS *Gumtree*, USCG Buoy Tender *Cactus*. These vessels stood by. In the meantime, the Coast Guard motor life boats that had attempted to reach the vessel were forced to return owing to the state of the sea. Upon receipt of the message from the master of the *Empire Knight* that he would abandon ship at daybreak 12 February, all vessels stood in as close as practicable. The *Falcon*, however, had difficulty owing to the Quandrant [sic] room and after hold being flooded.

"At daybreak on 12 February, the ship was sighted on Boon Island Ledge headed north. Apparently, one-third of the vessel was on the ledge and two-thirds in the open water with heavy seas breaking over her and around her. At or about 0820 the *Empire Knight* attempted to abandon ship. The first life boat lowered, however, capsized and almost immediately after that the ship was seen to buckle about 115 feet from the bow throwing men and stores into the sea. The *Firm*, *Gumtree*, and *Cactus* attempted to rescue the survivors in the water and while engaged in this operation, the stern fell off clear of the ledge but was immediately covered by a snow squall. After the living survivors in the water were picked up, an immediate search was instituted for the stern of the *Empire Knight* which had apparently floated clear and on an even keel. This search was immediately unsuccessful. Having no proof, however, that the stern had sunk, the search for the missing stern of the *Empire Knight* was continued with all available vessels and aircraft until 1900 14 February. By this time, it was clearly evident that the stern had sunk very shortly after leaving the bow. Wreckage coming to surface 14 February indicated its approximate position.

"There was only a very short period during which a boat could get close enough to the bow of the *Empire Knight* to inspect it and to make certain that no survivors were aboard the bow. As late as daylight Sunday, 13 February, the seas were breaking over the bow masthead high. The shift of wind to the northwest gradually beat down the sea enough for ComSur (Commander L.C. McEwen) to make a close inspection of the bow in a small boat at or about 1500. Orders had been issued to make certain that no survivors were still alive in the bow of the *Empire Knight*. A further inspection was made shortly after by the Coast Guard motor life boat from the Island of Shoals. No survivors were aboard.

"Inasmuch as the tug *Resolute* was the duly assigned Salvage tug acting under the Bureau of Ships this vessel remained to conduct salvage operations after the search for the stern was discontinued, and the rescue vessels had returned to bases. The AM-98, however, was ordered to remain with the *Resolute* in order to be of assistance.

"Owing to the heavy seas and bad weather with consequent interference to the vessels arriving or remaining at the scene, it was necessary to change the ComSur at intervals.

"In answer to the inquiry as to why one vessel did not remain as near as practicable to the stern once it had broken loose from the bow, the ComSur (at that time Lt. I.B. Warner, U.S.N.R.) replied that his immediate concern was the rescue of men already thrown into the icy waters; he further stated that with the heavy breaking of seas and with boxes, debris, and flotsam on the surface of the sea, it was very difficult to pick out living survivors. Consequently, he felt that all three ships in the area were required for the rescue of survivors actually sighted in the water. The stern had, in his opinion, apparently floated clear so that the men aboard the stern should have been temporarily safe.

"The commanding officer of the *Firm*, who was also acting as ComSur at the time the ship buckled, is deserving of special mention for his part in the rescue operations. He was the first to arrive at the scene and remained nearest to the *Empire Knight*, and he rescued most of the survivors by good seamanship and by his foresight in rigging floating trailing life lines. Three of his men jumped overboard to save three helpless sailormen which further complicated their final rescue. The AM-98 picked up 13 living survivors; *Cactus* picked up seven. Special mention should also be made of the *Cactus* which proceeded at once to the scene from Rockland with 150 tons of buoys aboard and took an active part in the rescue operations although forced at one time to seek shelter in order to restow her shifted cargo.

"Although considerable general information has been secured from the survivors of the *Empire Knight* as to the courses previous to its grounding, the only reliable information can be summarized as follows:

The magnetic compasses had not been compensated since September.

The last Atlantic Coast land mark sighted was at approximately 0900, 11 February. This had not been definitely identified.

Ship had had a quartering and following sea from the northeast for about twenty-four hours with bad visibility conditions.

Boone Island Ledge buoy was sighted off the port beam at or about 1410, distance one-half to one mile. Ship was making revolutions for seven knots.

The *Empire knight* slowed down very shortly after sighting the ledge buoy and proceeded to turn to port finally striking the ledge headed in a northerly direction with the Boone Island Ledge buoy on the starboard side.

The record of soundings taken and the bearing and distance of Boone Island Ledge buoy when firs sighted indicated the that *Empire Knight* was not on the course reported by the survivors (probably due to the compasses) and also not at the position they thought they were when Boone Island Ledge buoy was first sighted."

I should like to mention that this is the longest and most complete action report that I have ever encountered in the War Diary of the Eastern Sea Frontier. It must have been a slow day – or a slow year – and the author (Captain John S. Barloon) had nothing better to do with his time as Acting Commander.

There was one short official follow-up that is of interest: "On February 20 a patrol plane from Brunswick sighted a lifeboat which was apparently empty but with tarpaulin and some lumber aboard. Since it was sighted in the area of 42-55N, 69-25W, the wreckage was very likely from the *Empire Knight*. The *K-9* [a blimp] on a special mission also reported tires, wheels, and boxes in the area. The *Migrant* was dispatched on a special mission to search for the lifeboat and to recover as much as practicable. The results of the search for the lifeboat were negative and she was ordered to discontinue the search on the morning of the 21st.

"However, in the vicinity of 43-02N, 69-22W the *Migrant* picked up seventy-three truck tires mounted on wheel rims and a carton of ether addressed to Chunking, China. The tires, which had been made in Canada and which were stamped 'Military' were taken to Pier #1, East Boston where they were to remain until orders for their disposal might be forthcoming from CESF [Commander of the Eastern Sea Frontier]."

Oddly, attached to the War Diary was a newspaper clipping that presented a photograph of the bow of the *Empire Knight*, high and dry on the ledge. The caption read, "All that was left of 7,000-ton British merchantman that went aground on Boon Ledge, off Portsmouth, N. H. in blinding snowstorm last Friday. Photograph taken from U. S. Coast Guard plane. Ship broke in two and stern section sank out of sight of rescue vessels standing by. Twenty of crew were rescued and bodies of 13 others recovered. Eleven, including master, are missing."

Note that in accordance with standing orders, information released to the press from the ESF excluded the name of the vessel.

The daily log of the War Diary of the ESF offered a more succinct account than the special report, but contained additional information: "Another month passed with no positive proof of enemy submarines operating in Frontier waters during the entire period. Unfortunately, however, winter storms and high winds of blizzard proportions resulted in a series of groundings and collisions which caused some loss of life and one sinking. The worst of these was the case of the British cargo vessel SS *Empire Knight* which ran aground on Boon Island Ledge about twelve miles off York, Maine, during the heaviest snowstorm of the winter on 11 February. At 1500 on that day, Radio Amagansett intercepted distress messages from the *Empire Knight* stating that she was aground, taking water and laboring heavily under the pounding of heavy seas. Several rescue vessels and three tugs were soon on their way to the scene. At 2114 on 11 February, the *Empire Knight* reported she had taken 14 feet of water and did not believe she could be refloated. Later she reported that she would have to abandon ship by daylight or earlier. At 0400 the USS *Firm* (AM), which had been on patrol in the area, reported that she was within one mile of the vessel. She was unable to approach too close because of the fifty-foot rollers building up along the ledge on which the *Empire Knight* was being battered. At 0830 on the morning of 12 February, the ship buckled and broke in two, the stern falling off clear of the ledge while the bow remained fast aground. 'We jumped just as the ship broke in two between the saloon and the third hatch,' one of the survivors stated. The rescue vessels which had been unable to offer assistance immediately proceeded to the rescue of those swimming in the water or holding to lifebelts and flotsam. Out of the crew of 44, only 20 were recovered before the icy water numbed and killed them. Fourteen bodies were picked up and were subsequently given burial in the Navy Yard Cemetery at Portsmouth."

The forward section posed as a visible reminder of the midwinter catastrophe until 1954, at which time a storm knocked the wreck off its rocky perch and scattered the parts down the slope of the ledge. Hull plates sloughed off like leaves in autumn. The cargo in the forward hold spilled out, and through the action of the sea was tossed helter-skelter over the uneven surface from a depth of 20 feet to 120 feet.

Today the bow is a popular dive site because there is so much wreckage to explore and so much cargo to investigate. At the time of her loss, the *Empire Knight* was transporting a mostly military cargo, the majority of which consisted of two steam locomotives, automobile and jeep parts, rifles, munitions, artillery shells, tank treads, copper coils, canned milk, ammonium sulfate fertilizer, and whiskey (remember that this was a British vessel). Divers commonly find large shell casings and grindstones in a debris field that is the size of an elongated baseball field. The locomotives are extant but hardly recognizable.

In the summer of 1990, I had to good fortune to meet Bob Higgins. He was the organizer of the "The *Empire Knight* Project" for which he incorporated an outfit that was named Atlantic Marine Research and Recovery. According to his prospectus, he started intensive research of the stern of the *Empire Knight* in 1983, the location of which at that time was unknown. This was by far the largest section of the wreck, comprising everything from the wheelhouse aft, or some two thirds of the hull that included three of the five cargo holds.

Higgins began actively searching for the stern wreckage in 1985. His search equipment consisted of a depth sounder installed on his 43-foot vessel which was appropriately named *Prospector*. In 1987 he ran over a target that fit the search parameters of the missing section of *Empire Knight* with regard to size, shape, and location. In 1988 he obtained the services of Garry Kozak, of Klein Associates, to conduct a side-scan sonar survey of the suspect site. The resulting imagery confirmed that the target could be nothing other than the long-lost stern.

Higgins immediately hired a remotely operated vehicle (ROV) from the University of New Hampshire. Mounted on the "mini-rover" was a video camera. Throughout the remainder of 1988 and in 1989, the video camera recorded footage that provided the layout of the wreck. He also conducted additional side-scan sonar surveys of the wreck and its surroundings. These various surveys confirmed that diving operations and salvage recovery were feasible.

The wreck was in remarkably good condition. The hull was basically intact with most of the steel plates in place. A lifeboat hung in its davits atop the port side of the wheelhouse. Despite the sharp list – the wreck lay nearly on its side – the smokestack was still standing. Deck-mounted cargo booms angled down into the seabed. The after doghouse retained its shape and structure if not its integrity.

Most important of all, the hatch covers were missing: likely blown off by air that was compressed as the hull dived to the bottom and filled with water. Through the

Ice coating the bow of the *Empire Knight*. (Courtesy of the National Archives.)

openings the cargo was plainly visible and easily accessible.

At the time I met Higgins, he had lost the mini-rover when it got entangled in fishing nets that shrouded portions of the wreck. It was located at cargo hold number two. He told me that it was worth $25,000. I offered to retrieve it for him. I wanted no compensation. I wanted only to dive on the wreck and take photographs.

So far Higgins had been overly friendly. At my suggestion he became guarded. He did not doubt my ability or experience on scuba because he already knew my reputation. I was in top shape for a dive to the depth of the *Empire Knight*, for within the previous three months I had made two dives on the *Ethel C* (at a depth of 190 feet), four dives on the *Araby Maid* (210 feet), four dives on the *Monitor* (230 feet), one dive on the *Rhein* (240 feet), five dives on the *Andrea Doria* (240 feet), and four dives on the *Wilkes-Barre* (250 feet). Two weeks later I dived on the German battleship *Ostfriesland*, at 380 feet.

What cooled Higgins' ardor had nothing to do with me personally. I did not learn the truth until later. Higgins' sudden caution had to do with a competing salvor. He did not want to take a chance that I might have some association with his competitor, and give the location of the wreck to him. I did not have any association with his competitor, did not know who it was, and did not know anything about the legal battle that was brewing.

The competitor was known as Strategic Salvors. Owner Jerome Burke claimed that he "bought information pinpointing the wreck in 1979," filed for salvage rights in 1988, but so far had not commenced salvage operations.

Not to take sides, but I cannot refrain from pointing out that buying information that supposedly pinpoints a wreck site is not the same as positively locating and identifying that wreck, and side-scanning and videotaping that wreck. To bolster this contention, Burke admitted that he knew only the "approximate location" of the wreck.

Furthermore, according to Admiralty law, a potential salvor cannot simply roam around the world laying claims to abandoned shipwrecks to stick in his back pocket as a way to prevent other outfits from salvaging them; a court-appointed salvor must *work* a wreck – continuously – or lose his salvage rights by dint of lack of performance of his duty as a court appointed custodian.

Further still, to establish an Admiralty claim, a salvor must take a piece of wreckage into the courtroom in order to prove that he has taken possession of the wreck. Burke's legal position was specious at best.

By 1990, Strategic Salvors had not done any salvage work on the *Empire Knight*. And by the end of that year, Bob Higgins' divers had begun recovering copper coils: more than $7,000 worth.

Meanwhile, Higgins' affirmative action and the resulting court battle with Strategic Salvors triggered a response that put both salvage outfits out of business with regard to the *Empire Knight*. His divers located canisters of mercury that were worth far more than coils of copper wire.

In Higgins' prospectus, he noted that the stowage plan listed not only 3,000 copper coils that weighed 250 pounds each, but mercury in "221 cast iron, glass lined, sealed flasks, each about 9" tall and 5" in diameter, and weighing about 76 lbs. each."

The Coast Guard had a fit when it obtained this information. The agency did not give a wit about 375 tons of copper (worth about a million dollars), but it was very much concerned about eight tons of mercury (minus the weight of the flasks). Both salvors wanted to recover the mercury for the profit it would entail. But government agencies objected to letting them do so. Ironically, those agencies also objected to leaving the mercury on the bottom.

What followed was a boondoggle of immense proportions. Or perhaps it should be called a Boon Island Ledge doggle.

The Coast Guard, the Environmental Protection Agency, and Maine's Department of Marine Resources employed standard scare tactics to raise a ruckus which completely obviated ongoing litigation over salvage rights, whining that mercury was considered to be a toxic substance which, if ingested, could work its way up the food chain. They ranted about the possibility of birth defects, brain damage, adverse neurological effects, and so on.

In its wisdom, the government decided that neither commercial salvage outfit should be allowed to recover the mercury, and that instead the government should hire a different commercial salvage outfit to do the job. In other words, instead of letting one of the con-

Side-scan sonar image of the stern of the *Empire Knight*. (Courtesy of Garry Kozak, of Klein Associates.)

tending outfits do the job at its own expense, and at no cost to American taxpayers, the government hired a commercial salvage outfit and *paid* to have the mercury recovered.

One official boneheaded attitude was that eight tons of mercury was an awful lot toxin to let loose in a prime fishing area, should there be a catastrophic spill during its recovery. These deskbound quarterbacks must have assumed that the entire eight tons of mercury would be raised in one fell swoop that could be spilled or dispersed by accident, thus poisoning the entire coast of Maine. It seems never occurred to them that a commercial salvor would raise only one flask at a time.

Another gross misconception of officialdom was its Hollywood vision of shipwrecks: that wrecks sat on the bottom as if they had docked there, upright and intact like a newly constructed building or, in this case, a hardware store, waiting for someone to walk through the doorway and grab items off the shelves. Every wreck-diver knows and accepts that shipwrecks are found in various degrees of collapse and decay; that the ocean is a reducing chemical bath which rots and rusts the components of a wreck and everything on or inside the wreck.

The Coast Guard's first action was to order Higgins "to refrain from further salvage activity until the situation could be more thoroughly assessed.

"Over the next year, the COTP [Captain of the Port] convened an incident Specific Regional Response Team (RPT) consisting of representatives from the Maine Department of Environmental Protection, the New Hampshire Department of Environmental Services, the Maine Department of Marine Resources, the New Hampshire Department of Fish and Game, the U.S. Environmental Protection Agency, and the U.S. Coast Guard to gather information about the M/V *Empire Knight* and its cargo, and to identify possible courses of action.

"During the summer of 1991, the Maine Department of Marine Resources collected samples of bottom sediment around the stern portion of the *Empire Knight* to determine if mercury was present and, if so, to what extent. Laboratory analyses of the samples revealed levels of mercury consistent with background levels with some exceptions, rendering them inconclusive on whether mercury had been on board the M/V *Empire Knight* at the time of its sinking."

After two years of typical bureaucratic inaction, "In the spring of 1993, the COTP, in consultation with the RRT, determined that the possible presence of mercury on board the M/V *Empire Knight* constituted an imminent and substantial threat to the environment."

This despite the fact that only background levels of mercury surrounded the wreck.

"The RRT agreed that an on site assessment of the stern section of the *Empire Knight* was necessary to determine the presence of the mercury, and to assess whether it would be necessary, feasible, and safe to remove it if on board. In August, 1993, the COTP, as the Federal On Scene Coordinator, initiated a $6.8 million emergency site assessment and removal operation. The presence of mercury on board was quickly confirmed."

This should have come as no surprise, as Higgins had already informed the Coast Guard that his divers had spotted the mercury flasks, and told them where to look. Commercial divers from a New Orleans, Louisiana company called Subsea International descended from the company's 290-foot salvage barge *LB-278*. The barge housed, fed, and lodged more than ninety crewmembers, scientists, and Coast Guard personnel. Equipment on the barge included cranes, laboratories, and a machine shop.

Operational costs averaged $90,000 a day. The money was provided by a so-called Superfund: a hazardous waste abatement program that was administered by the EPA.

"All 221 manifested mercury flasks were located in cargo hold number 5 and subsequently recovered, but they were found in badly deteriorated condition and were nearly empty. Loose mercury was discovered throughout cargo hold number 5, and approximately 1,230 pounds were recovered. Nearly 2,200 pounds of mercury-contaminated debris and cargo residue were also recovered.

"Extensive sampling and analysis was conducted throughout the operation. Samples included bottom sediments in the vicinity of the stern section of the wreck and various species of fish and shellfish from the area around the vessel. From within cargo hold number 5, samples of the sediment, scrapings off the cargo, and fish and shellfish were taken.

"In October, 1993, the operation was suspended due to deteriorating weather conditions. At that time, an estimated 15,000 pounds [seven and a half tons] of mercury remained unaccounted for and is believed to have settled into the sediment, and may have come to rest at a low point of cargo hold number 5."

Less than ten percent of the mercury was recovered.

"In February, 1994, the RRT was reconvened by the COTP to consider the results of the sample analyses and to determine the best course of action. The sample analysis results showed that concentrations of mercury were elevated inside cargo hold number 5, but dropped off quickly to background levels in the bottom sediments outside the hold. No contamination of fish or shellfish was identified with the exception of those specimens collected from within cargo hold number 5. The key issue then became the long term fate of mercury in a marine environment. The RRT decided to submit the sample results to NOAA and an independent scientist with a request for an analysis of the available data and scientific literature and to develop a forecast of the long term behavior of the mercury site.

"In August, 1994, a commercial salvage company that had remained prohibited from conducting salvage operations by the Captain of the Port Order, submitted to the COTP a request to list the order. The company also submitted a request to conduct salvage operations on the wreck of the *Empire Knight*.

"In September, 1994, the RRT was reconvened to consider the reports submitted by NOAA and the independent scientist. While the reports differed in details, they both concluded that the site was currently stable and that the mercury did not pose a substantial threat to the environment. Both reports were written, however, under the presumption that the wreck of the *Empire Knight* would remain essentially undisturbed with the exception of its gradual decomposition from natural forces. Both reports further agreed that the probability of a catastrophic release of mercury to the environment as a result of activity on or near the *Empire Knight* was low. The RRT reached the conclusion that the wreck of the *Empire Knight* did not meet the condition of 'imminent and substantial' threat under CERCLA [Comprehensive Environmental Response, Compensation, and Liability Act] and that additional emergency response operations would not be conducted. The RRT further agreed to develop a plan for long-term monitoring of the site with the intent of detecting any changing conditions."

Another year passed while the wheels of officialdom spun in limbo.

Finally, in November of 1995, the Coast Guard published a rulemaking proposal to establish "a Safety Zone in the waters of the State of Maine prohibiting all vessels and persons from anchoring, diving, dredging, dumping, fishing, trawling, laying cable, or conducting salvage operations within a 1000 yard radius of the stern portion of the wreck of the M/V *Empire Knight* except as authorized by the Captain of the Port, Portland, Maine."

The proposal was duly passed and remains in effect today.

In 2010, treasure salvor Greg Brooks – famous (or notorious) for his involvement in the *Port Nicholson* scam (which see) – asked the Coast Guard lift the ban so that he could recover the mercury, copper wire, and a secret cargo of coins that he believed to be on board. His request was denied, but it offers the perfect segue to an interesting speculation of mine.

The British government intervened in the *Port Nicholson* case, arguing that all British vessels during World War Two operated under the authority of the Ministry of War Transport, which subsequently paid insurance claims for hull and cargo losses, and therefore still owned whatever treasure existed on the shipwreck. By that line of reasoning, the British government should also have been liable for damage caused by cargoes that it claimed to own. That means that the British government should have paid for the clean-up of mercury from the *Empire Knight*, and should be held responsible for any biological contamination that may result in the future.

The British government cannot have it both ways: claiming cargoes on one hand while evading responsibilities on the other. It is interesting to note that the British government kept a low profile with respect to the *Empire Knight* by not intervening and bringing notice to itself.

In March of 2013, the National Oceanic and Atmospheric Administration published a superfluous, misinformed, and totally useless Screening Level Risk Assessment Package on the *Empire Knight's* potential for accidentally discharging oil from the bunkers. By that time the Coast Guard had already ascertained that the only environmental hazard on the wreck was its cargo of mercury.

Nonetheless, "NOAA recommends that this site be noted in the Area Contingency Plans as necessary to answer future questions about the pollution risks associated with this particular vessel, and that if a mystery spill is reported in the general area, this vessel could be investigated as a source. Should additional information become available that would suggest a greater level of concern, then an active monitoring program could be implemented or an assessment undertaken."

This stupidity was compounded by the following hilarious statement: "The oil volume risk classifications refer to the volume of the most-likely Worst Case Discharge from the vessel and are based on the amount of oil believed or confirmed to be on the vessel. The *Empire Knight* is ranked as High Volume because, the best estimate is that the vessel could have the potential to carry up to 10,000 bbl [barrels] based on the size of the vessel, although some of that may have been lost at the time of the casualty due to the breakup of the vessel. Data quality is low because the actual bunker capacity of *Empire Knight* is not known."

The actual bunker capacity *was* known, but not to NOAA personnel who gathered information about the *Empire Knight* without ever leaving the office. The bulk of their research was done via the Internet, using secondary sources. One would think that the dunderheads that were keeping their chair seats warm should have realized that the Coast Guard had the situation well in hand, and that the 43-page NOAA document was redundant.

F. C. PENDLETON

Built: 1882
Previous names: None
Gross tonnage: 409
Type of vessel: Wooden-hulled three-masted tern
Builder: Crosby Brothers, Bangor, Maine
Owner: Pendleton Brothers, Belfast, Maine
Port of registry: Belfast, Maine
Cause of sinking: Foundered
Location: Seal Harbor

Sunk: 1925
Depth: 50 feet
Dimensions: 145' x 33' x 12'
Power: sail

Lat/lon: 44-19-38 N /68-54-27

Not every vessel had a noteworthy history or dramatic end. The *F. C. Pendleton's* 43-year career can best be described as lackluster: much like a tractor-trailer that did yeoman's work in delivering freight without being involved in any traffic incidents. Her final mention – and the only mention that I could find – appeared on October 19, 1925. It read:

"The schooner *Pendleton* which sent out distress signals last night, was reported safely in tow of the coast guard *Mohave*, en route to Vineyard Haven by naval communications here [New York] today. The boat was disabled but no details of the mishap were received. The *Pendleton* has a cargo of railroad ties. She left Jacksonville, Fla. For Portland, Me., about 24 days ago."

The 1925 edition of the *Record* of the American Bureau of Ships noted that her registration had expired. Merchant Vessels of the United States stated that she "foundered about 1925 in Seal Harbor, Maine."

And that's all she wrote.

The *F. C. Pendleton* was rigged as a tern: not a feathered relative of the gull but a Maine shipping term for a local three-masted schooner.

Today the wreck is a popular dive site.

The *F. C. Pendleton* looking much the worse for wear, with her starboard hull badly damaged. (From the collection of Bill Carter.)

GARDINER G. DEERING

Built: 1903
Previous names: None
Gross tonnage: 1,982
Type of vessel: Wooden-hulled five-masted schooner
Builder: Gardiner G. Deering, Bath, Maine
Owner: Boston Ship Brokerage Company, Boston, Massachusetts
Port of registry: Unregistered
Cause of sinking: Abandoned
Location: Smith Cove, West Brooksville

Sunk: 1930
Depth: Visibly exposed
Dimensions: 251' x 44' x 25'
Power: sail

GPS: 44-22.916 / 68-46.476

Gardiner G. Deering – the person, not the vessel – had a long and distinguished career in the shipbuilding business. First in partnership with William Donnell, then on his own, he built ninety-nine vessels over a career that spanned six decades. Additionally, he held partial ownership in many of the vessels he built.

In the late 1800's and early 1900's, the construction cost of many vessels was paid by selling shares to investors. Shares were usually sold in sixty-fourths; that is, an investor generally bought a minimum of one sixty-fourth of the total cost of the vessel. After the vessel was completed and started earning profits, the investor received a dividend of one sixty-fourth of the net (the gross minus wages, expenses, maintenance, repairs, and so on).

The sixty-fourth shares might also be subdivided into one hundred twenty-eights, or half shares. Sometimes an investor bought only a quarter share. Conversely, an investor might purchase two or more (or partial) shares.

Instead of buying an entire vessel on his own, Deering – as well as other investors – bought one or more shares in a large number of vessels. This was a way of amortizing losses in case a vessel was lost at sea. Or, to put it another way, investors never put all their eggs in one basket. This financial management system operated the same way as modern day mutual funds, whose portfolios are spread across a broad range of companies that are involved in a broad range of products and services. If any one investment goes bust, the loss to the fund is minimized.

If Deering could not obtain subscribers at the beginning of a project, he started with his own money and picked up investors along the way. Even though Deering might be listed as the principal owner, as in the case of the *Gardiner G. Deering*, he was never the sole owner. By way of example, at one time the Deering-built five-masted schooner *Henry O. Barrett* had sixty-seven owners, or investors if you will. This was sound financial planning for all concerned.

As for the *Gardiner G. Deering* – the vessel, not the person – she was the second vessel to be so named; the first one was wrecked in 1891. The new namesake slid down the ways of the Deering yard in 1903, much the way tractor-trailers are produced in assembly line plants today. Deering was a teetotaler, so instead of being christened with a bottle of wine, Deering's daughter Emma broke a bottle of spring water on her stem.

She was built at a cost of $84,984.78, or $1,326.48 per share.

She immediately started her career in the freight business. Her principal cargoes

The *Gardiner G. Deering* in her glory days. (From the collection of Dave Clancy.)

throughout the years were ice (carved out of the Kennebec River in winter), coal, lumber, phosphate, and railroad ties. She worked primarily as a coastal schooner, seldom venturing far from the American eastern seaboard, although she visited some of the Caribbean islands, and transported coal as far south as Brazil.

Her usual complement was eleven men: skipper, two mates, engineer (for the steam windlass and gaff hoisting machinery), cook, and a handful of able-bodied seamen.

She had her fair share of mishaps. In 1904, she collided with the Merchants and Miners steamship *Essex* off Point Lookout, in Virginia's part of the Chesapeake Bay. According to the newspaper, "The prow of the steamer caught the schooner above her second mast and almost cut her in two. The *Essex* had two holes stove in her starboard side ten feet above the waterline. Captain Ross and his crew of eleven men including five Japanese were saved by the boats of the *Essex*, and were taken aboard by that vessel."

The bilged schooner quickly filled with water and rolled over onto her beam end with her masts lying nearly flat against the brackish water. Deering traveled post haste to the site of the collision to determine if the vessel could be saved. He thought she could, so he hired a salvage outfit to raise the hull. They were successful. Afterward, the schooner was towed to Baltimore, Maryland for repairs.

In 1913, she had the maritime equivalent of a fender-bender off Nantucket, Massachusetts. That is, what amounted to a fender-bender for the steel-hulled steamer *Sloterdyk* was nearly fatal for the wooden-hulled *Gardiner G. Deering*. The schooner's stem was smashed down the middle when wood met steel. Only constant working of the bilge pumps saved her from sinking before she reached safe harbor.

Christmas day in 1921 found the schooner in Santos, Brazil. To spark off Yuletide festivities, her cargo of coal caught fire and did significant damage to her innards before the flames could be extinguished. She was ordered to return home for lengthy repairs – the cost of which was shared by her multitudinous investors. But the worst was yet to come as she hopscotched from island to island through the Caribbean Sea.

Traveling light, the schooner first stopped in Barbados then proceeded to Nassau, the Bahamas. Catastrophe struck between the two islands. The schooner was fine but her skipper was not, for the cook shot and killed Captain Chester Wallace when an argument escalated to deadly proportions. Gallows humor aside – much could be said about the quality of food aboard sailing vessels, and the imagination that was required to make it palatable – murder was a serious matter. At least one of the mates had sufficient training and skill to navigate the vessel to Nassau, where the circumstances of the captain were related to the United States consul.

After filing a report, the *Gardiner G. Deering* continued her fateful journey to Maine. The peculiar incident was radioed ahead from Nassau. The schooner made a way stop in Portland, where authorities piled aboard and escorted her – and the shooter, Harry Wilmot – to Bath. There a formal arrest was made by a United States marshal.

Wilmot pleaded self-defense. After the whole story was told, he was released without prejudice. It turned out that Captain Wallace suffered a mental aberration in which he entertained a paranoid delusion that a stowaway had sneaked aboard. For some reason he believed that Wilmot was harboring this imaginary stowaway. He paced the deck with a handgun, waving it at Wilmot and shooting wildly.

Then the captain went below deck forward into the compartment that housed the steam machinery for the windlass and winches. The first mate was close on his heels. Wallace fired three shots at the engineer, but the mate shouted a warning so the engineer was able to dodge the bullets by hiding behind the mast.

Still acting crazy, Wallace again confronted Wilmot in the mess room, and managed to wound him before the terrified cook was able to squirm through a port. Wilmot then produced a pistol of his own. When Wallace next came after him, the cook retaliated with two shots of his own. He wanted only to wound the captain but one of his bullets struck Wallace in the chest. He expired soon afterward.

The mate confirmed his participation in the strange events concerning a skipper gone mad. The rest of the crew stood by Wilmot's testimony. And Wilmot had a bullet wound as evidence to strengthen his declaration.

The *Gardiner G. Deering* was duly repaired. In dry-dock her hull was scraped clean of barnacles, and painted. The schooner again went to sea.

Shortly afterward, Gardiner G. Deering – the person, not the vessel – passed away at the age of 88 years.

In 1925, the *Gardiner G. Deering* – the vessel, not the person – was sold to the Boston Ship Brokerage Company. She was working in the coal trade in October 1926 when she ran afoul of a storm that tore her sails to shreds. In a spectacular display of superhuman endurance, an unnamed crewmember spent hours clearing coal dust from the clogged bilge pump by lying on his stomach and scooping up handfuls of black sludge. The lighthouse tender *Ilex* eventually towed the schooner to the nearest safe harbor.

Afterward, she was towed to Belfast, Maine, where the shifting cargo of coal was offloaded. That proved to be her final voyage. She had outlived her usefulness, and was sold at auction for $525. Her registration was suspended.

One problem with aging wooden-hulls was gradual loosening of their timbers. The space between planks constantly had to be recaulked as a way to keep the hull waterproof. In their off-duty hours, sailors at sea engaged in the time-honored pastime of picking oakum. Oakum is the "coarser part of hemp or flax." Scrap rope was "teased" apart and mixed with pine tar to produce caulking material so that cracks and leaks could be repaired whenever they occurred between lay-ups.

Another problem was the hull "working" or bending under way whenever it encountered rough seas. The longer a vessel's hull, the greater the inherent instability in maintaining a straight keel. Over time a hull tended to either hog or sag, depending on how the cargo was distributed in the holds. Hogging occurred when the ends of the hull drooped so that the center became somewhat arched. Sagging occurred when the middle of the hull slumped so that the ends angled upward. Either of these actions stretched the hull and created more gaps between planks.

The reliable workhorse ended her career by being put out to pasture. After thousands of miles of sea had passed under her keel, the schooner was abandoned at an anchorage in Smith Cove: still a thing of beauty whose graceful lines were gradually obscured as she settled ever deeper in the water.

The last straw was ignominious even if it was momentarily splendiferous. On July 4, 1930, a group of partiers torched the rotting schooner in celebration of Independence Day.

Today, a few rotting and seaweed-covered timbers protrude above the surface of the sea to mark the grave of one of the grand five-masters of yesteryear.

Although the wreck lies only a couple of hundred yards from shore, the nearby land is privately owned, making the site difficult to reach. The best place to put a boat in the water – motorboat, canoe, or kayak – is from the public boat launch at the end of Town Landing Road.

Use a local road map to find your way to Bucksport. From there go east on Route 3 for two to three miles, then turn south onto Route 175. Five miles past Penobscot the road forks, with Route 176 leading straight ahead, and Route 175 leading to the right to North Brooksville. Here is where the directions get confusing. Route 175 continues south at the T (to the left), while another segment of Route 176 leads north (to the right). Turn right, go for a hundred feet, and turn left (west) onto Varnum Road. After two and a half miles, Varnum Road ends at Route 176 (which completed a semicircle to reach this point.) Turn left (south), go three-quarters of a mile, and turn right onto Town Landing Road. This road ends half a mile later at the public dock.

Hug the peninsula on the starboard side of your boat. After you pass the point, continue past the southern one of the Henry Islands, then veer slightly to starboard and head toward the house on the opposite shore. The wreck site is almost directly off the house.

At extreme high tide, you might have trouble spotting the wreck because its high points could be submerged. At low tide some of the timbers of the starboard hull protrude above the water like the posts of a picket fence. Approach the wreck carefully in a motorboat because the lower hull is intact and contiguous, spreading southward of the visible timbers, and some of the other timbers lurk barely beneath the surface. Bumping into these timbers in a slow-moving canoe or kayak will probably not upset the boat, but could damage a propeller, rudder, or outboard motor.

The close-up view above shows the highest relief of the wreck. Draped seaweed indicates that some if not all of this prominent part of the starboard side can be under water at higher tide levels. Boaters should be aware that the entire lower hull extends outward from this exposed fragment, as shown in the view below. Approach the wreck slowly and carefully so your canoe or kayak does not tip over from striking a submerged projection, or so the propeller or rudder of a motorboat does not get snapped off from collision with same.

GEORGETOWN

Built: Unknown
Previous names: *C-12705*
Gross tonnage: Unknown
Type of vessel: wooden-hull, possible Coast Guard cutter
Builder: Unknown
Owner: Unknown
Cause of sinking: Ran aground
Location: Southward beach of Stratton Island, off Prout's Neck

Sunk: September 27, 1942
Depth: Unknown
Dimensions: Unknown
Power: Engine

Serendipity sometimes accompanies research. I stumbled across a secret and confidential account of the loss of the *Georgetown* while doing research for *The Fuhrer's U-boats in American Waters*. Neither the Naval History and Heritage Command nor the U.S. Coast Guard Historian's Office has any knowledge or documentation about the existence of this possible ex-cutter, much less about her loss.

During World War Two, the U.S. Coast Guard was placed under the command of the U.S. Navy. Some Coast Guard cutters retained their names or numbers throughout this temporary assignment; others were given different names and classifications. According to official documents, the *C-12705* was renamed *Georgetown*. The alphanumerical designation seemed to me to indicate that the *Georgetown* had previously been a Coast Guard cutter.

The Naval History and Heritage Command no longer answers query letters, and no longer allows civilian researchers into the Naval Historical Center or the Naval Photographic Center, so my request to that Command met a dead end. The command now devotes all its efforts toward writing legislation to take control of 17,000 abandoned wrecks worldwide. (See *The Great Navy Wreck Scam* for more information in this regard.)

I wrote to the Coast Guard and asked for statistical information: "I am looking for construction information about Coast Guard cutter *C-12705*, which during WW2 was transferred to the Navy and renamed USS *Georgetown*. The Navy has no information about this vessel. I want to know her vital statistics (and class of vessel): length, beam, depth, tonnage, date of construction, name of builder, hull material (wood or steel). Can you please help me in this regard?"

By contrast, the U.S. Coast Guard Historian's Office answered my email query overnight. The responding Coast Guard historian speculated thus: "If the vessel was an emergency acquisition during World War II, the name you have provided is not consistent with the standard identification for such vessels. Further, if this vessel were an emergency acquisition, they were not standardized, in other words, they were not part of a class. They were civilian craft of varying types acquired for short-term usage as ad hoc patrol craft. As such, we have no technical information to provide to you."

A researcher can be only as good as his sources. If official records are lacking, then a researcher cannot do anything about it. The information that I have is from a Navy Investigation Report, from which I will quote extensively, as that is the only known source so far for the existence and loss of the *Georgetown*.

The first notification of trouble was a radio message that was intercepted by the Navy's Portland Section at 7:39 on the morning of September 27, 1942: "We ran aground off Cape Elizabeth. The ship is breaking up."

According to the transcript, "No further word was received from the vessel and repeated efforts to contact her by radio thereafter were unavailing."

Nevertheless, the Navy dispatched the USS *Ave Maria* to search for the beleaguered vessel. As another oddity in this saga of absent historical information, like the *Georgetown*, the online database of the Naval History and Heritage has no mention of any such vessel named *Ave Maria*. Perhaps this incident occurred in an alternate universe.

Be that as it may, "At 0800 Q [8 a.m. Queentime, or local time], Lieutenant Commander Rowland, accompanied by the Medical Officer, Portland Section Base, and several other officers and enlisted men, drove to the Cape Elizabeth Coast Guard Station, taking with them blankets, hot coffee, and other supplies.

"Lieutenant Commander Rowland said: 'We found, upon arrival, that the Coast Guard people already had their patrols out and had sent a lifeboat out in the direction of Richmond Island. It was very thick at that time and blowing hard. The Captain of the Station and I both felt that the crew of the ship might be on Richmond Island and that that was the most likely place to look for them. So we got a lobster fisherman to take us out to the Island in a small boat, with the Medical Officer, and we searched the shore without finding any trace of the men.

" 'Between 1330 and 1400 Q, after we got back to the Station – other stations having been alerted, of course, as well as Army patrols along the shore, we got word from the Coast Guard Station at Biddeford Pool that the men from the *Georgetown* had been found on Stratten [sic] Island, off Prout's Neck, by a Coast Guard boat, and were being brought ashore.'

"Meanwhile, at 1000 Q, the USS *YMS 5*, of the Portland Section Base, which was patrolling Sector #1, had been ordered by Commander, Portland Section, to proceed to the Portland Sea Buoy and stand by to render any possible assistance.

"At approximately 1415 Q word was received from the Fletcher's Neck Coast Guard Station that the men had been taken to Biddeford Pool and the USS *YMS 22* and the USS *Ave Maria* were ordered by Commander, Portland Section, to proceed to the Southeast side of Stratten [sic] Island, where the *Georgetown* had gone aground, and to "assist if possible."

"The *Ave Maria* anchored at the scene, outside the *Georgetown*, resuming patrol of Sector #3 at 1745 Q, September 27 and continuing through the night, but remaining within sight of the *Georgetown* at all times.'

"Lieutenant Commander Rowland today dictated to Operational Intelligence Officer the following report of his findings as to the circumstances of the grounding of the USS *Georgetown*:

" 'The petty officer-in-charge – Graham, Philip, BM1c – who is a native of Boothbay Harbor, and a fisherman with considerable experience along this coast, was on Patrol in Sector #3, which extends from Portland Sea Buoy to Whistling Buoy 2-CP, off Cape Porpoise. There were five enlisted men in the crew, besides himself.

" 'Graham stands deck watches, and he had had the deck from 1600 Q to midnight on Saturday, September 26.

" 'At 0155 Q, the morning of the 27th, the vessel was in the neighborhood of the

Portland Sea Buoy. He (Graham) had instructed the leading hand who had the deck at the time of the accident, to return to the 2-CP buoy, off Cape Porpoise, in continuing the patrol. That course is 246 P.S.C. Owing to the fact that the wind was onshore, however, this man actually steered 230 P.S.C. I checked with him and also with the petty officer who relieved him at 0400 Q, and they both stated that they steered that course. But it shut in thick before they had actually picked up the Portland Sea Buoy so that the point of origin (just when and where the course was changed from 246 to 230) is in doubt. In other words, they were going by dead reckoning entirely and didn't actually make the buoy.

" 'The wind started to pick up between 0200 Q and 0300 Q and blew hard. It was very thick and visibility was practically zero.

" 'They said that steering was difficult and that it was not possible to judge what course they were actually making good. But they felt that they were making sufficient allowance for leeway, although they had no way of making sure because they were able to see nothing at all.

" 'About 0600 Q, the wind increased to gale force and the vessel was virtually hove to. Graham slept through, and was not called, and he was just on the point of getting up at about 0730 Q, when he felt the vessel strike and came up on deck. It was breaking water all around him, and he saw that the vessel was on a reef and he could land about 100 yards directly to leeward. The direction of the wind at this time was about Southeast.

" 'The first thing Graham did was to jump into the pilothouse and make an urgent priority call over the radio. His impression was that he was ashore on or near Cape Elizabeth, or Richmond Island, which is right off Cape Elizabeth, and that was the message he gave. He had barely time to make this one call before the radio went dead. He saw right away that she wasn't going to last in the heavy sea.

" 'Then he immediately gave his whole attention to saving his men. They wanted to jump overboard and swim, but he stopped them from doing that and he got his life raft overboard with a long sea painter – all the rope he had on board – on it. He sent his men ashore, one at a time, on the raft, and they landed on a rocky point, it being about dead low water then.

" 'The last man to leave the ship before Graham was Favazzia, the leading hand, and Favazzia insisted that Graham would not be able to pull the raft back to the ship alone, so they got on it together and cut it adrift.

" 'Graham picked up a box which he thought contained the codes but on his first attempt to get aboard, the raft turned over with them and he lost it, but at the same time, before he lost it, he discovered that it was a signal searchlight box that was about the same size and shape, so he was not able to get the confidential papers and no trace of them has been found. But they were unquestionably washed out of the wheelhouse as it was completely gutted by the waves, and they must have sunk, in deep water, between the reef and the island.

" 'All hands got ashore safely, without any injuries. About 10 to 15 minutes later the ship drove over the reef into the deep water inside, and lay on her side before righting. Then she drove in on the rocky point of the island, where she now lies.

" 'Before leaving the ship, Graham attempted to get his anchor overboard, but he was swept off the deck, and couldn't do anything about it. The seas were making a clean breach over the ship and it is felt that Graham did an excellent job in getting his crew ashore safely.

"'When the men got ashore they found an empty cottage on the island, to which they gained entrance and dried themselves out. They built a fire in the stove and made hot soup, using food that they found in the cottage. Although they were wet and cold when they got ashore, they suffered no lasting ill effects.

"'As to salvaging the ship, I went down again this morning (Monday, 28 September) with Lieutenant (jg) Elmer, Ensign Barton and Chief Machinist's Mate Wiggin of the Section Base. We took along Graham and his crew to act as guards for the wreck. We salvaged all movable material, such as the radio, compass, machine guns and ammunition, and brought it back. We made plans for the salvaging of the machinery and everything else of value that can be saved.

"'The Coast Guard left a detail on the island over night, and they were there this morning when we arrived.

"'The vessel is lying on the outside shore of the island, on the rocks, and at low tide we could walk right up to her. Her back is broken and her frames and planking are – well, I would say this: on her starboard side she has a hole in her from 10 to 15 feet long, amidships, at the turn of the bridge, and the frames are broken and the plank is all gone. She is also holed on the port side, but as she was lying on that side, it was not possible to tell the extent of the damage. It is felt that the hull is a total loss.'"

An addendum noted, "The log book and confidential papers were lost overboard in approximately 40 ft. of water. A diligent search around the exposed edges has been made and nothing found."

As a result of losing his vessel, the following "letter of admonition" was given to Graham: "The Commandant, First Naval District considers that the loss of the U.S.S. *C-12705* (Ex-*Georgetown*) was due to your failure to properly indoctrinate those under your command who stood watch, to notify you promptly of changes in weather conditions. This is a flagrant example of operating in waters on a 'lee shore' with a change of weather from fair, with practically no winds, to zero visibility and a gale, during which time no report of these changes in weather conditions were made to you by the men on watch. You are hereby admonished to exercise the proper supervision over members of your command in the future.

"A copy of this letter will be placed upon your official record."

The above letter spelled out the skipper's name as Philip Alvin Graham, Boatswain's Mate, First Class, U.S. Naval Reserve. More interesting, it reverses the name and ex-name of the vessel as given in the Investigation Report.

Homarus americanus.

GEORGIA

Built: 1863
Previous names: *Japan*
Gross tonnage: 690
Type of vessel: Iron-hulled screw steamer
Builder: William Denny & Brothers, Dumbarton, Scotland
Owner: Quebec & Gulf Ports Steam Ship Company, Quebec City, Quebec
Port of registry: Quebec City, Quebec, Canada
Cause of sinking: Ran aground
Location: Triangle Ledge, 7 miles east of Tenant's Harbor

Sunk: January 14, 1875
Depth: Unknown
Dimensions: 206' x 27' x 14'
Power: Coal-fired steam

Lat/lon: 43-55-39 N / 69-01-40 W

It is unusual for there to be two vessels of the same name in the same navy at the same time. The condition creates confusion. Yet during the Civil War the Confederate navy had two vessels named *Georgia*, and their operational times overlapped.

In written texts, one was referred to as either the C.S.S. *Georgia* or the C.S.S. Floating Battery *Georgia*. This ironclad vessel was a failed attempt to build an armed warship with inferior propulsion machinery. Her speed was described thus: "For want of locomotive power, the *Georgia* was a fixture, her steam power scarcely adequate to propel her at the slowest speed."

Despite this major shortfall, she served suitably at her wharf for two and a half years as her guns prevented Union naval incursions into Savannah, Georgia. When Savannah finally fell to overwhelming Union forces, the Confederates scuttled the armed fixture in the Savannah River. As this book goes to press, the remains of the floating battery are being recovered piecemeal by the Army Corps of Engineers, as part of a multi-million dollar project to deepen and widen the channel in the river.

This chapter is about the other Confederate *Georgia*: the one that served as a commerce raider, and that went under the cognomen C.S. Cruiser *Georgia*. The Confederate States of America had no navy when it seceded from the Union. In order to prosecute the war at sea, the South had either to charter existing vessels or build new ones. The Confederates lacked the resources to build vessels from the keel up, as proven by the so-called floating battery mentioned above, so it relied on Great Britain to build vessels for them.

One hull that William Denny & Brothers already had on the ways on the River Clyde, at Dumbarton, Scotland, was the *Japan*: a wooden-hulled screw steamer that was designed to provide service between Great Britain and Singapore. The hull was propelled by a pair of geared steeple engines for which steam was provided by four boilers, each boiler having two furnaces. There was also an auxiliary cylindrical tubular boiler. Somehow the South came up with enough money to woo the vessel away from her intended owner.

Wrote Erik Heyl, "The *Japan* left Greenock, Scotland, on April 1, 1863 and proceeded to Ushant, France where she met the steamer *Alar*. The *Japan* had ostensibly departed Great Britain for the East Indies. The *Alar's* cargo of cannons, rifles, ammunition and naval stores were transferred to the *Japan*, which was then commissioned as the CSS *Georgia* on April 9, 1863 and left on a cruise which was to last seven months."

From *Illustrated London News*.

The newly commissioned *Georgia* was now armed with five guns: two 100-pounders, two 24-pounders, and one 32-pounder. "Pounder" refers to the weight of the shot or shell that a gun could fire.

In command of the raider was Lieutenant William Maury. He was immediately disappointed to learn that the *Georgia* did not meet his expectations with regard to speed and mechanical reliability. Nonetheless, he proceeded on a cruise to capture or destroy commerce vessels that were registered to the United States (of North America). The advantage of this was twofold: a reduction of imports and exports for the North, and stretching the North's naval resources. The Union was forced to dispatch warships to search for Confederate commerce raiders, which left fewer vessels available for blockading Southern ports.

The *Georgia* raided Union commerce in the South Atlantic Ocean, and was credited with capturing, burning, or bonding nine vessels: *Dictator, George Griswold, Good Hope, J.W. Seaver, Constitution, City of Bath, Prince of Wales, John Watts,* and *Bold Hunter*. ("Bonding" was a condition in which a captured vessel was released on the promise that the owners of the vessel and cargo would pay the Confederacy the value of that vessel and cargo after the cessation of hostilities.) Other vessels were stopped and released because they belonged to neutral nations and their cargoes were not consigned to Northern ports.

On October 28, 1863, the *Georgia* put in at Cherbourg, France and went straight into dry-dock for much needed maintenance and repairs. So much work was required that it took three months to complete. According to International Neutrality Laws, the vessel of a belligerent nation was permitted to remain in the port of a neutral nation for more than twenty-four hours only if she needed more time for supplies or repairs, but not if she wanted safe harbor from her enemies.

In the meantime, on December 27, Maury wrote to Flag-Officer Samuel Barron in Paris: "Sir, in your communication of yesterday's date (already acknowledged) you require my report as to the unfitness of this vessel as a cruiser against the commerce of the enemy. In reply I have the honor to state that the propelling power of the sails is so small that she can not cruise advantageously and capture enemy's vessels under them. She has to chase always under steam, which necessarily causes great consumption of fuel, and to cruise actively it is necessary for her to coal frequently."

The most frustrating problem on the *Georgia* was the continuous breakdown of her propulsion machinery. The propeller shaft was fitted with iron teeth that meshed with wooden cogs in the gearbox. The cogs kept sheering off and flying around the compartment like missiles.

On January 11, 1864, Barron decided that the *Georgia* was no longer fit for duty. Her arms and ammunition were to be transferred to the *Rappahannock*, which was also docked at Cherbourg. Neutrality laws forbid the transfer to take place in French waters. A meeting between the two vessels was planned in the Mediterranean Sea off the coast of Morocco, but Napoleon III foiled the works because he believed that supporting the South would put him in disfavor with the North, which he expected to win the war. He refused permission for the *Rappahannock* to depart.

The *Georgia* waited for three weeks at the designated rendezvous. The skipper let the crew have shore leave. They rowed ashore only to encounter "hundreds of Moors armed with spears and old-fashioned guns." A blood bath was avoided only because the sailors made a hasty retreat. Once on board, a broadside was fired at the bloodthirsty natives, who made an even hastier retreat into caves in the shore-side cliffs. Afterwards, in lighter moments, the victorious sailors called the engagement "the Confederacy's only foreign war."

When the *Rappahannock* did not arrive, the *Georgia* proceeded to the French port of Bordeaux. She was expelled after twenty-four hours, as per international law.

Heyl: "She slipped past two Federal men-of-war on blockade just off the mouth of the Garonne River, and went on to Liverpool [England] and interned herself. On May 10, 1864, the Confederate commissioner ordered her decommissioned and her flag hauled down. The CSS *Georgia* was turned over to the British authorities, who on June 1, 1864 sold her to a Liverpool merchant, Edward Bates."

Bates retained the vessel's name minus the CSS. Under new command, the *Georgia* returned to her old stomping grounds in the Atlantic Oceans as a cargo vessel in merchant service. On August 15, 1864, the Union steam frigate *Niagara* stopped the *Georgia* off the coast of Portugal. When the Union skipper learned that the vessel was the same one that used to be the Confederate raider *Georgia*, he arrested the crew and claimed the vessel as a prize of war.

The capture was obviously illegal: one of a long list of illegal actions that the Union navy committed during the War of the Rebellion. At the time of her capture, the *Georgia* was no longer active as a Confederate commerce raider, but belonged to a private citizen of a neutral nation, in which she was lawfully registered.

Nonetheless, Bates was divested of his newly purchased property, and the *Georgia* was confiscated in the name of the United States. A prize crew took her to Boston, Massachusetts, where she was sold at auction. Under U.S. prize rules, the money that was realized by auction was distributed among the officers and crew of the *Niagara*: an incentive that led to more than a few injustices.

Be that as it may, on August 15, 1865 (a year after her capture), the *Georgia* was bought by John Williams, who registered her at New Bedford, Massachusetts. Williams and his later partner Stephen Guion operated the *Georgia* for five years, although in what capacity is uncertain.

In 1870, they sold the *Georgia* to the Quebec & Gulf Ports Steam Ship Company, of Quebec City, Canada. The new owners modified her by removing one mast and altering the deck houses to better enable her to work in the passenger service. She operated primarily between Montreal, Quebec and St. Johns, Newfoundland.

On January 14, 1875, the *Georgia* was on a passage from Halifax, Nova Scotia to

Portland, Maine when she encountered thick snow that reduced visibility dramatically. Worse, because the sounding lead fell into 420 feet of water where the depth should have been shallower, Captain McKenzie suspected that his compasses were out of calibration. He adjusted both of them.

Now uncertain of his location and bearing, he misinterpreted lighthouse signals. To make up for his confusion, he decided to idle until daylight, when he could firmly establish the position of his vessel with respect to the various islands and submerged rock reefs that dotted the area. The set of the current carried the *Georgia* onto what was later determined to be Triangle Ledge, where she stranded at the worst possible time: at high tide that was ebbing.

Aggravating matters were high rollers: not rich gamblers with hot dice but non-breaking seas with tall crests and deep troughs. The iron hull was alternately lifted and dropped with increasing intensity. Rivets popped and plates fractured. Soon the interior was flooded from nearly stem to stern. Both the baggage compartment and the machinery spaces were inundated by the sea. Then the hull started to break apart.

Captain McKenzie ordered abandon ship. By this time the passengers and crew had been chased out of the lower decks and were standing next to the lifeboats. Three boats were launched successfully, although the one with the skipper and the women and children was nearly swamped when two men leaped into it from the weather deck. The fourth boat capsized when it fouled the davits. No one was in the boat at the time, but six men were left on the ship with no means of escape. The other boats refused to return for them because their occupants feared that they were already overloaded.

Two boats rowed seven miles Tenants Harbor: one in charge of the captain and the other in charge of the engineer. The other one rowed to Whitehead, where the mate informed the lifesaving station keeper of the accident. Under the command of the station keeper, named Norton, a lifeboat was launched and the lifesavers rowed to the ledge on which the *Georgia* perched.

By this time the hull had broken in two. The stern sank. Fortunately, the men who had been left on the wreck had made their way to the bow before the hull separated.

The rollers made it extremely difficult for the lifeboat to approach the wreck without being smashed against the hull or slammed down on the rock in the trough of a giant wave. The lifesavers were forced to wait for a safe opportunity before rowing hard to the side of the wreck. It could remain only long enough for one person to leap aboard. Then the lifesavers backed away into deeper water to await the next safe opportunity. In this fashion they made six dashes to the wreck, until finally they had all the stranded sailors onboard the lifeboat.

One person was overcome by exposure to the elements. He was taken to a private residence on Hewitt Island – which was closer than the lifesaving station – where he soon revived in the welcome heat. Then the people were taken to the lifesaving station where they were comforted throughout the night. The next day they were taken to Tenants Harbor to join the other survivors.

There was no loss of life. The revenue cutter *Dallas* transported the *Georgia's* passengers and crew to Portland.

The wreck was a total loss. Some of the cargo was later salvaged. The exposed bow was stripped its anchors, chains, and rigging. Two donkey engines were recovered. The financial loss was estimated to be between $75,000 and $100,000, but the amount of insurance coverage was only $60,000.

HARTWELSON

Built: 1902
Previous names: *Burbo Bank, Freida Leonhardt, Astoria*
Gross tonnage: 3,078
Type of vessel: Freighter
Builder: J. Blumer & Company, Sunderland, England
Owner: Hartwelson Steamship Company, Boston, Massachusetts
Port of registry: Boston, Massachusetts
Cause of sinking: Ran aground
Location: Bantam Rock, south of Damariscove Island

Sunk: March 5, 1943
Depth: 30 feet
Dimensions: 319' x 46' x 21'
Power: Coal-fired steam

Lat/lon: 43-43-47 N / 69-37-26 W

The *Hartwelson* may be unique as the only vessel to have been sunk in both World Wars. The vessel in question began her career in 1902 as the *Burbo Bank*, hauling commodities for the Fenwick Shipping Company. She was a standard steel-hulled freighter that was propelled by a triple-expansion reciprocating steam engine whose boiler furnaces were fueled by coal.

In 1914, the British vessel was sold to the German company of Leonhardt & Blumberg, which renamed her *Freida Leonhardt* and changed her hailing port to Hamburg, Germany. She did not serve for very long under her new owners; or, at least, not in any useful capacity.

War started brewing in Europe after the assassination of Archduke Franz Ferdinand and his wife Sophie, on June 28, 1914, at Sarajevo, in the country of Bosnia and Herzegovina. Combat forces mobilized over the following month. Embroiled in the conflict were Germany, Austria-Hungary, Serbia, Russia, the Ottoman Empire, Luxemburg, France, and Belgium. On August 4, the United Kingdom declared war on Germany in protest over the German invasion of Belgium.

The Great War was on!

The very next day, when the *Freida Leonhardt* was on a passage from Gulfport, Mississippi to Italy with a cargo consisting of 2,350,000 board feet of timber, the British cruiser *Berwick* spotted the German freighter off the Florida Keys, and instantly gave chase. Captain Lestner, master of the *Freida Leonhardt*, knew that he could not outrun the cruiser, so he hugged the American coastline – such as it was, consisting of numerous small islands or keys – in order to stay inside the three-mile territorial limit.

The United States was a neutral country. In accordance with International Neutrality Laws, her waters constituted neutral territory in which belligerent nations were not permitted to fight.

The *Berwick* overtook the *Freida Leonhardt*, but respected the neutrality laws by steaming abreast of her a mile off her starboard side, and by not firing on the unarmed freighter. The chase endured for twelve hours. Predator and prey rounded the southern tip of Florida and headed north. Finally, Captain Lestner steered his vessel into safe harbor at Jacksonville. The *Berwick* lingered outside the port in international waters.

Another Article of the International Neutrality Laws proclaimed that vessels of belligerent nations were not permitted to remain in neutral ports of a sovereign nation for more than twenty-four hours. If they did, they were interned by the host country

Official U.S. Coast Guard photo.

for the remainder of the war.

Captain Lestner had two choices: depart within the allowable time limit and chance having his vessel blown out of the water, or stay put and have his vessel and crew interned for the duration of hostilities. The latter course would prevent both the sinking of the vessel and the deaths of crewmembers. Lestner remained.

Life aboard an interned vessel was safe but boring. The crew had to live on the vessel, but were allowed to roam freely on shore. After all, they were not enemies of the sovereign state in which they resided. They could send and receive mail, purchase food and supplies in nearby communities. They could visit local shops and bars. But, they could not leave the country by any means. In short, they were like prisoners on house arrest.

This situation endured for nearly three years. The *Freida Leonhardt* idled at the dock. The crew idled.

Finally, on April 6, 1917, the United States declared war on Germany. The declaration made the *Freida Leonhardt* an enemy vessel, and made the crew enemy civilians. The declaration meant that the United States could claim the interned freighter as a prize of war. To prevent the U.S. from taking over the vessel, the crew sabotaged the machinery, destroyed the boilers by draining the water and stoking fires in the furnaces, and scuttled the ship at the dock.

The crew was arrested. The vessel was raised and towed to the Charleston Navy Yard in South Carolina. The Navy made repairs with the idea of using the ex-German freighter as a supply vessel. On November 15, she was commissioned into the U.S. Navy as the USS *Astoria*. She was armed with four 3-inch deck guns and two machine guns. She was assigned to the Naval Overseas Transportation Service

After a trial trip to Gulfport and back, the *Astoria* steamed Hampton Roads, Virginia, where she was loaded with military supplies for shipment to Brest, France, in support of the U.S. Army. That was her only passage as a military supply ship because on February 15, 1918, she was accidentally rammed by the French vessel *La Drome*. The damage was extensive and required extensive repairs.

She went to sea again in May as a collier. For the rest of the year and into 1919, she transported coal from Cardiff, Wales to various French ports. Her Naval service lasted until 1921, and included a trip through the Panama Canal in order to work with the Pacific Fleet. On April 20, 1921, she was decommissioned at the Boston Navy Yard, in Massachusetts, and was transferred to the United States Shipping Board, which sold her to Richard Green for merchant service on December 20.

Green established the Astoria Steamship Company. The "USS" was dropped from the vessel's name. As a cargo vessel, the newly ordained *Astoria* operated under that appellation until 1929, at which time she was sold to H.N. Hartwell & Sons, of Boston, Massachusetts. In deference to the owners of the latter company, the *Astoria's* name was appropriately changed to *Hartwelson*.

The *Hartwelson* remained with the Hartwelson Steamship Company for the rest of her career. She operated almost as a conveyor belt, transporting coal from mostly from Norfolk, Virginia to various ports in Maine.

The only recorded incident of note during the next decade and a half occurred in November 1935, when a man was washed overboard while the collier was riding out a storm.

In 1943, the *Hartwelson* delivered a load of coal to Stockton Springs, Maine. She encountered a fierce storm on her return passage to Norfolk. Wisely, Captain G. Beranger, master, decided to duck for cover. He dropped anchor in the lee of Damariscove Island at around four o'clock in the morning of March 5. As the ship swung around on the anchor chain, she grounded on Bantam Rock. Pounding seas shoved the hull farther onto the rock until it was stuck like a moth on an automobile radiator.

The Coast Guard maintained a lifeboat station on the Island. At 6:45, a lookout noticed a freighter that was anchored a mile and a half south of the station. After a while he realized that the freighter was not anchored, but stranded. He called Portland, Maine to report the situation. Portland called the Coast Guard, which immediately dispatched the lighthouse tender *Ilex*.

Meanwhile, the Damariscove Island Lifeboat Station launched *Motor Lifeboat No. 36345* to render assistance. The lifeboat reached the *Hartwelson* at eight o'clock, "but sea conditions and shallow water around the freighter made it impossible to get alongside until the sea was calmer. By blinker message the freighter reported that those aboard were all right. *Motor Lifeboat No. 36313* from the Kennebec River Lifeboat station arrived at 1000; later *Motor Lifeboat No. 36380* from the Burnt Island Station and a naval vessel joined them.

"Heavy seas were causing the *Hartwelson* to disintegrate and it was still impossible to get near enough to her to use the Lyle gun. When the seas diminished an attempt was made to use a shoulder line throwing gun, but the line broke and the projectile was lost."

Meanwhile, the hull broke in two between the fire room and engine room. The stern slipped into deep water.

Lifeboats stood by all day. When the *Ilex* arrived, she positioned herself on the windward side of the stranded steamer "and fed oil to smooth the sea." When darkness fell, the *Ilex* played her searchlight on the besieged vessel.

A restricted telegram that was sent the following day described subsequent events: "Boat of the *Ilex* manned by CBM Melcher Seal CBM Ray Hamilton and 4 others proceeded as close as possible to leeward side and shot a line aboard the *Hartwelson* with shoulder line throwing gun X 35 men and a dog were taken off X The crew of the *Hartwelson* used the new style life preservers X Some of the effects of the crew were left aboard X Some of crew came off without shoes X The crew was removed at 2350 yesterday Friday and the *Ilex* left the scene shortly thereafter arriving at South Portland Base at 0450 today Saturday X 3 crew members of *Hartwelson* were taken to the Marine Hospital suffering from exposure X The others were taken to the Seamens Friends Society X Capt G Beranger of the *Hartwelson* is aboard *Ilex*."

Today the wreck is a popular dive site.

HELEN B. CROSBY

Built: 1906
Previous names: None
Gross tonnage: 1,776
Type of vessel: Wooden-hulled four-masted schooner
Builder: E.S. Crosby, Bath, Maine
Owner: Crosby Navigation, Richmond, Virginia
Port of registry: Bath, Maine
Cause of sinking: Ran aground
Location: Inner Bay Ledge, Penobscot Bay

Sunk: October 11, 1906
Depth: Unknown
Dimensions: 227' x 42' x 24'
Power: Sail

There is not much to write about this four-masted schooner because her career was so short. She was built and lost in the same year. Captain Chester Wallace must have been dismayed when his brand new command encountered fierce weather. A White Head Lifesaving Service report provided a succinct account of the catastrophe:

"During fresh SW. wind and heavy rain squalls, vessel got out of her course and stranded on Bay Ledge 14 miles ENE. Of station at 8 p. m., she at the time being hidden from the station by intervening land. Upon being notified of the disaster by telephone the keeper and his crew boarded schooner and found her hull stove in and full of water and the crew, with the exception of the master and mate, having gone ashore in a small boat. The master decided to abandon ship, and the life-savers landed him and the mate and transferred them to a tug bound for Rockland. The vessel afterwards proved a total loss."

The best that can be said about the incident is that no lives were lost.

Newspapers reported that the schooner ran aground on Drunkard's Ledge, but I am more inclined to accept the word of the Lifesaving Service.

In the few months prior to her loss, the *Helen B. Crosby* had been under contract to Lind & Company, transporting coal from Newport News, Virginia to the Navy base at Culebra, Puerto Rico.

Final moments of the *Helen B. Crosby*. Note the people who are leaning against the starboard rail amidship. (From the collection of Paul Sherman.)

HESPER / LUTHER LITTLE

Hesper built: 1918
Previous names: None
Gross tonnage: 1,348
Type of vessel: Wooden-hulled four-masted schooner
Builder: Crowninshield Shipbuilding Company, South Somerset, Massachusetts
Owner: Wiscasset Industrial Development Corporation, Wiscasset, Maine
Port of registry: not registered
Cause of sinking: Abandoned
Location: Used to be on the Sheepscot River, east of the Route 1 bridge

Sunk: 1932
Depth: Exposed
Dimensions: 210' x 41' x 20'
Power: Sail

Luther Little built: 1917
Previous names: None
Gross tonnage: 1,234
Type of vessel: Wooden-hulled four-masted schooner
Builder: Crowninshield Shipbuilding Company, South Somerset, Massachusetts
Owner: Wiscasset Industrial Development Corporation, Wiscasset, Maine
Port of registry: not registered
Cause of sinking: Abandoned
Location: Used to be on the Sheepscot River, east of the Route 1 bridge

Sunk: 1932
Depth: Exposed
Dimensions: 204' x 40' x 19'
Power: Sail

I cannot decide which of two words best describes these two historic schooners with regard to Maine's maritime heritage: iconic or symbolic. Perhaps both.

Although neither one was built in Maine, both of them spent the majority of their careers there: as tourist attractions rather than as work boats.

First built was the *Luther Little*, in 1917. Actually, two of them were built. The first *Luther Little* was burned to a crisp while still on the ways when a fierce conflagration swept through the shipyard of Read Brothers and destroyed the entire complex of buildings. From the ashes rose the Crowninshield Shipbuilding Company, which completed and launched the second *Luther Little* by the end of the year.

This four-masted schooner was immediately put to work in the freight trade, the way a tractor-trailer is employed today. She hauled any cargo that came her way.

She was barely a year old when crewmembers saw a balloon crash into the ocean off the New Jersey coast. The sighting was fortuitous – for the pair of balloonists. Had they not been rescued by the *Luther Little*, they likely would have drowned before they could have swum to shore.

In 1920, the *Luther Little* almost came to an untimely end. She was transporting logwood to Pennsylvania when she ran aground at Haiti, outside Fort Liberte Harbor. Two agonizing weeks passed, with the schooner rolling in the surf, before she was successfully pulled off the bar. Damage was minor.

The *Hesper's* career was equally as lackluster, and as dramatic. She was not even off the ways when, during the launching ceremony, her hull crashed through the timbers that she was supposed to slide down into the water: a maritime version of Caesarean birth that delayed her launching.

This postcard picture from the early 1970's shows the location and contemporary condition of the *Hesper* and *Luther Little*. The ocean lies toward the lower right.

Transatlantic voyages were common. Her holds were often filled with coal, lumber, fertilizer, case oil in barrels, and other miscellaneous cargoes. Like every work boat of her day, she had a few accidents that curtailed her voyages: she had her sails blown out in a storm, and got stuck in the mud in Boston Harbor. Another storm blew her away from the wharf; the dock lines did not break: instead she took the wharf with her as she careered across the harbor until she stranded on the beach.

In short, working on a schooner was no more glamorous than driving an eighteen-wheeler across the country, although adverse weather conditions and accidents they had were more trying. Plus, their voyages lasted for months instead of days, and the food that crewmembers ate consisted of salt beef and hardtack instead of the scrumptious meals that teamsters find at truck stops.

The glamor comes only in retrospect: from modern day landlubbers who look back on the "glorious" days of sail as if hauling freight was fun and exciting instead of uncomfortable drudgery.

The end of the 1920's found the sailing business in decline. By that time most windjammers had been dismasted and converted to barges. The *Hesper* and *Luther Little* did not suffer such an ignominious fate. Instead they were laid up awaiting future cargoes – which never came.

Although sailing vessels were inexpensive to operate because the fuel was free, time and timeliness became valuable commodities. Metal-hulled steamships were fast and reliable, and did not rely on the vagaries of wind for propulsion. They gradually took cargoes away from the windjammers until there was little or no work for them.

According to Alice Larkin, "In June, 1932, *Hesper* and *Luther Little* were auctioned off by a U.S. marshal to settle claims against the vessels. Frank W. Winter of Auburn, Maine, bid them in, paying $600 for *Hesper* and an amount close to that for *Luther Little*. He then had them towed to Wiscasset."

And there they stayed – for the next sixty-six years.

Alton Sweet added some reminiscences to the post-layup history of the schooners. He lived and worked on them during the winter of 1933, painting and doing all-around repairs so that Frank Winter could utilize them in the logging trade. He planned to transport lumber by rail from upper Maine to Wiscasset, then ship the logs to Boston and New York.

At that time a skipper, his wife, and his daughter lived aboard the *Luther Little*, which lay next to the wharf. Sweet and his father took over the forecastle of the *Hesper*, which lay outboard. Sweet was paid a dollar a day for maintenance work.

Sweet: "It took me a while to get used to stepping over the high thresholds, about 15 inches high, on the doors of the galley and forecastle. They were built that way to keep seas from flooding in. There were no big waves coming on deck where we were tied up, but I cracked my shins and stumbled a good many times on the thresholds before I learned to lift my feet.

Some of the masts were still standing when I first saw the Wiscasset schooners in 1990.

"To get to the captain's and officers' quarters one walked toward the stern and up four or five steps to the poop deck. There were also steps leading down into the main cabin which was finished in natural oak. The ship's wheel was in another cabin on the deck.

"In addition to the caretaker aboard the *Luther Little*, there was another man who worked on the schooners. His job was to scrape and oil the masts, which towered 80 feet above the deck, with topmasts another 20 feet higher in the air. I worked the lines for hoisting his bo'sun's chair, and climbed aloft myself to the crosstrees to paint the sail hoops on the topmasts. . . .

"During my stay on the *Hesper* I came across her logbook in a cupboard in the captain's cabin, and spent evenings reading it by lamplight. From it I learned that the schooner had made trips to Le Havre, France; Liverpool, England, and to Central and South America.

"There was one entry that told of a sailor with a grudge who got hold of a gun and took a shot at the captain. He missed and was overpowered by the mate. They locked him up and later took him back to port to stand trial.

"Another entry described how a sailor at the winch head had caught his arm between the winch and the line passing around it. His life was saved, but he lost his arm.

"I often wonder what became of the *Hesper's* log. I wish I had it now."

Frank Winter passed away before he could put his logging plan into operation. The two schooners languished and slowly fell into disrepair. Eventually they sank, or settled into the mud that clogged the riverbed beneath their keels. Decay and degradation occurred slowly, almost infinitesimally. Over time the masts were removed or came crashing down, the cabins collapsed, the decks gave way, small fires ran rampant, and the erstwhile majestic schooners turned into rotting hulks.

During this constantly changing sculpturing process, the Wiscasset schooners were a photographers delight. Hundreds, perhaps thousands of photographers – both amateur and professional – took pictures that graced postcards, magazines, and newspapers. Many of these pictures are still in circulation, and preserve the image that came to be associated with Maine in general and Wiscasset in particular.

By the 1990's the derelicts were little more than eyesores: flattened remains that barely protruded above the surface of the water, and that no longer resembled the graceful hulls of yesteryear. What nature started, mankind finished.

In 1998, a crane barge was placed adjacent to the wreck sites, and reclamation commenced. Throughout the months of May and June, the clamshell bucket bit into the debris, swung a clutch of splinters to shore, opened its steel jaws, and deposited the remains. Some parts, such as masts and their hardware, were saved. Most of the litter was hauled to a landfill site. Nearly three hundred dump truck loads were required to transport the refuse. The cost of the demolition project was $70,000.

Then, astonishingly, people came from all over New England to collect souvenirs from the landfill. Stan Lucien took small chunks of wood from which he planned to make ballpoint pens. The owners of Sarah's Café recovered beams and timbers from which they intended to frame a mural of the schooners in their glory days. Large sections of wood were used to appoint a kitchen. Countless other souvenir collectors kept tiny pieces of wood as mementoes.

John Gardner built a diorama to one-eighth scale, depicting the schooners the way they used to appear during the early stages of their decomposition.

Because of these saviors, and published photographic records, the *Hesper* and *Luther Little* – the Wiscasset Schooners – will remain in mankind's memory forever.

By 1997 the schooners were slumped in a sad state of collapse.

HOWARD W. MIDDLETON

Built: 1883
Previous names: None
Gross tonnage: 590
Type of vessel: Wooden-hulled three-masted tern
Builder: S.W. Tilton, Camden, New Jersey
Owner: S.H. Crawford
Port of registry: Philadelphia, Pennsylvania
Cause of sinking: Ran aground
Location: North end of Higgins Beach, Scarborough

Sunk: August 10, 1897
Depth: Exposed at low tide
Dimensions: 145' x 35' x 15'
Power: sail

GPS: 43-33.679 / 70-16.361

You will notice in the statistical sidebar that the *Howard W. Middleton* was rigged as a tern. Although tern is mostly commonly used to describe a seabird that is related to gulls, in this instance the word refers to an old-time Down East (or coastal Maine) usage for a three-masted trading schooner.

The best story about the loss of the tern came from Emma Bray David, whose reminiscence was published in 1967. She was a young girl when she witnessed the stranding. This is her recollection in full:

"The old wreck down by the river has been a part of the scenery here at Higgins Beach so long that most folks just take it for granted. But there are some of us who can remember when it wasn't there and when it came. Way back in 1897, August 11 [sic], that was a bad, bad night-foggy! It was so thick it looked as if the space between earth and sky was stuffed with gray-white cotton.

"A bunch of 'us kids' rode over to Bowery Beach on our bicycles to a square dance that evening. It was clear when we started; but when the dance was over and we set out for home, it was so foggy we were afraid of running into each other on the river coming down Meeting House Hill and across Spurwink. However, we made it without a mishap. About two o'clock my mother was awakened by loud curdling noises out towards the water, but she could see nothing. When morning came and the fog cleared, we saw a three-masted schooner stationed well inshore near the first point in the river. It was a beautiful ship – majestic – setting there as if at anchor. She didn't look at all like a wreck with a big hole in her hull.

"It was the *Howard W. Middleton*, strongly built of white oak and yellow pine in 1882 [sic] at Camden, New Jersey – a really noble ship. It had left Philadelphia on August 2 with 894 tons of coal for Peter Nickerson and Company in Portland. Captain Shaw was trying to make Richmond Island Harbor inside the breakwater to lay over till morning. Instead, he ran onto that rock near the mouth of the Spurwink. On our geodetic map that rock is charted simply as 'obstruction' and it is only about 28 feet (8.5 m) deep there. If you stand at the foot of Champion Street at a very low tide, you may see the top of the rock beneath a breaker. You can always see a breaker there a couple of hours before and after dead low water.

"Well, there was lots of excitement! The crew came ashore and talked with the residents. Tugs from Portland Harbor plied the water for days taking off coal. She had soft coal in her lower hold and hard coal between decks. On August 12th, she was de-

A postcard picture of the *Howard W. Middleton* after she ran aground.

clared a total loss and was placed in the hands of the underwriters. People began to pick up coal on the beach by the buckets and barrels. Mrs. Kenney remembers that her father drove over from Westbrook with a cart and got two tons of coal for winter.

"People were eager for souvenirs, of course, and many of us remember when some big boys stole the ship's bell. But the Captain or the Sheriff made them return it to the Captain.

"There she stayed on the rocks, pretty as a picture (although she was really broken in two), all the rest of August and was there when we left in September. Sometime that following winter a storm broke her up and washed her ashore where she now lies. There is a piece of it in the river, too, which can be seen at low tide. There are always changes around the old wreck. Years ago there was quite a big swimming pool around the ocean end of it with water as deep as eight feet near the boat. A twelve year old boy was drowned there one summer.

"Some years the ribs of the hull stand up head high above the beach and perhaps the next year they will be buried in the sand. For years we picked up beautiful iridescent pieces of coal showing red, green, and blue; and even now you may find a lone piece from the old *Howard W. Middleton*. A few people have a picture of this boat on paper weights. These pictures were taken from the beach and showed this proud, three-masted vessel in her last days of beauty.

"P.S. In talking with several people, I found that my memory did not agree with theirs. I had the date wrong and I couldn't think of the name, but I did remember the number of tons of coal. However all the facts herein have been verified by the old newspaper records of August 11 and 12, 1897."

Today, the bottom of the hull is exposed at low tide. It is a popular subject for photographers who venture onto the sandy beach.

IRVINGTON

Built: 1907
Previous names: None
Gross tonnage: 398
Type of vessel: Steel-hulled tug
Builder: Burlee Dry Dock Company, Richmond, New York
Owner: Lehigh Valley Transportation Company, Jersey City, New Jersey
Port of registry: Perth Amboy, New Jersey
Cause of sinking: Ran aground
Location: Pond Island Ledge

Sunk: October 29, 1914
Depth: 50 feet
Dimensions: 140' x 26' x 15'
Power: coal-fired steam

GPS: 44-00.799 / 69-02.135

A tugboat has often been described as a large and powerful engine surrounded by a hull. This attribute fit the *Irvington* perfectly. Her hull was propelled by a 3-cylinder triple-expansion reciprocating steam engine that developed one thousand horsepower: the kind of engine that was employed to propel large tankers and freighters. The *Irvington* was engaged in the occupation of towing strings of anthracite-laden barges from Perth Amboy, New Jersey to various northern ports. There was little glamor in the job but it provided an adequate livelihood for the members of the crew, with some profit leftover for the stockholders of the company.

Some barge strings contained as many as four barges, or dismasted schooners that had outlived their usefulness under sail.

On her final voyage, the *Irvington* departed from Gloucester, Massachusetts at 9:15 on the morning of October 29, 1914. Her destination was Rockland, Maine. The stalwart tug was commanded by Captain Harry Herbert. Fifteen crewmembers attended to duties other than navigation. By the time tug and tow neared their destination, the sun had set and the weather had turned "misty." Yet they continued to maintain a speed of 12 knots.

In some manner that was never explained, the *Irvington* got off course and "took wrong departure when running for Rockland, Maine." Without warning she struck the "Pond Island Ledge inside Muscle Ledges, about 10 miles from Rockland," and there she remained. The time was 7 p.m., about one hour before high tide.

There was no loss of life and no injuries were reported. The barges stayed afloat; later they were taken in tow by another tug, and were delivered to their destination where people eagerly awaited their home heating fuel.

The *Irvington* was valued at $75,000. She was insured for $64,600.

At first there was hope that the tug could be pulled off the rocky bar on the morning high tide by a pair of Revenue Cutters. That was not to be. So the T.A. Scott Company, a respected salvage outfit that was located in New London, Connecticut, was hired for the job. (The T.A. Scott Company later merged with the Merritt & Chapman Derrick & Wrecking Company to form Merritt-Chapman & Scott.)

In accordance with orders from Captain David Chase, the marine agent of the Lehigh Valley Transportation Company, Scott's workers loaded pumps, anchors, pontoons, chains, and salvage gear onto the salvage barge *Salvor*, and proceeded for the site of the stranding under tow of the tug *Neptune*. In addition to the crew, also on board

From the collection of Steve Lang.

the *Salvor* were divers, riggers, engineers.

By the time of their arrival – late in the afternoon of October 30 – the *Irvington's* crew had already lightened the tug's load by offloading everything that was movable. A bevy of vessels surrounded the stranded tug.

Scott's salvors "arranged for day light start to the wreck and for Mr. Perry to send one of the tugs down to assist us in case of need. Mr. Fenwick made arrangements with George W. Turny with his motor boat to act as official watchman and for him to get all of the coal out of her bunkers that he could."

Salvage operations started in earnest at daybreak, November 1. An 8-inch pump was installed in the fire room: "found that she would lower the water rapidly." Half an hour later, a southwest "wind and sea rose so fast that we were obliged to disconnect and tow in under the lee of the islands. Sent *Neptune* to town for coal and water. All hands onboard *Irvington* in surf boat working all possible coal out of bunkers. During this 24 hours got out nearly 100 tons of coal."

After the storm passed, an inspection during low tide revealed a long crack in the hull outboard of the garboard strake. "Got diver in dress and pine wedged this opening." Meanwhile, crewmembers resumed the discharge of coal.

High swells prevented work the following day. When the seas moderated, another 8-inch pump was installed. The crew continued to throw coal overboard.

On November 4, the *Salvor's* windlass was cabled to a 2,800-pound anchor, and other cables were stretched to the *Irvington* in preparation for an attempt to pull the tug off the rocks "if opportunity presented itself." In addition to the *Neptune*, three other tugs were positioned to help: the *Perth Amboy*, *Cumberland*, and *J.C. Morrison*. All hawsers were in place by the noon high water. The sea churned as all four vessels strained to pull the *Irvington* off the ledge . . . and failed.

A couple of days later, kelp was found flowing in the engine room. Examination found "her hull crushed and broken." Although the tug lay completely exposed at low water – resting on the ledge as if in dry dock – salvors were unable to locate the leak. At high tide, seawater ebbed and flowed throughout the lower hull.

November 7: "Decided the proposition of floating her impractical at this season of the year. Took our pumps and gear off of her [the *Irvington*] and proceeded to Rockland."

For its services, the T.A. Scott Company submitted a bill in the amount of $3,005.14.

The Snow Marine Company, of Rockland, then attempted to strip the hulk of its valuables. John Snow, president and manager of the company, reported to Scott: "We started operating on the *Irvington* the 13th but the weather was rough and the hull got considerable hammering before we got there in the storm preceding the Sunday nights gale. We got nothing off her worth mentioning and were driven away Sunday afternoon in the beginning of the Southeast gale. It has been so rough since that we have not been able to do anything except take pictures, one of which I will mail with this letter. Apparently the sea threw her ahead so that her stern is about where the lighter laid alongside in the deep hole, the forward end having slewed to the westward having followed the valley in the ledge. Apparently she has shoved her bow into the mud. . . .

"Sunday at low water the rock forward of her engine room bulkhead in line with the air pump was up through her three feet and a half. Close to her keel in the corner of the coal bunker and after end of the fireroom alley, a similar rock was up through far enough to reach the planking of the bunker floor. . . .

"Since you left there has not been a day when it has been fitting to lay a lighter alongside with the exception of two or three hours on the ebb tide."

The wreck was officially abandoned to the underwriters.

On November 16, it was reported that "high seas tossed the tug off a ledge into deep water."

The phrase "They don't make them like they used to" clearly applies to the *Irvington*. For example, the deck railing was made of solid brass. A steam whistle that measured four feet nine inches in height adorned the smokestack that stretched forty-eight feet above the boat deck. During summer operations, an awning was spread over the foredeck for the comfort of the crewmen who lived in the forecastle. The *Irvington* was as stately a workboat as could be built, equivalent to the fancy tractor-trailers that you see on the Interstates.

Today the *Irvington* is a popular dive site for those who care to explore a towboat from yesteryear.

JESSICA ANN

Built: 1979
Previous names: None
Gross tonnage: 173
Type of vessel: Steel-hulled commercial fishing vessel
Builder: Master Marine, Bayou La Batre, Alabama
Owner: Zenon Gogola, Quincy, Massachusetts
Port of registry: Boston, Massachusetts
Cause of sinking: Struck Alden Rock
Location: 2 miles south of Cape Elizabeth

Sunk: February 20, 2000
Depth: 156 feet
Dimensions: 81' x 22' x 11'
Power: diesel engine

GPS: 43-32-06.80 / 70-12-14.10

Nowadays, large vessel losses are few and far between. The news media tends to make the most of the few that occur, thus giving a false impression to the public that they are common events. Most of the vessel losses that do occur involve fishing vessels, for no other reason than the fact that there are so many of them plying coastal seas. The law of averages catches up with such vessels the way traffic crashes seem to plague Interstate highways: not because they are dangerous but because so many vehicles travel on them.

In the instant case, however, there were mitigating factors; or, to be precise, there was *one* mitigating factor: alcohol. And not the kind that fuels lamps or rubs out sore muscles.

The owner and operator of the fishing vessel *Jessica Ann* was Zenon Gogola. He went under the corporate name of Gulf of Maine Trawlers, of which he was the "sole officer and sole shareholder." His crew consisted of Ken Davis, Mike Patterson, Mike Williams, and Marina Ames.

According to court documents (with citings omitted), "Beginning sometime in the afternoon of February 19, 2000 and continuing until sometime around midnight of the same day, Gogola and the entire crew gather[ed] at a tavern in Portland to eat and drink beer. . . . At approximately midnight on February 19, 2000 Gogola and the crew left the tavern and went to the F/V *Jessica Ann*. . . . After returning to the F/V *Jessica Ann*, Davis went to bed and slept, while Gogola drank an additional 3 or 4 beers and worked on the nets."

A planned eight or nine day trip began when "Gogola had Davis roused from his bunk and told Davis to get the F/V *Jessica Ann* underway and proceed to the fishing grounds while Gogola went to his bunk to sleep. . . . The weather at the time was fine, with good visibility, no wind and a ground swell from the east."

Davis cleared Portland Head and "set the autopilot on 150 Magnetic. . . . There was a compass deviation card in the pilot house of the vessel, the purpose of which was to state the deviation between the magnetic readings of a compass and known magnetic direction, but Davis did not know if the card was dated or when the compass was last adjusted. Davis did not manually take fixes nor mark the vessel's position on a chart while operating the F/V *Jessica Ann* on February 20, 2000. Davis visually observed the flashing red #4 and green #3 buoys marking the channel through West Cod Ledge. He observed two unlighted aids . . .

"There were two main obstructions in the path of the F/V *Jessica Ann*: Old Anthony Rock and Alden Rock. Both are charted on . . . Survey Chart Number 3290. Alden Rock is marked by a red flashing buoy. The buoy marking Alden Rock was on station and working properly on February 20, 2000.

"At approximately 4:00 a.m. on February 20, 2000, while proceeding at approximately 8 knots, Davis heard a loud 'wham' as the F/V Jessica Ann struck something in the water, which Davis believed was Alden Rock. Gogola heard the noise and went to the pilot house. Soon after Gogola arrived at the pilot house, a high bilge level alarm sounded. Gogola went to the engine room and discovered a cracked weld in a seam that was located below the starboard fuel tank. The compartment was flooding rapidly. Gogola started all four bilge pumps but they did not keep up with the flooding. Gogola returned to the pilot house to call the Coast Guard but the VHF radio was inoperative. At approximately 4:30 a.m. on February 20, 2000 Gogola gave the order to abandon ship. After donning survival suits, Gogola and the crew boarded the life raft. Williams shot off three flares."

The Coast Guard station at South Portland received "a telephone notification that a flare was sighted off Cape Elizabeth." A patrol boat was dispatched immediately and soon "reported seeing a life raft near Alden Rock and recovered Gogola and the crew of the F/V *Jessica Ann* from the raft. The F/V *Jessica Ann* sank in approximately 130 [sic] feet of water about 1 nautical mile southwest of Alden Rock, in the vicinity of Old Anthony Rock. Because the patrol boat reported that the crew appeared to be intoxicated," Coast guard personnel "calibrated the station's Alco-Sensor III, a device that measures BAC [blood alcohol concentration]."

All but Ames registered some concentration of blood alcohol. Gogola "failed two of the field sobriety tests."

In court, Davis pleaded guilty to a misdemeanor charge of "one count of operating a commercial fishing vessel under the influence of alcohol." He was fined $1,000 and sentenced to a year and a half of "strict probation." "Strict probation" meant that if he drank alcohol or went to a bar he could be put in prison for a year.

Gogola pleaded guilty to "one count of operating a commercial fishing vessel in a grossly negligent manner" by allowing Davis to pilot the boat. He was sentenced to one year of "strict probation."

But for Gogola, the worst was yet to come. First, on account of the circumstances under which the *Jessica Ann* was lost – "willful misconduct," but read "drunkenness" – his insurance company refused to pay his claim for $300,000: the appraised value the fishing vessel before she sank.

Second, at the wreck site, the Coast Guard "reported a slight sheen, presumably coming from the vessel's fuel vents." The Coast Guard then initiated a "removal action" pursuant to the Oil Pollution Act. It was estimated that the *Jessica Ann's* fuel tanks contained approximately 12,000 gallons of diesel fuel, which was at risk of leaking into the surrounding seawater.

The Coast Guard's first action in this regard was to hire divers to examine the wreck. Divers "verified that the fuel tanks were intact and the diesel was leaking from the vents. It was estimated that 1 gallon per hour was leaking out of the tanks."

The next step was to stop the leakage. As a temporary expedient, on March 1, 2000, contract divers again descended to the wreck and plugged the vents.

On April 4, 2000, the Coast Guard established a safety zone of 1,000 yards in diameter around the site of the wreck, "to protect the environment from a diesel fuel spill which may occur from the disturbance of the sunken vessel F/V *Jessica Ann*." The safety zone was effective until July 1, 2000.

This meant, "All vessels and persons are prohibited from anchoring, diving, dredging, dumping, fishing, trawling, laying cable, or conducting salvage operations in this zone except as authorized by the Coast Guard Captain of Port, Portland, Maine. Innocent transit through the area within the safety zone is not affected by this regulation and does not require the authorization of the Captain of the Port."

Finally, the Coast Guard decided that the diesel fuel had to be removed from the tanks. Foul winter weather precluded immediate fuel recovery operations.

Containment contractors did not start work until late spring. The Coast Guard's plan was "to have the divers drill holes in the tanks, attach valves, open up the fill/vents, and oil would flow through a line to the surface. The first day this was attempted only 800 gallons were recovered, most of which were water."

Rough seas intervened, so "the job will be completed in the summer, during more favorable sea conditions." Not until July 25, 2000 was all the fuel oil removed. The total cost for the removal operation amounted to nearly one million dollars, or $930,510.09 to be exact.

"On January 15, 2003, GMT [Gulf of Maine Trawlers, or Zenon Gogola, who was the sole owner of the corporation, whose only asset had been the *Jessica Ann*] paid the United States $80,906.21, leaving an unpaid balance of $849,603.88. On January 27, 2003 the United States filed suit against GMT to recover the remaining $849,603.88 expended from the Oil Spill Liability Trust Fund to respond to the sinking of the F/V *Jessica Ann*."

Court records noted, "On August 6, 1999 GMT had purchased a one-year marine oil pollution insurance policy covering F/V *Jessica Ann* against liability arising under the Oil Pollution Act from a discharge of oil or the substantial threat of discharge of oil from the *Jessica Ann*. WQIS [Water Quality Insurance Syndicate] underwrote the policy, which bears policy number 29-07458 (the 'Policy'). WQIS provided coverage to GMT following the sinking of the F/V *Jessica Ann* until sometime in June 2000. On June 30, 2000 WQIS informed GMT that coverage for the government's claim was excluded under the Policy because the sinking of the F/V *Jessica Ann* arose from the willful misconduct of Gogola, who was intoxicated when the F/V *Jessica Ann* got underway and who knew that Davis was intoxicated when he ordered Davis to get the vessel underway."

In other words, Gogola's insurance company left him twisting in the wind; or, as the case may be, in an alcoholic effluvium.

In fact, the policy contained exclusions to which WQIS pointed: "Notwithstanding any provision in this Policy to the contrary, this Policy does not provide coverage for any liability, loss, damage, cost or expenses arising from . . . (6) The willful misconduct of the Assured, or the willful misconduct of the owner or operator of the Vessel if within the privity or knowledge of the Assured."

Both plaintiff and defendant cited prior decisions to bolster their claims for summary judgment against the other. Secondary aspects apart, ultimately the divisive point involved the definition of "willful misconduct," which was also referred to as "recklessness" and "negligence." The case that seems to have had the most relevance was on in which a drunken sailor was injured aboard a vessel, in which the court noted, "A seaman who suffers injury as a result of intoxication has no claim against the vessel or her owners."

Five years passed before the final opinion was rendered. In the final analysis, the court ruled:

"It therefore becomes necessary to decide whether the intoxication of Gogola and Davis constituted willful misconduct, in the absence of definitive federal or New York case law on point. It seems logical to me that if a seaman has no cause of action for injuries incurred on a vessel while he was intoxicated, then it is reasonable to conclude that voluntary intoxication of a vessel's captain and the man he put at the helm of a fishing vessel constitutes willful misconduct by both individuals which may be ascribed to their employer. Accordingly I recommend that the court grant the motion of WQIS for summary judgment and deny that of the government."

To be clear on this point, Gogola and Davis were found by sobriety tests to be inebriated when the *Jessica Ann* put to sea. The fishing vessel struck a submerged rock and sank after Gogola ordered Davis to take the helm. Gogola was covered by insurance against the spillage of contaminants. The insurance company afterward denied coverage on the grounds of willful misconduct, citing intoxication. The court upheld the policy's exclusion. Payment for the clean-up was taken out of the Oil Spill Liability Trust Fund.

To reduce this train of events to a mathematical formula, you may recall from high school algebra that if A equals B, and B equals C, then A equals C. It therefore follows that a straightforward translation to a real-life scenario signifies that the American taxpayers paid the bill when Gogola had one beer too many.

Joseph S. Zeman. (From the collection of Dave Clancy.)

JOSEPH S. ZEMAN

Built: 1919
Previous names: None
Gross tonnage: 1,956
Type of vessel: Wooden-hulled five-masted schooner
Builder: Percy & Small, Bath, Maine
Owner: Stanley Navigation Company, Delaware
Port of registry: New York, NY
Cause of sinking: Ran aground
Location: Metinic Island, Penobscot Bay

Sunk: February 3, 1922
Depth: 50 feet
Dimensions: 253' x 43' x 23'
Power: sail

The usage of schooners for the transportation of bulk cargoes was going strong at the end of the nineteenth- century and in the beginning of the twentieth-century. Gradually they were being replaced by steamships, which did not have to rely upon the fickle wind for propulsion. By the 1910's, schooners were in decline as the main means of transport.

Instead of sailing, many schooners were dismasted and towed by tugs in strings that resembled elephants on parade – and white elephants at that. With the coming of the Great War, sailing vessels of all kinds underwent a resurgence as the need for bottoms increased dramatically. The lull in shipbuilding ended in an explosion of hull construction, both sail and steam. Freight rates soared, and there was money to be made by building anything that could float, however temporarily. Shipyards were created from the ground up in order to meet the industrial demand.

The offshore trade collapsed with the signing of the Armistice. Those who climbed onto the bandwagon too late found themselves possessing vessels for which there was no need. Literally hundreds of wooden-hulled steamships were laid up due to lack of cargoes to transport. Against this dire economic situation, schooners hardly had an opportunity to survive.

Construction of the *Joseph S. Zeman* was completed in this mercantile vacuum, in 1919. Her owners immediately found themselves holding a nearly useless appendage. It was impossible to earn a profit and pay off investment debt and maintenance costs.

In January 1921, the Beaver Trust Company brought suit against the Stanley Navigation Company and the Zephyr Navigation Company for failure to pay their mortgage debts. The trust company had floated bonds for the two navigation companies in the amount of $250,000, so they could purchase the *Joseph S. Zeman*. The trust company held title to the schooner, which was used as collateral in order to procure the loan. The outstanding debt was $120,000.

The schooner continued to operate under receivership . . . but knot furlong, er, not for long.

Merchant Vessels of the United States noted that on February 3, 1922 the *Joseph S. Zeman* stranded on "Matinin Ledge, Penobscot Bay, Me." I presume that "Matinin" was meant to be "Metinic." No fatalities were recorded among the eleven people on board at the time she ran aground.

The wreck is supposed to be diveable.

MARY F. BARRETT

Built: 1901
Previous names: None
Gross tonnage: 1,833
Type of vessel: Wooden-hulled five-masted schooner
Builder: Gardiner G. Deering, Bath, Maine
Owner: Joe Totman
Port of registry: Unregistered
Cause of sinking: Abandoned
Location: Robinhood Cove, Georgetown

Sunk: 1929
Depth: Visibly exposed
Dimensions: 241' x 43' x 24'
Power: sail

GPS: 43-50.664 / 69-43.951

The *Mary F. Barrett* was a flush-deck schooner. This means that her weather deck was surrounded by posts and a top rail (much like a handrail on a staircase) instead of a bulwark (which was equivalent to a low wall). Vessels of this design were uncommonly wet in rough seas because, without the barrier of a bulwark, waves readily washed between the posts and rolled across the deck. Of course, the water washed out just as fast.

To compensate for the lack of a bulwark, the deck was slightly humped in the middle, the way macadam roads are built to shed rainwater to the sides. Also, the forward deck curved upward so that the elevated stem prevented the bow from dipping beneath upcoming wave tops.

It was believed that the flush-deck design added character to a vessel's contours, whereas bulwarks presented a boxlike configuration that appeared strictly utilitarian.

The *Mary F. Barrett* suffered her share of misfortunes. On January 21, 1906, she was making her way through thick fog and heavy seas when collided with the *Alice E. Clark*, "striking the port side about 3 feet abaft the main rigging, damaging same, carrying away mainmast, and other damage. Damage estimated at $5,000. No one injured; no loss of life."

At the time of the collision the wind was southwest, the *Alice E. Clark* was southbound on the starboard tack, while the *Mary F. Barrett* was southbound on the port tack. The resulting convergence occurred off the coast of Delaware.

The *Mary F. Barrett's* bowsprit was sprung, carrying away her stays and damaging her stem. As she was already bound in ballast from Boston, Massachusetts to Norfolk, Virginia, she continued southward and into the Chesapeake Bay, where she put in to a shipyard for repairs.

Investigators concluded, "On receipt of detailed reports from masters of schooners, we found that schooner *Mary F. Barrett*, the vessel required to keep out of the way by the international rules for preventing collisions, owing to the direction of the wind did not clearly hear the fog signal of the other vessel, until such time as collision was inevitable, when every endeavor was made to avoid same. Both reports agree in stating that fog signals, lookouts, etc., were strictly complied with, as required by international rules."

On September 13, 1918, crewmember Ronald McDonald was knocked overboard and drowned when the *Mary F. Barrett* collided with the schooner *Lottie G. Merchant*

Maine

From the collection of Paul Sherman.

off Monhegan Island.

In a subsequent incident, the *Mary F. Barrett* was transporting logwood from Jamaica to Chester, Pennsylvania when the master got off his course and ran aground on a reef off the coast of Cuba. The crew turned to, and by herculean efforts were able to jettison enough cargo to let the schooner float free and continue on her way with considerably less weight. That might have been the end of the matter if everyone had acted honestly and responsibly. Unfortunately, underwriters and their lawyers tried their best to muddy the Caribbean waters.

The instigation for shameless events to follow was the conjuration of an insurance clause called "general average." According to this clause, when a vessel and/or her cargo was damaged, the financial loss should be shared equally among those who incurred a loss. The underwriters argued that the *Mary F. Barrett* also suffered financial loss because some of her property was jettisoned as well. Their argument was in accordance with the doctrine that the sacrifice was made for the common benefit of all.

In the instant case, not all of the cargo that was shipped by the American Dyewood Company was delivered in accordance with the company's contract with the vessel owner. It sued for payment for the portion of the cargo that was jettisoned in order to save the schooner from destruction.

Attorneys for the American Dyewood Company invoked the Harter's Act of 1893, which read, "It shall not be lawful for the manager, agent, master, or owner of any vessel transporting merchandise or property from or between ports of the United States and foreign ports to insert in any bill of lading or shipping document any clause, covenant, or agreement whereby it, he, or they shall be relieved from liability for loss or damage arising from negligence, fault, or failure in proper loading, stowage, custody, care, or proper delivery of any and all lawful merchandise or property committed to its or their charge. Any and all words or clauses of such import inserted in bills of lading or shipping receipts shall be null and void and of no effect."

The case was decided on January 20, 1921. In rendering its opinion, the most salient features that the court noted were as follows: "As the master admits the schooner was 10 miles out of the course he meant her [the *Mary F. Barrett*] to have taken, an error in navigation was undoubtedly committed. . . . The law has long been established in this country that shipowners cannot contract themselves out of liability for the negligence of the master or crew, which in law is their negligence. . . . Ship and cargo owner had the like right and owed like duty, but the right did not belong to one to whose negligence the necessity for the sacrifice was due.... We see no escape from the conclusion that the necessity for the sacrifice of the part of this cargo which was not delivered arose out of a dangerous situation resulting from the negligence of the master, which was in law the negligence of the shipowners, and that the defense that the case is one of general average must be denied them.... Our conclusion is that the proximate cause of the loss of cargo was not any error in navigation, but the throwing of the cargo overboard ... and the libellant is entitled to recover its whole loss undiminished by any general average contribution."

Later in 1921, the *Mary F. Barrett* was lying at her wharf in Portland, Maine, when a pack of thugs beat their way up the gangplank and, with racial motivation, physically assaulted black crewmembers. One James Walker was cast overboard to his death.

The beginning of the end of the *Mary F. Barrett's* most productive career commenced in 1925, when Deering sold her and the *Gardiner G. Deering* (which see) to the Boston Ship Brokerage Company. She lingered in the coal trade for two more years, then was laid up at Bath, Maine. There were notions of converting her to a schooner barge by dismasting her and towing the hull at the end of a hawser, but that scheme never materialized.

Joe Totman purchased the idling hulk with the intention of salvaging any useful parts. In 1929, she was towed to Robinhood Cove and partially dismantled. Then the hull was left there to rot. She is rotting there today.

The wreck is easy to spot because some of the timbers protrude above the surface of the water. Getting there is another matter. Head east from Bath on Route 1 across the Kennebec River. Turn right (south) on the other side of the river onto Route 127. Proceed five miles or so, through Arrowsic, across the Back River, and turn left (northeast) onto Robinhood Road. This leads to the Robinhood Marina a mile and a quarter later. Pass the marina and dogleg into the parking lot of the Osprey Restaurant. Park at the far (south) end. From there it is about half a mile south along the Sasanoa River to the wreck site, just past the east headland and near to the dock of a house.

Motorboats must be launched at the marina, but canoes and kayaks can be put-in on the rocks past the parking lot. Proceed downstream. Hug the left bank at the narrows. The wreck is tucked into the small cove, with a northwest heading.

You can also reach the wreck by land. Instead of turning onto Robinhood Road, keep going straight for several miles on Route 127. Cross the bridge over the Sasanoa River. A couple of miles later take Old Schoolhouse Road on the left (north). Shy of half a mile, take North End Road on the left (north). This road is unpaved but the dirt surface is compacted. Close to two miles later you will enter a Nature Conservancy called Loring Conant Preserve. Park in the lot.

Now bushwhack through the boggy forest for a quarter mile on an easterly heading. When you reach the water, determine if you are upstream or downstream of the cove, or walk a short distance in either direction until you see the wreck tucked into the cove. If your heading was too far southerly, you will bump into a house; the wreck lies upstream (north, to your right). If your heading was too far northerly, you will see nothing but trees in either direction, and no cove if you look north (to your right); then go the other way to the wreck.

Admittedly this is a long way to carry scuba, but it is not too far to take snorkeling gear and a wetsuit. The lower hull is contiguous on the bottom, ripe for exploration.

The picture above was taken from the end of the Osprey Restaurant parking lot, looking south. Canoes and Kayaks can be launched from the rocks. Paddle straight ahead for half a mile while hugging the left bank. The picture below shows the wreck from shore. More of the hull is exposed when the tide is lower.

NORTH AMERICA

Built: 1839
Previous names: None
Gross tonnage: 296
Type of vessel: Wooden-hulled side-wheel steamer
Builder: William and Richard Wright, Courtney Bay, St. John, New Brunswick, Canada
Owner: M.B. Almon, Halifax, Nova Scotia
Port of registry: Unknown
Cause of sinking: Blown ashore off Long Island, Mount Desert

Sunk: November 25, 1846
Depth: Unknown
Dimensions: 155' x 25' x 13'
Power: coal-fired steam

Courtesy of Erik Heyl.

The *North America* had a number of owners during her short career. She did valuable freight and passenger service for all of them, operating for the most part between St. John, New Brunswick and Boston, Massachusetts, and stopping at ports in between.

This early steamer was equipped with two vertical beam engines, each with its own boiler and linkage. The paddle wheels measured twenty-two feet in diameter. According to Erik Heyl, "It is reported that her engines were brought from England in the *British Queen*."

Heyl: "On November 25, 1846 the *North America* left Eastport for Boston about 10:00 AM, some two hours before the departure of the *Portland*. At dusk the people of the *Portland* saw the *North America* going into Moosepecca Harbor, when it had started to blow and snow very hard. The *Portland* made for shelter for Mt. Desert, as the wind hauled around from N.E. to S.E., blowing hurricane force.

"In the meanwhile the *North America* was doing her best to reach safety; she was laboring hard in the wild and confused seas, when her steam pipes burst and left her helpless. The bursting of the steam pipes was in all likelihood caused by the working of the hull. When the unfortunate steamer had drifted to within half a mile of the shore both anchors were let go and apparently held. But the *North America* was straining so badly in the high waves that she soon became waterlogged, and it became imperative to cut the cables and allow her to drift ashore on Long Island, Mt. Desert, Me.

"The passengers and crew were all saved with the exception of one fireman, but the steamer, her cargo and much of her baggage became a total loss. The survivors were taken to Boston in the *Penobscot*."

The location of the wreck is presently unknown. According to the National Park Service, "David Farley of Bass Harbor reported finding a large anchor off the southwest side of Long Island, Frenchboro, while scuba diving in sixty feet of water." The NPS speculated on the possibility that the anchor could be one of those that the *North America* cast off, but added this caveat: "It could also have been an anchor from other reported wrecks in the vicinity such as *Ricochet* or *Union*, or from another vessel entirely."

NOTTINGHAM

Built: Unknown
Previous names: Unknown
Gross tonnage: 120
Type of vessel: Wooden-hulled two-masted galley
Builder: Unknown
Owner: Jasper Dean, London, England
Sunk: December 11, 1710
Depth: 20 feet
Dimensions: Unknown
Power: Sail

Port of registry: London, England
Cause of sinking: Ran aground on the east side of Boon Island

    The first misconception that I would like to correct is the name of the vessel. In the old days, it was common to denote the rig of a vessel by appending it after her name. A vessel might be a ship, brig, brigantine, bark, barkentine, galley, and so on. Differences were distinguished by the rig: that is, the number of masts, the type of sails (quadrilateral or lateen), and how the sails were rigged or stepped on the masts. There were also hybrid rigs.

    Note that in old-time nautical terms, "ship" was not a generic word for any vessel afloat; it was a sailing vessel that sported three or more masts, each of which had a topmast and a topgallantmast, and all of whose quadrilateral sails were square-rigged: that is, spread athwartship, or perpendicular to the centerline.

    In this context, the vessel that is the subject of this chapter was not named *Nottingham Galley*. Her name was given as *Nottingham* galley, meaning that the *Nottingham* was a galley: a commonly accepted short form or abbreviation that people of the day understood.

    The word galley has been applied to several type of vessels throughout the millennia, going all the way back to Greek and Roman times. In the 1700's, a galley was an armed sailing vessel (naval or commerce) with lateen (triangular) sails that were rigged fore-and-aft (as in a schooner). The *Nottingham* carried ten guns on her top deck for protection against pirates.

    The second misconception deals with the facts that surround the grounding and subsequent occurrences on Boon Island. The most popular account was written by Kenneth Roberts in 1956. Appropriately enough, it was entitled *Boon Island*. This is the most widely read version of the *Nottingham* catastrophe, and it is a spectacular read that is in keeping with Roberts' previous novels. Although the book adheres closely to the facts, author's license – which Roberts openly acknowledged – enabled him to tell a story that was more dramatic than actual incidents. In addition to a story of survival, Roberts created conflict among the participants and added dialogue that he had no way to know or corroborate. This literary form is called historical fiction, in which real happenings provide the basis of a story to which the author adds dialogue and imaginary trappings.

    Two contemporary accounts were published by survivors: one written by Captain John Dean, master of the *Nottingham*, and a refutation written by Christopher Langman, the *Nottingham*'s mate and second in command. The relationship between these two men was rather like that between William Bligh and Fletcher Christian, of *Bounty* fame. With regard to the *Bounty*, Bligh condemned Christian as a base mutineer, while Christian castigated Bligh as a brutal and abusive slave driver.

At this remove it is difficult if not impossible to know which account was true (on the *Bounty* as well as on the *Nottingham*). Therefore I am taking the liberty of relating both sides of the *Nottingham* story. The first body of text is taken from Dean's point of view. In order to preserve the narrative flow without interruption, I have appended a second body of text that is taken from Langman's point of view, but only those portions that constitute additional information and disagreements with Dean. Keep in mind that neither account may be perfectly accurate. Each author may have inserted his own bias.

Caveat lector: let the reader beware.

Both accounts agree that onboard the *Nottingham* at the time of departure were "fourteen men, John Dean, commander." I have interpreted this phrase this to mean "fourteen men *including* John Dean," but in the interest of historical accuracy I must note that others have interpreted this phrase to mean "fourteen men *plus* John Dean."

In either case, the *Nottingham* departed from London, England on September 25, 1710. A cargo of cordage lay packed in her holds. She made a stop in Ireland for an additional cargo of butter and cheese, then proceeded toward her final destination: Boston, Massachusetts. Foul weather and contrary winds followed her across the Atlantic.

For eleven days rain, hail, and snow prevented stellar observations. The *Nottingham* proceeded westward by relying on compass and dead reckoning. "I saw the breakers ahead, whereupon I called out to put the helm hard to starboard, but before the ship could wear we struck upon the east end of the rock called Boon-Island, four leagues [twelve statute miles] to the eastward of Piscataqua."

Boon Island was an inhospitable chunk of bedrock that measured two football fields in length by one football field in width. No one lived there. Nothing grew there.

The howling wind and fierce seas threatened to tear the galley apart on the submerged ledge. The fog was so thick that the men could not see the island. Dean ordered the men to cut down the shrouds. "The force of the sea soon broke the masts, so that they fell right toward the shore."

One of the men crawled out on the bowsprit, from which he thought he could see land through the darkness. He and two others (one being the Mate), leaped overboard and swam onto the island. Dean tried to save some things to carry to the island, but "the ship bulging, her decks opened, her back broke, and her beams gave way, so that the stern sunk under water, I was, therefore, hastened forward to escape instant death."

Dean and the rest of the men soon followed their companions. They splashed and crawled and clawed their way up the slippery rocks until they were clear of the breakers, and joined the three men who had preceded them. There was no shelter from the wind and snow. The rock was so uneven that they could not walk to create body heat.

Daylight brought revelation about their isolation and plight. The galley had gone to pieces during the night. Flotsam was washed ashore, but the only food the men found were pieces of cheese. They collected everything they could find. A canvas provided scant shelter. They had a steel and flint, but the wood from the wreck was so water-soaked that they could not start a fire. One man died in the sub-freezing conditions, from what today is called hypothermia. They commended his body to the sea.

"After we had been in this situation two or three days, the frost being very severe, and the weather extremely cold, it seized most of our hands and feet to such a degree as to take away the sense of feeling, and render them almost useless, so benumbing and discoloring them as gave us just reason to apprehend mortification. We pulled off

Woodcut from *The Mariners' Chronicle* (1835)

our shoes; and cut off our boots, but in getting off our stockings, many, whose legs were blistered, pulled off skin and all, and some, the nails of their toes. We then wrapped up our legs and feet as warmly as we could in oakum and canvass."

As more flotsam came ashore, they were able to build the semblance of a tent from sails. They hoisted a piece of cloth on a staff as a signal for passing fishing vessels. They managed to scavenge a few tools: a hammer, a caulking mallet, knives, and a cutlass. They built a small boat out of planks, used sheathing nails to keep them together, erected side panels on stanchions, and caulked the bottom and sides with oakum.

The cold was so severe that they were able to work no more than four hours a day, "and some days we could do nothing at all." They scrounged some beef bones "which we ate, after beating them to pieces."

After about a week they spotted three boats on the horizon. The men screamed and waved their makeshift flag, but "they neither heard nor saw us."

Small fortune came to them when the waves tossed the carpenter's ax on the rock, "by which we were enabled to complete our work [on the boat], but then we had scarcely strength sufficient to get her into the water."

On the tenth day of their confinement, seven of the strongest men waded into the water and attempted to launch the boat into the surf. The venture was short-lived. A large swell "heaved her along shore and overset her upon us, whereby we again narrowly escaped drowning. Our poor boat was staved all to pieces, our enterprise totally disappointed, and our hopes utterly destroyed."

In addition to being starved, the men were now wet and colder than they were before. Their hands and feet were frozen, and their legs were covered with deep ulcers, "the smell of which was highly offensive to those who could not creep into the air" outside the tent. When they finished the cheese, they resorted to eating "rockweed and a few muscles [sic]."

"As a slight alleviation of our faith, Providence directed toward our quarters a seagull, which my mate struck down and joyfully brought to me. I divided it into equal portions, and though raw, and scarcely affording a mouthful for each, yet we received and ate it thankfully."

Next they decided to build a two-person raft. The finished product measured four feet square. Side boards were attached to keep out spray. "We fixed up a mast, and out of two hammocks that were driven on shore we made a sail, with a paddle for each man, and a spare one in case of necessity."

Another vessel was spotted in the distance, but again the men were unable to attract its attention.

The raft was launched with the same result that befell the boat: a huge swell overturned it. When the raft was launched a second time, it got away from the island and headed west. By sunset, the raft was halfway to the mainland. "Two days afterward the raft was found on shore, and one man dead about a mile from it, with a paddle fastened to his wrist; but the Swede, who was so very forward to adventure, was never heard of more."

Another man died toward the end of December. He was a large person, and the stranded men were so enfeebled by starvation that they were unable to haul the body out of the tent. Only by tying a rope to the body were they able to drag it outside. It was then that "the men began to request my permission to eat the dead body, the better to support their lives."

"After mature consideration of the lawfulness or sinfulness on the one hand, and absolute necessity on the other, judgment and conscience were obliged to submit to the more prevailing arguments of our craving appetites. We at length determined to satisfy our hunger, and support our feeble bodies with the carcass of our deceased companion. I first ordered his skin, head, hands, feet, and bowels to be buried in the sea, and the body to be quartered, for the convenience of drying carriage; but again received for answer, that, none of them being able, they entreated I would perform that labor for them. This was a hard task; but their incessant prayers and entreaties at last prevailed over my reluctance, and by night I had completed the operation.

"I cut part of the flesh into thin slices, and washing it in salt water, brought it to the tent and obliged the men to eat rock-weed with it instead of bread. My mate and two others refused to eat any that night, but the next morning they complied, and earnestly desired to partake with the rest.

"I found that they all ate with the utmost avidity, so that I was obliged to carry the quarters farther from the tent, out of their reach, lest they should do themselves an injury by eating too much, and likewise expend our small stock too soon.

"I also limited each man to an equal portion, that they might not quarrel, or have cause to reflect on me or one another. This method I was the more obliged to adopt, because in a few days I found their dispositions entirely changed, and that affectionate, peaceable temper they had hitherto manifested, totally lost. Their eyes looked wild and staring, their countenances fierce and barbarous. Instead of obeying my commands, as they had universally and cheerfully done before, I now found even prayers and entreaties vain and fruitless; nothing was now to be heard but brutal quarrels, with horrid oaths and imprecations, instead of that quiet submissive spirit of prayer and supplication they had before manifested."

By this means the desperate survivors were saved.

Ultimate deliverance arrived on the twenty-second day after their shipwreck. A shallop (a small sailboat equipped with oars) dropped anchor off the southwest corner of the island. The swells prevented the rescuers from approaching any nearer. Finally, around noon, when the seas settled somewhat from a change in the tide, the sailboat advanced close enough for Dean and the rescuers to hold a conversation.

One man came ashore in a canoe. He was aghast at the deplorable state of the survivors. "Our flesh was so wasted and our looks were so ghastly and frightful, that it was really a very dismal spectacle."

The rescuer was able to make a fire that helped to warm the survivors. Dean importuned the rescuer to take him off the island, "and to send for the rest, one or two at a time. . . . but the sea immediately drove us against the rock with such violence that we were overset, and being very weak, it was a considerable time before I could recover myself, so that I had again a very narrow escape from drowning. The good man with great difficulty got on board without me, designing to return the next day with better conveniences, if the weather should permit."

A sudden squall arose, and the wind "blew so hard that the shallop was lost, and the crew, with extreme difficulty, saved their lives. Had we been with them, it is more than probable that we should all have perished, not having strength sufficient to help ourselves."

The next day was so stormy that no one could venture from the mainland onto the ocean. The following day was calm enough for the shallop to return with a much larger canoe, "and in two hours got us all on board, being obliged to carry almost all of us upon their backs from the tent to the canoe, and fetch us off by two or three at a time."

Ten men survived the terrible ordeal on Boon Island, although "my apprentice lost the greater part of one foot; all the rest recovered their limbs, but not their perfect use; very few, excepting myself, escaping without losing the benefit of fingers or toes, though otherwise all in perfect health."

Langman started his version by stating that four of the ten guns were useless, and that only six of the men onboard were capable sailors. He then started his timeline before the *Nottingham's* departure from London, stating that Dean unnecessarily fought the galley through a gale, after which he attempted first to surrender his command to a pair of French privateers, and second to run the galley ashore, both because Dean's brother Jasper, who owned the *Nottingham*, had over-insured the hull and cargo and could make a good profit if she were hijacked or lost. Langman and the crewmembers managed to talk him out of surrendering and stranding.

Dean's treatment of the men who disagreed with his wishes was so barbarous that he beat them so severely that two of them were unable to work for a month.

In addition to cordage, the rest of the cargo consisted of thirty tons of butter and three hundred cheeses.

Dean limited food and water to salt beef and one quart of water per day. The men got so thirsty that they had to lap rain water off the deck.

When one man took an extra quart of water to quench his thirst, Dean knocked him down and left him for dead.

Off the Banks of Newfoundland, Dean tried to surrender his vessel to another privateer, but the vessel proved to be a British galley.

Instead of heading straight for Boston, the *Nottingham* cruised along the coast for a week, searching for a place to crash.

After Dean and Langman exchanged harsh words, Dean's brother struck Langman with a water keg, and Dean struck him three times with a block on the back of the head, so that Langman fell to the deck unconscious and covered in blood.

When the *Nottingham* approached Boon Island in the dark, Dean did not see the breakers ahead because he was below deck undressing for bed. Dean then cowered in his cabin and cried in fear of losing his life. Langman took charge of cutting down the mainmast and foremast.

By this time waves were rolling right across the deck. Langman and two others reached the island by crawling over the foremast, which had fallen forward and landed on exposed rock. They spent the night in the open. After daybreak, they entreated the rest of the crew to use the mast to reach the island, then to crawl along the rocks until they got above the reach of the waves.

Although Dean claimed this the spit of rock was Boon Island, Langman stated that the captain did not know their location. Langman estimated the distance to the mainland as one league, not four. [In reality, the distance is two leagues, or six miles, so that neither Dean nor Langman was correct.] Langman spotted houses on shore and boats passing to and fro.

In addition to cheese, the survivors had four or five pieces of beef, and one neat's tongue (the tongue of a bovine).

The boat that they knocked together measured twelve feet by four feet, and could hold six men. It had neither mast nor sail. This boat was destroyed the way Dean described it, so the men built a raft. A Dutchman and one other proceeded in it to the mainland. No corpse was found with a paddle secured to his wrist.

Feats such as procuring mussels were performed not by Dean alone, but also by George White.

Dean was the one to suggest eating the flesh of the man who died. The head, hands, feet, and skin were not deposited into the sea, but were left on the island when the survivors abandoned it. Nor did the seamen quarrel with horrid oaths and imprecations. Only the captain, his brother, and Charles Whitworth indulged in such vulgarity.

On January 4, after twenty-four days on Boon Island, "several" sloops made the passage from the mainland to the island to effect the rescue of the survivors, whose number Langman gave as ten: "Two of us having died on the Island, and Two being lost that were sent off on the raft." This confirms my count: that the *Nottingham* started with a total of fourteen men.

The survivors were "John Dean, Captain; Christopher Langman, Mate; Christopher Gray, gunner; Nicholas Mellan, Boatswain; George White, Charles Whitworth, Henry Dean, Charles Graystock, William Saver, and the Captain's Boy, who had Part of his Foot cut off to prevent a Mortification, and several others were lame."

Although Langman signed the captain's deposition, he stated that he signed under duress and the fact that he was "very ill of a Flux and Fever," and was not in his right mind to know what he was doing.

Langman declared numerous other deficiencies in Dean's account, the most recurring of which was that he exaggerated his own efforts and dangers.

So there you have it.

According to modern media, sea urchin divers discovered the *Nottingham's* cannons in 1980. It then took archaeologists from the University of Maine fifteen years to get around to salvaging them. Little else was found in the vicinity other than cannon balls and lead shot. The cannons were preserved by catalytic reduction for several months. Then began the painstaking five-year process of conservation. Eventually one of the cannons was displayed in the Maine State Museum. The rest were put in storage.

OAKEY L. ALEXANDER

Built: 1915
Previous names: *Nevadan, Franklin*
Gross tonnage: 5,285
Type of vessel: Collier
Builder: New York Ship Building Corporation, Camden, New Jersey
Owner: Pocahontas Steam Ship Company, New York, NY
Port of registry: Wilmington, Delaware
Cause of sinking: Broke in two off High Head, Cape Elizabeth
GPS (bow): 43-31.823 / 70-10.312

Sunk: March 3, 1947
Depth: 20 (stern), 190 feet (bow)
Dimensions: 368' x 55' x 30'
Power: coal-fired steam

The *Oakey L. Alexander* led a long, useful, and unblemished career that came to a dramatic and miraculous end on the shore of Cape Elizabeth. She even survived World War Two without a scratch from Nazi U-boats.

To set the stage, during the first week of March 1947, a tremendous snowstorm swept across New England with a vengeance, spreading death and destruction in its wake. On shore, 40-knot winds with 50-knot gusts blew snowflakes sideways for thirty-seven hours straight, with accumulations as much as two and a half feet in certain areas. Schools were closed, vehicular traffic was snowbound, motorists were stranded, trains were delayed by high drifts, and aircraft were grounded.

The conditions at sea were worse. Hurricane-force winds whipped the sea to a froth with wave heights reaching monstrous proportions. "The 100-foot dragger *Vandal* broke from her moorings at Rockland, carrying away a 4-foot section of pier, collided with another ship and sank. At Old Orchard Beach, wreckage bearing the name *Pe-*

The *Oakey L. Alexander* in her wartime guise. (Courtesy of the National Archives.)

Three views of the *Oakey L. Alexander* in extremis against a hostile shore. Note the mammoth surf striking the hull in the middle picture. (All official U.S. Coast Guard photos.)

Joe Cushing discovered the bow in 190 feet of water. According to him, the remnant measures some 120 feet in length. The hull sits upside down on a hard bottom. The keel rises to 140 feet, giving the hull a relief of 50 feet. The anchors are still snugged in their hawse pipes. The cut - where the forward section separated from the after section - is jagged.

maquid came ashore. The 48-foot *Pemaquid 2d*, with a two-man crew, had put out of New Harbor on a fishing trip. The barge *Cullen No. 5* was stranded in Rockland Harbor, the *Freddie B*, a sixty-five-foot mail and freight boat, piled up on the rocks at Owl's Head, near Rockland, and a Navy barge was grounded in Portland Harbor."

Farther at sea, the *Novadoc* (which see) disappeared with all hands. The *Portland* lightship was dragged five miles off station. And the *Oakey L. Alexander* snapped in two like a dry stick.

The collier was on route from Norfolk, Virginia to Portland, Maine with 8,200 tons of bituminous coal. She threaded her way through the Cape Cod Canal in order to avoid the raging open ocean. She poked her nose out of Boston Harbor but hugged the coast on her northbound passage. She was only eight miles from her destination when the steering gear "went out of kilter." The time was 4:46 in the morning, in the dark.

With no way to control his vessel in 70-knot winds, Captain Raymond Lewis immediately ordered Lorenz Connelly, the ship's radio operator, to transmit an SOS. Minutes later the "ship took a dive and the bow ripped apart" with a loud *crack*. The bow kept diving and was never seen again. The truncated stern remained afloat . . . but for how long?

Now 130-feet shorter, and 5,000 tons of coal lighter, the *Oakey L. Alexander* bobbed and rolled in the howling northeaster. Lewis: "A huge sea engulfed the whole ship. It carried off all the lifeboats, hung forty feet above the waterline."

"I thought we were goners," said Third Engineer Manuel Pardo. "I thought we would never get on land again. I got to the deck about ten minutes after the bow went, but noticed the engine was still running. I cut into the dynamo, and so we had heat and light until about 8 a.m."

With the engine still working, somehow Captain Lewis managed to drive the after section to shore, where it ran aground a couple of hours later. The situation of the crew was only slightly less precarious, for solid ground lay a quarter mile away. Yet the men remained calm despite their fear for the worst as the waves and offshore wind drove the wreck closer to safety.

The Coast Guard intercepted the SOS and alerted lifesavers along the coast to keep a lookout for the drifting collier. "At 7 a. m., Bosun E. B. Drinkwater, in charge of the Coast Guard station two miles away from Cape Elizabeth, was able to put a fix on the stricken vessel. He and six other Coast guardsmen got into a tractor and beach wagon loaded down with breeches buoy equipment and made for High Head.

"It took them forty-five minutes to set up their equipment and a line was shot from a Lyle gun, which is similar to a small cannon. The line landed right over the pilot house, 1,200 feet from shore, and was made fast. Ashore the ropes were suspended from crossed poles which gave elevation for the operation. Working with pulley effect the ropes were used to draw seamen in the basket-like chair built into a life ring."

Drinkwater gave a personal account of rescue operation: "The only time I ever saw one of those Lyle guns was during training drills with the Coast Guard. If it had been luck, it would have been because I closed my eyes and let her go, but it was darn good judgment, considering the wind."

In another account, Drinkwater's rank was given as Warrant Officer, and the distance from ship to shore was given as 150 yards, which, looking at the photographs, appears more accurate.

Over the course of two hours, the men were pulled to shore one at a time. Drinkwater: "Only three of the crew men doused in waves as they rode along the line from ten to thirty-five feet above the water."

Every man was saved. Captain Lewis was the last one to be brought ashore.

Eventually the hull was pounded to pieces.

In the official U.S. Coast Guard photo at right, coastguardsmen have established a breeches buoy on the rocks in order to haul the men from ship to shore. In the postcard picture below, a crewmember is splashed by waves as he hangs from the bottom of the catenary while coastguardsmen pull him to safety.

POLIAS

Built: 1919
Previous names: None
Gross tonnage: 2,564
Type of vessel: Concrete-hulled freighter
Builder: Fougner Ship Building Company, Long Island City, New York
Owner: United States Shipping Board (operated by Porto Rican Steamship Company)
Port of registry: New York, NY
Cause of sinking: Ran aground
Location: Old Cilley Ledge, off Port Clyde, near Rockland

Sunk: February 6, 1920
Depth: 10 feet
Dimensions: 267' x 46' x 23'
Power: coal-fired steam

Lat/lon: 43-53-16 N / 69-15-24 W

Most people laugh at the mention of a hull constructed of concrete, or make some obvious ethnic slur about the nationality of the designer. "Concrete doesn't float," they will state with strong derision. "That is why the Mafia makes concrete shoes." While it is true that a concrete block will sink like a stone, the same can be said of a steel I-beam. Yet hulls are made of steel. What allows a hull to float is its form, not the material of which it is made. As long as a hull displaces more weight of water than the weight of the material of which the hull is constructed, the hull will float. Ferro-concrete is an extrapolation of iron and steel hull construction. ("Ferro" means iron, and refers to the reinforcing rods that form the crosshatch grid pattern on which the concrete is poured. The iron reinforcing rods (called "re-bars" in the trade) add strength to the completed structure once the concrete has set, or solidified.)

The first ship made of ferro-concrete was the *Namsenfjord*, the brainchild of Norwegian engineer Nicolay Knudtzon Fougner. The *Namsenfjord* successfully completed sea trials in 1917. Lloyd's of London, the insurance syndicate and vessel classification society, had no standard for such construction, but gave the ship a provisional rating for the purpose of writing insurance. Fougner then brought his innovative (some said strange) concept to the United States. The U.S. had only recently joined the war effort on the side of the Allies, and was already feeling the crunch from the lack of raw materials with which to produce the machines of war. Fougner either had a good idea, or he had a bad idea at a time when desperation made it appear good.

The United States Shipping Board created the Emergency Fleet Corporation to procure "bottoms" by either the purchase of existing vessels or the construction of new ones. The EFC was persuaded to make a trial effort of Fougner's oddball construction method. Contracts were authorized for forty-two experimental vessels whose hulls were to be molded of ferro-concrete. These were to be constructed in half a dozen shipyards on both coasts of the country.

According to history professor Fred Hopkins, "Proponents of the concrete ship claimed that the material required was easily available and did not cause a drain on necessary war material; much of the work [of construction] could be performed by unskilled labor; the cost would be less than steel or wooden vessels of similar size and design; the carrying capacity of a concrete ship was eight percent more than a wooden ship and only five percent less than a similar steel vessel; and no maintenance was required on concrete ships. Arguments to the contrary included studies that showed the cost of a concrete hull would be higher than estimated; the concrete ship would be 30 percent heavier than a similar steel vessel; skilled carpenters would be needed to craft the wood forms and skilled steel workers would be needed to form the steel reinforcing rods; no machinery would be available for the hulls when completed; there would be a maintenance problem since the poop, bridge, forecastle, main decks, and ceilings of the cargo holds were of wood; there were questions concerning claims of simplicity to repair hulls and general concern of lack of experience with large concrete vessels over a lengthy period of time."

Elsewhere it was noted that concrete hulls vibrated less than steel hulls underway, and that the period of roll in rough seas was increased by comparison with steel. "The increase in the period of roll is undoubtedly due to the fact that these vessels have a relatively large moment of inertia around a longitudinal axis, even when loaded with cargo. This is due to the mass of the concrete shell, which is considerably greater than the mass of the shell of a steel ship." Increase in the period of roll meant that they rolled more slowly; in other words, they manifested greater stability.

The *Polias* was one of twelve ferro-concrete ships that actually made it from the drawing board to the launching platform. The remaining contracts were canceled after the Armistice was signed. In retrospect, it was fortuitous that the other thirty ships were never built, for the design did not prove to be commercially successful. "The great hull weight compared to their cargo carrying capacity made them financially unable to compete with traditional steel ships on postwar routes." Despite this knowledge, another twenty-four ferro-concrete ships were constructed during World War Two. They were just as unsuccessful.

It is interesting to note that the American Bureau of Ships could not determine how to classify the radical hull design of these concrete ships. The ABS avoided the issue by designating the *Polias* and her sisters as "class contemplated."

During the first week of February 1920, a blizzard of tremendous ferocity struck Maine and New Hampshire, dumping huge quantities of snow for forty-eight hours nonstop. Six-foot snowdrifts forced the States to a standstill.

The *Polias* was caught in the middle of this blinding snowstorm. She was on a passage from Searsport, Maine to Norfolk, Virginia. The end came suddenly when the *Polias*, proceeding onerously at 9 and a half knots, ground to a halt on a submerged rock bar called variously Old Cilley Ledge or Old Gilley Ledge or Calley Ledges.

The concrete bottom was stove in, and water quickly filled the empty holds. The time was six o'clock in the evening: far after dark at that time of year. No amount of engine power would back her off the rock. The Coast Guard was notified by radio of her predicament.

All night long the waves bashed against the concrete hull. But the vessel incurred no additional damage. Thirty-eight crewmembers were safe and sound, although obviously unsettled.

At 9:30 in the morning, nine or ten or eleven men (accounts differ) launched a lifeboat in an attempt to reach land. They were never heard from again. An oar and three life preservers washed ashore on Monhegan Island. It should be noted that the skipper gave no order to abandon ship at the time the men left; they disobeyed his command to stand pat.

Captain Richard Coughlan and the rest of the crew waited patiently until help arrived in the form of Coast Guard lifeboats from Stations 10 and 11, which transferred

From the collection of Bill Carter.

them to the cutter *Acushnet*; or the crew left in the ship's lifeboats and were towed to the *Acushnet*. No matter how it happened, those who stayed aboard the *Polias* lived to sail again.

The concrete ship was pinned to the ledge like a moth to a radiator. The U.S. Shipping Board put the hulk up for auction "as is" and "where is." The highest bid (amount undisclosed) was posted by Aironautical Engineers. Try as they might they were unable to float the vessel off the ledge. Eventually the *Polias* was abandoned where she lay.

In the July 1922 issue of *Popular Mechanics*, an anonymous writer penned these words about the *Polias*: "In July of that year [1920] I went aboard and carefully inspected the entire vessel. The ship was as solid as the rock on which she rested: not a break or a crack above or below decks, except where a sharp rock came through the bottom. Standing on the bridge 40 feet above the waterline, I could feel no tremor when the heavy seas struck her. An inspection a year later showed the same conditions, except that the paint was beginning to wash from her sides. The superintendent of the wrecking company declared either a steel or wooden hull in the same position could not have withstood the seas three months. Efforts during two summers to float her with air, however, proved a failure, and after removing the machinery, etc. other salvage was abandoned. It will be interesting to note how many years the hull will last."

In the 1999 Winter issue of *Stem to Stern*, the official organ of East Carolina University, it was noted that the college had scheduled a two-week archaeological study of the concrete ship *Polias* for the following summer, claiming, "Historical data on these ships is spartan at best."

University archaeologists must not have done their homework. The construction of concrete ships was such an innovative concept that it was extremely well articulated in contemporary professional journals, right down to the placement of the last rebar, and complete with cutaway drawings of all facets of the hull, construction diagrams, and photographs of the *Polias* that included shell framing, iron reinforcement, interior forms, concrete pouring, and exterior finishing with a cement gun.

In-depth articles about concrete ships appeared in *The Shipbuilder*, *International Marine Engineering*, and *The International Steam Engineer*. After the war, Fougner himself wrote an entire book about concrete ships, in which he expounded upon the whole gamut of concrete ship construction and management from keel laying to launching and follow-up transport service. The 232-page book was published in 1922. It started with a history of concrete ships, then expressed every aspect of design and construction, including mathematical calculations, formulas and equations, tables of wages and cost estimates, plan and sheer diagrams, strengths and capacities, even the kind of concrete to use and the best method of mixing it – everything that was known or knowable about concrete ships, and a heck of a lot more than I want to know.

I found no intermediate records about the persistence of the *Polias* to resist nature's advances. Today, the bottom is littered with chunks of concrete and reinforcing rods.

ROYAL TAR

Built: 1835
Previous names: None
Gross tonnage: 400
Type of vessel: Wooden-hulled passenger-freight steamer
Builder: William & Isaac Olive, Carleton, New Brunswick
Owner: John Hammond, Daniel McLaughlin, Mackay Brothers
Port of registry: ?
Cause of sinking: Fire

Sunk: October 25, 1836
Depth: Unknown
Dimensions: 146' or 160' x 24' x ?
Power: wood-fired steam

Location: Off Fox Island

The steamboat *Royal Tar* had an unfortunately short career, being in active service for slightly less than a year. The hull was launched on November 9, 1835. It was outfitted over the winter, then put into service the following spring. The primary ports on her route were St. John, Nova Scotia; Eastport, Maine; Portland, Maine; and Boston, Massachusetts.

On October 31, 1836, the *Royal Tar* departed from St. John with Portland as her destination. She carried an unusual cargo: a traveling menagerie that consisted of aviaries, a collection of snakes, small animals in cages, several horses (to pull the display wagons when traveling on the road), two camels, two lions, a leopard, a Bengal or Siberian tiger, a gnu, and an elephant. One can only imagine how the twenty-one crewmembers and seventy-two passengers must have felt about sharing the deck of this reincarnation of Noah's *Ark* with a herd of wild animals. This live zoological collection was known as Burgess' Collection of Serpents and Birds.

Also on board was a sideshow called Dexter's Locomotive Museum; that is, a traveling museum, not one about train locomotives. In addition there was a brass band and all the circus personnel, plus a number of non-associated passengers and crew, totaling some ninety-three men, women, and children.

Fair weather soon yielded to increasing wind and mounting waves. Before long, the steamboat found itself weathering a full-blown gale. Captain Thomas Reed, master, wisely decided to change course for safe harbor at Eastport, Maine. When the tempest abated on October 25, Captain Reed proceeded cautiously to sea. The abatement was only a lull, however, and the *Royal Tar* was soon plowing through waves of monstrous proportions. Again Captain Reed ran for cover, this time to the lee of Fox Island, where he dropped anchor to wait out the storm.

Meanwhile, the engineer discovered that the water had run out of the boilers. No water meant no steam to propel the engine. While the engineer was refilling the boilers, "the boilers became red hot, setting fire to nearby woodwork." The flames spread rapidly through the deck. "The wooden steamer blazed with fierce intensity, the two funnels falling overboard, and causing much havoc. Soon there was terrible panic, in which human beings and animals struggled together to reach some place of safety."

The *Royal Tar* was in extremis.

"The engineer, with 15 others, immediately jumped into the largest boat, and made for the nearest land to leeward, which they reached in safety in about four hours. Captain Reed promptly took possession of the only remaining boat, and took a position at

From *Steamboat Disasters and Railroad Accidents* (1846).

a short distance to the windward. Three gentlemen passengers, good swimmers, committed themselves to the water, and were taken up by Captain Reed.

"The cable was slipped and sail made on the boat, with the hope of reaching shore, but the flames spread so rapidly from aft to forward that her mainmast was consumed in a few minutes, and, her tiller ropes being burnt away, she drifted, broadside to the wind, directly out to sea.

"A signal of distress had been made, and it was fortunately discovered by the revenue cutter stationed at Castine, then about 4 or 5 miles to windward, and she promptly bore up to her relief. Captain Reed put on board of her the persons in his boat, and then immediately commenced taking off those remaining on board the *Royal Tar*.

"At this time she was a mass of flames nearly from stem to stern; a small space forward, which had not yet taken fire, with the bowsprit, bobstay, &c., was crowded with the survivors. Those on the quarter-deck were driven overboard by the flames, and such as survived were hanging to the davit tackles, chains, and ropes attached to the rudder.

"Many were suspended by ropes, secured on deck, but as the fire reached them were precipitated into the sea and drowned. The cutter unfortunately had no boat of sufficient size to render any assistance in taking off the sufferers, and having gunpowder on board, Lieutenant Dyer, in command, did not deem it prudent to approach very near the wreck, so that the work of rescue was unavoidably very tedious.

"Captain Reed, however, firmly and resolutely persevered with his boat, thought it was with some difficulty that he could obtain an efficient boat's crew to approach the wreck, fearing the elephant would go overboard and destroy the boat.

"The last boat left the wreck a little before sunset, with one solitary frantic female, the last on board, whose sister and child had both perished before her eyes. The loss of lives is estimated at from 26 to 32, there being some small children on board, who had not been inserted on Captain Reed's passenger list – the precise number cannot be ascertained.

"The prompt and praiseworthy decision of Captain Reed, in securing the boat, was the only means by which the life of an individual could have been saved. The elephant, camels, and horses, jumped overboard, and all the animals in the cages were burnt.

"None of the passengers or crew's baggage was saved. Many of the trunks, &c., were thrown overboard, in the hope they might be picked up.

"The cutter landed the survivors about 8 p.m. at the Isle of Hunt, where they received the most hospitable treatment from the inhabitants. We learn there was a large amount of specie on board the *Royal Tar*."

In case you do not know the meaning of the word, specie is not the singular form of species: the category in taxonomic classification that refers to organisms that can interbreed. Specie refers to coined money: generally gold, sometimes silver.

Elsewhere it was noted, "The amount of specie and notes lost is not less than 60,000 dollars. One of the caravan keepers tied 500 dollars in specie about his person, jumped overboard, and was drowned. The scene on board beggars description: many passengers were so much frightened that they jumped overboard, some of them mothers, with their infants lashed to them. Only one person, an elderly Irish woman, was burnt: she had not been seen at all on deck; the remainder of the 32 were drowned. One gentleman, Captain Edward Waite, of Portland, had about 5,000 dollars intrusted [sic] to him, which were lost. It is said that Captain Waite secured himself and trunk on the steps of the boat, until the raft to which they were attached burnt off, when, still retaining possession of his treasure, he swam to another part of the vessel, where he sustained himself and property until a cabin passenger, a lady, floated near him, when he let go his trunk, and seized and sustained the woman until they were both saved."

Yet another account noted that the man who jumped overboard and drowned with money on his person was carrying silver dollars. "Six horses, belonging to the caravan, were backed overboard; three of them instinctively swam towards the nearest land; the other three swam around the boat until they sank exhausted. A large elephant, belonging to the menagerie, having retreated to that part of the boat which the fire had not reached, mounted his fore feet upon the rail, in which position he remained till about 4 o'clock, apparently calculating with the characteristic sagacity of the animal, the prospects of escape, until it became too hot for him, when he leaped overboard, carrying with him, as he slid down the vessel's side, several of the passengers who were still clinging there. His immense weight probably carried him to the bottom ere he rose, as he re-appeared, after some time, at a considerable distance. This animal also instinctively swam towards the nearest land; but, as the boat was by this time drifted four or five miles out to sea, he must have perished. The rest of the menagerie, consisting of lions, tigers, and other animals of a like nature, were allowed to become a prey to the flames, as, on account of their ferocity, it was deemed dangerous to loose them."

The abandoned steamboat drifted out to sea. At nine o'clock that evening the flames were seen to disappear. It was presumed that she had sunk "about twenty miles from the place where she took fire." The wreck has never been found.

"Capt. Reed behaved with great presence of mind and it was due to his efforts that so many people were saved. In recognition of his devotion he was presented with a purse containing 700 dollars by the citizens of St. John, and some years later he became harbour-master of the port."

S-21

Built: 1921
Previous names: *P.553*
Displacement tonnage: 854 (surfaced), 1,062 (submerged)
Type of vessel: Submarine
Builder: Bethlehem Shipbuilding Corporation, Quincy, Massachusetts
Owner: U.S. Navy
Cause of sinking: Scuttled
Lat/Lon: 42° 59' 48" North / 70° 20' 27' West

Sunk: March 23, 1945
Depth: 150 feet
Dimensions: 219' x 20' x 14'
Power: twin diesel engines, twin electric motors
Official designation: SS-126
Armament: 4 bow torpedo tubes

The career of a peacetime naval vessel is generally fairly tame. Except for one short interlude, the *S-21* was no exception.

Fifty-one S-class submarines were built in the aftermath of the Great War. They were actually divided into three types, but within the types quite a bit of individualizing was engineered, both initially and during subsequent refits. The S-class subs were powered by different engine types, operated by different kinds of machinery, armed with guns of varying sizes, and weighed in with different displacement tonnages. In short, no two S-class subs were identical.

Three prototypes were built. Generally, *S-4* through *S-17* followed the government design of the *S-3*, which measured 231 feet in length. *S-4* through *S-13* were built by the Portsmouth Naval Shipyard; *S-14* through *S-17* by the Lake Torpedo Boat Company.

S-18 through *S-41*, and *S-42* through *S-47*, were designed and constructed by the Electric Boat Company, after their *S-1* prototype. The length of the former group measured 219 feet; the length of the latter group measured 225 feet.

Lake Torpedo Boat Company designed the *S-2*, but the design was abandoned in favor of the other two types.

Then, the Lake Torpedo Boat Company received a contract to build four boats in a similar mold, but longer and with increased power. These were the *S-48* through *S-51*. At 240 feet in length, they could have been called a stretch-class submarine. They were the only S-class subs to possess a stern torpedo tube in addition to the four in the bow. No matter how big their external dimensions, S-class submarines were cramped and crowded inside. The men who served in them called them "pigboats."

If you want to know what an S-class submarine was like, read the 1931 Edward Ellsberg classic entitled *Pigboats*. Ellsberg was a Navy commander at the time he wrote the book; he continued his career throughout World War Two, and retired as a rear ad-

The wake indicates flank speed. Courtesy of the National Archives.

miral. Although he never actually served on an S-class sub, he was a hard-hat diver and salvage master who was the senior officer in charge of raising both the *S-4* and *S-51*. These operations gave him first-hand knowledge of their interior layout and workings.

For a more visual representation, view the 1933 movie that was based on *Pigboats*: it was called *Hell Below*, and starred Robert Montgomery, Walter Huston, Jimmy Durante, Robert Young, and Sterling Holloway. It is every bit as thrilling as the book, and set the trend for the submarine movies that followed World War Two.

Although construction of the *S-21* was authorized by an Act of Congress on March 4, 1917 – one month before the United States entered the Great War on the side of the Allies – the Armistice had long since been signed by the time she was commissioned: on August 24,

Control room of the *S-21*. Note the periscope in the upper right corner. (Courtesy of the Naval Photographic Center.)

1921. Her hull was designated SS-126; that is, the one-hundred twenty-sixth submarine that was ordered for construction since the inception of the Navy program in 1900.

Even at that late date there were teething troubles. After nearly a year of service she was returned to the builder, although existing records do not state why. After five months of extra work, the *S-21* was recommissioned on August 24, 1922.

For the next two decades she roamed along the eastern seaboard, visited the Caribbean islands, and spent time at the Canal Zone, where she was stationed at the submarine base and naval air station called Coco Solo. In the 1930's she passed through the Gatun Locks on her way to California, thence to Pearl Harbor, Hawaii, where she remained for several years in reserve.

The *S-21*'s most useful service occurred in 1928, when she conducted a special scientific cruise. According to *The Gravity Measuring Cruise of the U.S. Submarine S-21*, by F.A. Vening Meinesz and F.E. Wright, "Gravity measurements at sea are difficult to make because of the unsteadiness of the ocean surface; and, until recently, no satisfactory method was available by which this difficulty could be overcome. For gravity measurements on land the standard apparatus is a free-swinging pendulum of known length. On board ship the horizontal and vertical disturbances due to the ship's movements are so great that satisfactory records from a single pendulum can not be obtained. To meet this situation Dr. F. A. Vening Meinesz conceived the plan of using a pair of pendulums swinging in the same vertical plane. Any horizontal disturbance or acceleration then affects the angular position of each pendulum equally, so that, if the difference between the angular positions of the two pendulums is taken, the behavior of the combined pair is that of a simple pendulum free from the effect of the horizontal disturbances. This is the fundamental improvement which was introduced and which has made possible the use of a pendulum apparatus at sea for gravity measurements. Obviously it can be used on the surface only in calm weather. If measurements are to be made at any desired point, irrespective of the weather, rough seas must be avoided; this can be done on a submerged submarine. Dr. Vening Meinesz proved on three different voyages aboard Dutch submarines that his new method is feasible and yields reliable results. His voyages encircled the world and enabled him to occupy over 200 stations at sea."

The *S-21* was drafted for the continuation of these experiments. The gravity measuring apparatus was installed inside the submarine, "which set sail on October 2 [from Washington, DC] for Norfolk [Virginia] and thence to the Gulf of Mexico and the Caribbean Sea. Upon the return of the expedition to Washington measurements were again made at the gravity base station."

Eagle boats *35* and *58* accompanied the *S-21* on the two-month, 7,000-mile cruise. Some of the measurements were taken at periscope depth, but when the seas were rough the submarine submerged – usually to a depth of 80 feet – to take measurements. The submarine crept along at 4 knots so that vibration would not affect the apparatus. During this short cruise, the *S-21* added forty-six more gravity measuring stations to the total of approximately three hundred that had been made in the previous thirty-five years.

The authors noted, "Inasmuch as the value of gravity measurements increases with the number and spread of gravity stations over the surface of the earth, especially over the ocean surfaces, the contribution of the *S-21* cruise to the theory of isostasy and to fundamental geological theory is of lasting value and should form the starting point for other measurements of similar nature over more extended areas."

They also noted, "In spite of the novelty and interest of life aboard a submarine, it soon became evident to the scientists, that the crowded conditions aboard, the lack of adequate ventilation, and poor air resulting in part from the Diesel engine gases coupled with tropical temperatures, are not conducive to intensive intellectual work and that computations and the working up of results are not possible at sea."

Forty-seven officers, men, and scientists slept and ate in close confines on this cruise: four officers, thirty-five crewmembers, and eight scientists.

The *S-21* was overhauled in Philadelphia during the winter of 1938-1939. She then proceeded to New London, Connecticut, where she remained until the outset of war. She was then deployed to the Canal Zone to conduct defensive patrols on the Pacific side of the Panama Canal.

In mid-1942, the *S-21* returned to New London. She was decommissioned and transferred to the British navy, for which she operated under the name HMS *P.553*. The submarine was towed to Halifax, Nova Scotia, then relegated to anti-submarine training duty.

In 1944 she was transferred back to the U.S. Navy. She resumed her original name (or number). By that time, S-class submarines were obsolete, having been replaced by new classes of subs that were larger and that could go faster, dive deeper, and maneuver better.

According to the Naval History and Heritage Command, the *S-21* was "used as a target, she was sunk off northern New England on 23 March 1945." However, more reliable sources note that the sub was scuttled not as a gunnery target but was "sunk for experimental purposes 23 March 1945, depth 25 fathoms, 43-36-53 N, 69-59-24 W." Several official documents confirm the date and location, and add that the heading

of the hulk was 015 degrees true. The sunken hull was "laying on its side with hole in her bottom used for removal of engines." The submarine then became a test subject for a new breed of underwater detection devices such as sonar units.

Early New England salvage diver Burt Mason, with friend Robert Sullivan, located the resting place of the *S-21* in November 1963. The hulk lay three miles southeast of Halfway Rock. A wreck symbol marks the location on modern nautical charts. They were working on the wreck in 1964 when one of their divers, Albert Prejean, failed to return from a dive. Mason descended the anchor line and "found the victim lying face down three feet from the wreckage in 160 feet of water."

A month later, the Coast Guard fined Mason $250 "for unauthorized storage of explosives aboard the salvage tug *John Whooley* in Portland Harbor." Apparently, he was attempting to raise portions of the submarine the way he had salvaged the *G-1* in 1962. (For details, see *Shipwrecks of Connecticut and Rhode Island*.)

Oddly, after those incidents the *S-21* disappeared. By "disappeared" I mean that no one else could ever find it – and lots of people looked for it. In 1990, I personally spent a whole day searching for the submarine in the vicinity of its reported position. Others have spent far more time with the same result. Eighteen years passed before the wreck was finally relocated.

The ultimate discoverers were Joe Cushing and Bill Lussier. During the preliminary stages of their search process, Cushing contacted this author to request location information. I sent him copies of all the historical documents that were in my *S-21* folder, but Cushing had done his homework, and the documents that I sent him did not constitute much if anything different from what he already had in his possession.

Luck had nothing to do with Cushing's and Lussier's ultimate discovery. They found the wreck because they were persistent. They spent three years looking for the sub. Finally, after hiring side-scan sonar expert Garry Kozak, they hit the mark.

According to Joe Cushing, the *S-21* "lies on her port side in 170' of water. The bottom is hard pan mud with small rocks. The center section of the submarine is lying on [a] ledge. When approached from the bow the diver will first see a large steel cable dropping from the bow into the bottom and buried in the surrounding sediment. The

cable leads to a large mushroom anchor near the wreck site. The two starboard side torpedo tube shutter doors are deteriorated to the point of exposing the muzzle doors and corresponding linkages. Swimming further aft reveals the starboard side bow plane neatly tucked into its stowed position with its linkage and pivot bearing still in place. Due to reduced visibility this initial inspection gives the appearance of a completely intact submarine.

"Continuing aft the diver will encounter the weapons loading and torpedo room hatches and a mangled mess of steel plates and beams. The entire conning tower and control room area was destroyed by explosives during a salvage attempt in the early 1960's. Moving further aft the hull is again intact, the box keel is in place on the lower section of the hull and the engine room hatch is in place and closed, preventing entry into the cramped S class engine room. Moving aft the starboard dive plane stands tall after 70 years on the bottom. The linkage for the rudder is still connected to the rudder that lies flat on the bottom. The starboard propeller shaft is in place, the shaft taper is exposed and the propeller is no longer in place."

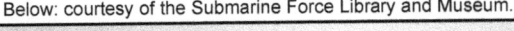

Opposite page top, and above: a pair of commemorative cachets that announce the *S-21's* decommissioning at the Philadelphia Navy Yard on June 1, 1939, and her subsequent recommissioning on September 1, 1940. Both cachets were franked at New London, Connecticut.

Below: courtesy of the Submarine Force Library and Museum.

SAGAMORE

Built: 1920
Previous names: *Lake Feodora*
Gross tonnage: 2,592
Type of vessel: Freighter
Builder: American Ship Building Company, Lorain, Ohio
Owner: Eastern Steamship Line, Boston, Massachusetts
Port of registry: Portsmouth, New Hampshire
Cause of sinking: Ran aground
Location: Prouts Neck, Cape Elizabeth

Sunk: January 14, 1934
Depth: 20 to 50 feet
Dimensions: 251' x 43' x 28'
Power: coal-fired steam

GPS: 41-28.701 / 70-32.981

On October 11, 1928, the *Sagamore* was steaming up the East River in New York City on her way to Portland, Maine, at the same time and place that the tug *Syosset* towing the barge *Car Float No. 15* was proceeding downstream: much like two vehicles driving in opposite directions on a dual-lane highway. The passing would have gone smoothly except that, with warning, a lighter decided at the last moment to cross ahead of the *Sagamore* in order to enter a dock on the other side of the river: like a vehicle pulling suddenly out of a driveway into a stream of moving traffic.

When the lighter executed this unannounced maneuver – her skipper did not sound his whistle – she was only seventy-five feet in front of the *Sagamore*. "Because of this unexpected movement of the lighter, the *Sagamore* was obliged to back, and, in so doing, swung her bow about two points [22.5 degrees] to starboard in the direction of the Brooklyn shore and thus got out of her course, which lay only a little east of the center of the stream. To break this sheer she started up her engines as soon as the lighter had crossed her bow and was carried forward into *Car Float No. 15*."

This kind of hull scrape is the maritime equivalent of a fender bender. The *Sagamore* was found solely at fault for causing the collision, despite the fact that her skipper reacted properly and responsibly, and did a skillful job of getting his vessel back on course against a flood tide that was trying to swing the *Sagamore* – which was no longer aligned with the current – broadside in front of two downbound vessels.

Some accidents happen while others are caused. The irresponsible skipper of the lighter that created the above situation was not cited in the resulting lawsuit. He got off scot-free. Go figure.

Another irony of the collision lawsuit was that it was not settled until nearly six years later – on June 18, 1934 – by which time the *Sagamore* had ended her career six months earlier. Nonetheless, the company still had to pay the cost of repairs to *Car Float No. 15*.

Her end came dramatically. The *Sagamore* was on route from Portland, Maine to New York City with 500 tons of cargo, "including many tons of newsprint paper in huge rolls and a quantity of general merchandise," when she ran into a severe snowstorm that was accompanied by pounding seas. "Officers on the bridge found that they were off their course when they were unable to pick up the buoys at Willard Rock or Pine Tree Ledge." This was cause for great concern.

Before Captain Ralph McDonough, master, could verify his position, the freighter ran aground on a submerged ledge that was known as Corwin's Rock (although he did not know this). The time was an hour and a quarter after midnight. The sharp pinnacle sliced open the bottom plates of the hull as if they were made of cloth instead of steel. Water flooded into the hull.

After several minutes, "high waves lifted her off and dropped her in deep water."

The vessel was no longer pinned to the ledge. Now she was sinking. And to make matters worse, her steering apparatus had been disabled when she struck. Even though Captain McDonough did not know his precise location, he had little choice but to make a run for it. He proceeded westward at full speed, toward the mainland.

"For an hour and a half she ran at her maximum speed, settling lower at each moment." Captain McDonough "drove her seven miles through the storm and breakers and ran her on the beach at Prouts Neck. . . . She was half filled when she ran up the rocky shore, and as the tide rose officers and crew were forced to the bridge for safety from the rising water and the breaking seas. Flares sent up at intervals were unanswered."

By this time it was three o'clock in the morning. Raging seas pounded the hull. After dawn, a resident spotted the distressed vessel in the breakers, and wasted no time in calling the Coast Guard. By now, high tide hid most of the hull so that only the upper deck and superstructure was visible, although green water washed through spaces in the bulwark as waves struck the hull.

The Coast Guard used a surfboat to rescue the twenty-six crewmembers, bringing them ashore three at a time. This dangerous rescue operation required expert boat handlers and split second timing to get the people off the ship while not getting the surfboat smashed to bits. By noon everyone was safe, sound, and soaked.

Although salvage operations continued for more than half a year, the wreck was too badly holed to refloat. Parts of the wreck still remain.

A postcard picture of the *Sagamore* aground.

SUSAN P. THURLOW

Built: 1872
Previous names: None
Gross tonnage: 460
Type of vessel: Wooden-hulled three-masted tern
Builder: Harrington, Maine
Owner: J.H. Weldon, master
Port of registry: New York, NY
Cause of sinking: Ran aground
Location: Cushing Island

Sunk: December 14, 1897
Depth: Unknown
Dimensions: 126' x 31' x 16'
Power: sail

The *Susan P. Thurlow* led a long and prosperous career for her various owners throughout the years. She was rigged as a tern: a term that Maine mariners applied to a three-masted schooner.

Her end came precipitously on December 14, 1897. She was on route from Hillsborough, New Brunswick to New York City with a cargo of plaster rock when she ran into a storm that Captain Helgersen, master, decided to weather out by pulling into Portland harbor for the hours of darkness. His decision was wise and, but for an unfortunate event, would have been a safe one for the schooner, her skipper, and her six crewmembers.

The rope that controlled the rudder broke at the worst possible moment. Instantly the schooner was thrown out of control by howling winds and heavy seas. Before the rope could be repaired and steering regained, the schooner struck a submerged outcrop with such force that all three masts cracked and crashed onto the deck.

Captain Helgersen's leg was snapped like a twig when he was struck by one of the topmasts. Ignoring the pain, he gave the order to abandon ship and did so himself. The men were swept away by the fury of the storm as the schooner was torn apart.

The only one to survive the ordeal by water was an able-bodied seaman named E. Reimann. He was able to grab a floating spar and hang on to it until it drifted ashore. Despite being drenched and suffering from the cold, he crawled to a nearby hut where the resident fisherman treated him for exposure.

Five of the six bodies were recovered later: captain, mate, and three crewmembers.

By morning, no part of the schooner was still standing where she stranded, but the beaches were littered with pieces of wreckage.

By fortuitous circumstances, the owner and master of the *Susan P. Thurlow* was not on board at the time of the catastrophe. Previous to her final voyage, Captain H.L. Weldon had gotten so sick that he relieved himself of command in Philadelphia, and appointed Helgersen to take his place.

Many people say that conversion to a schooner barge was a sad end for a windjammer. I disagree. Although it was an ignominious end to be dismasted and towed by the hawser of a tug, the truly sad end was to be shattered to pieces on a rocky reef and to cause the death of her crewmembers.

Above: The *Susan P. Thurlow* with all sails set. (From the collection of Paul Sherman.)

Below: A postcard picture of the *Wandby* that was taken soon after she ran aground.

WANDBY

Built: 1899
Previous names: None
Gross tonnage: 3,981
Type of vessel: Freighter
Builder: Ropner & Son, Stockton-on-Tees, England
Owner: Ropner Shipping Company, West Hartlepool, England
Port of registry: West Hartlepool, England
Cause of sinking: Ran aground off Walkers Point, Kennebunkport

Sunk: March 9, 1921
Depth: 20 feet
Dimensions: 336' x 46' x 25'
Power: coal-fired steam

Note: see photo on previous page

The *Wandby* was on a passage from Algiers to Portland, Maine when she ran aground on Walkers Point, near Kennebunkport. The best account of the disaster was given by Third Assistant Engineer William Gilbertson . . . but not until he wrote a series of letters thirty-six years after the event! What follows is a totally different kind of shipwreck story, especially when contrasted with the loss of the *Nottingham* (which see).

"On March the 9th, 1921, A British freighter was wrecked at Walker's Point, Kennebunkport, the name of the ship was the *Wandby*.

"At that time I was Third Asst. Engineer on board the *Wandby* and it was my first voyage to sea. My object in writing to you [the editor of the *Kennebunk Star*] is that I hope you may be able through your column to convey my very great appreciation of the kindness of all the people around Kennebunk which has stood in my memory for thirty-six years.

"When we were first wrecked on Walker's Point and the ship was considered dangerous we were invited to stay with many of the residents of Kennebunk. Myself, the Second Engineer and the Captain were the guests of Mr. and Mrs. Eldredge, who were most delightful people. They were the very essence of kindness and treated us as though we were royalty when we were 'Distressed British Seamen.' We stayed with them for three weeks before we embarked for home and every minute of those three weeks were filled with entertainment for us by the splendid people of your dear town and district. Cinemas, dances, socials, we were invited out to everywhere and everything. Car rides to Portland, jaunts into the forest of Maine and occasional dances at Cape Porpoise (I think that is the name). In fact everything was done by those splendid people to make us feel at home amongst you. We went digging for clams in the beach which Mrs. Eldredge converted into a most delicious clam chowder.

"Those good people, the Eldredges had two daughters at home while we were there. The elder was named Elise but the younger one who was still at school was always referred to as Honey Eldredge. Then there was a boarder living with them called George Cooper who had ambitions of becoming a garage proprietor. I often wonder if he achieved his ambition. I sincerely hope so. Many times during my retirement from the sea, I sit before my fire at home and think of the wonderful three weeks I spent over in Kennebunk. I think of the Eldredges taking me to worship on Sunday mornings.

I was a Protestant and I didn't know till the service began that I was in a Catholic Church, and couldn't understand the service.

"I remember the girl who used to slide down the emergency escape which we rigged from the ship's bow to a huge boulder on shore. This consisted of a boatswain's chair to which a pulley was attached and endless rope from ship to shore so that is [sic] was possible at high water to leave or go aboard the ship by this means. At low water one could walk over the rocks to the loader from the ship's deck to the rocks.

"When at last our sojourn among your people ended and we were ordered to embark at Portland, it was a very sad leave taking. Dear Mrs. Eldredge shed bitter tears and I had a very uncomfortable lump in my throat and neither my companion nor myself dare trust ourselves to speak for half an hour after we had said goodbye to those lovely people.

"Now perhaps you are wondering why I left it so long before writing. I have always cherished a hope that I would be able to visit Kennebunk again and surprise those splendid people who had been so very good to us, but although I have made many voyages to the United States since then, I have never been nearer to you than Baltimore and Philadelphia. I often hoped my ship would come to Portland, but this alas, never happened.

"So if you would give my letter a little space in your columns maybe some of the dear people who were so very kind to us will know that their great kindness was appreciated and still remembered by me.

"I am sorry to say that all of the crew of the *Wandby* with whom I was most friendly have passed on. Some gave their lives in this last war. My own home was blown down twice by German bombs but apart from losing our home twice, my wife and family suffered no hurt.

"I am now working as an engineer ashore, very happy as a dad and granddad and the only thing I could wish for would be a holiday in or around Kennebunk, but I am afraid this is out of the question.

"If you will publish my letter maybe some of the people will remember me. They used to call me Gilbert, that being an abbreviation of my surname. Should you consider favouring my request you will add youself [sic] to my already numerous friends in Kennebunk."

There was a curious follow-up to this letter. Maine author Kenneth Roberts, author of the fictionalized version of the *Nottingham* survivors called *Boon Island*, wrote to Gilbertson and asked him for particulars about the stranding of the *Wandby*. After joining the *Wandby* in England, she tramped across the Atlantic Ocean to Norfolk, Virginia, thence to Bahia Blanca, South America, thence to Rosario on the River Plate, thence to Genoa, Italy, thence to Algiers, thence to Maine.

"Thus we were crossing the Atlantic once more light ship. We were near the coast of America on Sunday the 6th of March, when we ran into dense fog. We slowed the ship down until she was just moving and crawled up the coast of Massachusetts and Maine in this manner until 10:00 on Wednesday on March 9th. During this long period our master, Captain [David] Simpson, never left the bridge although the 1st and 2nd mate kept alternate watches, the engineers kept their regular watch, 4th Engineer was on 8 to 12, 3rd Engineer 4 to 12 and 2nd engineer 4 to 8. So that I being 4th Engineer was on was on watch at 10:00 a.m. Wednesday, March 9th, 1921. At this time I received orders from the bridge to stop the engines which of course I did; and then after a lapse

of some twenty minutes, I got the order Full Ahead. I immediately complied with the order. The Captain left the Bridge for a well earned rest and as he passed the engine room he informed the Chief Engineer that we should be in Portland at about 1:00 p. m. as he had just picked up a buoy and from its markings we found from the Chart we were 40 miles due East of Portland. Just at that moment the lookout reported 'Breakers Ahead' and the Captain rushed back to the bridge and rang the telegraph to me, 'Full Astern'. Sensing something was wrong I swung the engines full astern without shutting down the steam at all, (bad practice) but I felt justified as I knew this must be an emergency. There was a terrific grinding and bumping going on and still the engines poundin [sic] over at Full Astern. At approximately 10:30 the Captain rang stop and finish with engines. The W. O. or Radio Operator asked me to start up the Dynamo to supply him with Juice to send out an S. O. S. This I did, and on turning round one of my firemen had entered the engine room to inform me that the ship was making water in the boiler room. I informed the bridge by speaking tube, but was unable to get any information as to what had happened till my watch ended at 12:00 noon, when my relief, the 3rd Engineer told me all about what had been going on on deck. I came on deck and found that we were still in dense fog, but the water was as smooth as a sheet of glass. At 3:00 p. m. the fog lifted and we could see a crowd of people not more than 20 yards away and could hear them talking. We spoke to these people and they assisted us to rig up a ship to shore emergency exit in case the ship broke her back. This was accomplished by putting a bosun's chair on a wire from the Forcastle [sic] head and moored to a large boulder on the shore.

"I think my narrative has answered all your questions.

"The Master of the *Wandby* was relegated to 1st Mate in another ship of the company and two years after the accident he was reinstated master in this ship. He retired from the sea, but came back when the last war started and was lost when his ship was torpedoed by a German submarine off the coast of America in 1942.

"Of course the *Wandby* was light [without cargo] when she grounded and it was right at the top of high water because at low water we could walk ashore from a ladder over her side, and one could walk right under her For'd end.

"It only now remains for me to explain how the accident occurred. They mistook the buoy, and its markings.

"Like yourself, many of the Fishermen around Kennebunkport marveled how we ran so far in before we grounded.

"The *Wandby* has a very distinguished career during the 14-18 war when her crew sank a German U boat single handed, while she was commanded by Captain Simpson. I was not on her then. I was a Soldier on the Italian front during the war."

So there you have it, from soup to nuts, stranding and aftermath of survivors. There remains only one aspect of the *Wandby* wrecking to cover, and that is done better in pictures that are worth a thousand words each. At first, Captain Simpson and the thirty crewmembers stayed on board, with the Coast Guard cutter *Ossipee* standing by. With the hull bilged and the wrecked steamer high and dry at low tide, she could not be pulled off her perch. Instead, she was sold for scrap and dismantled piecemeal. Today, very little remains that is recognizable as a shipwreck: a boiler being the most prominent feature in a field of steel debris.

About a block east of Sandy Cove Road, Ocean Avenue curves close to the water where a strip parking lot can hold about fifteen vehicles, facing southeast. Park there and enter the water, continuing southeast for about two hundred feet, passing a shallow rock ledge on the left. Then take a soft left turn so that you are heading slightly more than due east. Proceed for another couple of hundred feet until you encounter wreckage.

Be careful to take a soft left and not a soft right. A soft right will give you a southward heading instead of eastward: one that parallels the east side of the cape that is called Walkers Point. If you do that, not only will you miss the wreck site, but you might find yourself looking into the muzzles of guns in the hands of Secret Service agents who will either warn you away or take you dead or alive – probably the latter as they are fairly cool-headed. But you never know what the current threat level might be, or how intruders might be (mis)handled.

The house and grounds on Walkers Point are owned by President George Bush.

Opposite page and below: Two postcard pictures of the *Wandby* in diminishing states of salvage, as first the superstructure then the hull were dismantled and carted away by commercial salvors. Today, a boiler and scattered sections of steel plate constitute most of what remains.

WASHINGTON B. THOMAS

Built: 1903
Previous names: None
Gross tonnage: 2,638
Type of vessel: Wooden-hulled five-masted schooner
Builder: Washburn Brothers, Thomaston, Maine
Owner: Washburn Brothers, Thomaston, Maine
Port of registry: Thomaston, Maine
Cause of sinking: Dragged aground
Location: South end of Stratton Island

Sunk: June 12, 1903
Depth: 20 feet
Dimensions: 286' x 48' x 22'
Power: Sail

GPS: 43-30-12.30 / 70-18-22.17

The majestic five-masted schooner named *Washington B. Thomas* was only two months old when she was irretrievably lost within a stone's throw of the yard where she was built.

The schooner was transporting 4,000 tons of anthracite coal from Norfolk, Virginia to Portland, Maine along the coastal route. On board were Captain William Lermond, his one-year newlywed Hattie May, his daughter and son (the latter working as cabin boy), and twelve crewmembers.

The schooner was working her way northward when she ran into a gale from which Captain Lermond sought protection. He dropped anchor near Old Orchard in order to ride out the storm. When the anchor dragged, he dropped another anchor. As the schooner continued to drag, he and the crew raised sails on all the masts except the mizzenmast, in an attempt to claw off the nearby shore. They would have hoisted sails on the mizzenmast had there been more time before trouble arose.

A local correspondent wrote such a detailed account of subsequent events that it cannot be improved by rewording or interruption: "The *Thomas* was anchored, Friday night, off Stratton Island and at midnight drifted from her anchorage onto the island. Without a second's warning, there came a crash as the schooner tore her way over one rock to strike another a few minutes later and then to drive hard and fast on the reef on the southerly end of the outer side of Stratton Island.

"When the first shock came, Mrs. Lermond, her step-son and the first mate's son were in the cabin. They felt the shock and heard above the din of the storm the shout of the captain. Instinctively they struggled towards the stern companion-way and up to the deck, where at first they took refuge on the roof of the house.

"Mrs. Lermond was forward on the starboard side and clinging to the rail and iron work on a corner of the coach house. Her husband stood in front of her to protect her as much as possible. Great waves which swept the deck covered Mrs. Lermond and nearly tore her from her hold. The little group fought their way to the wheel house farther aft. From this they were soon driven, after one of them, young Bowdoin Lermond, had narrowly escaped being washed overboard. He was standing in the lee of the house where he supposed he was safe, when another sea, rushing toward the stern, picked him up and swept him along until he caught in the main sheet where he was held until the water ran from the decks.

"Mrs. Lermond, the two boys and the officers sought the cabin, hoping it would

The *Washington B. Thomas* in her days of grandeur. (From the collection of Bill Quinn.)

prove stout enough to afford safety. It was a vain hope, for they had been there but a few minutes when with a sickening crash a wave tore away the forward companionway, down which rushed a torrent of water. At this moment, Mrs. Lermond was with her husband in their stateroom aft of the main cabin on the starboard side of the ship. As the tons of water struck the bulkhead separating stateroom from saloon, it knocked it down.

"The partition fell into the stateroom and struck Mrs. Lermond on the head, rendering her unconscious. Capt. Lermond grasped her in his arms and tried to drag her to the companionway. The water was rushing in through the forward door and the skylight hatch and the narrow space where he stood was full of floating debris. As he slowly dragged her to the stairs he was struck across the face with such force that he was thrown backward and the unconscious woman was torn from his grasp. The water surged toward the bow again, carrying her body with it.

"The captain could not follow her, he could see nothing in the darkness and as the cabin filled in a twinkling he reached the deck in time to escape the fate of his wife.

"Driven from one place to another the officers and two boys climbed to the spanker boom which hung a few feet above the roof of the house where they remained five hours. Then the party discovered that the house beneath them was beginning to break up.

"The sea slacked its fury during the short time it took them to gain the bow. As they crept forward they supposed they would find the forward part of the vessel without tenants as they thought all on board had perished with the exception of themselves, but when they made their way to the forecastle, they discovered the seamen had reached it soon after the schooner struck and were safely sheltered there. In his bunk was Seaman Frank Eklund, who had managed to reach the place after his leg was broken. Finding the limb useless he had crept on hands and knees to the forecastle and improvised a splint which he secured with straws.

"When the schooner ran onto the reef her bow was forced high in the air so the waves did not break over it. The seas boarded her about midships and made terrific onslaughts on the after portions of the vessel. Much of the vessel was under water. The jigger mast, that one of the five which stood nearest the stern, was broken off but was held by the rigging. The after house and the wheel house had disappeared.

"The men were all removed after midnight, this morning, in two trips by a crew of two men from the Cape Elizabeth life saving station and a number of resident volunteers. After a line had drifted from the life boat to the wreck a 'trip line' was passed and used in drawing the men, one by one, through the seas after they had been lowered into the water. On the *Thomas*, one of the mates held an end of the trip line which was tied about the waist of the man whose turn it was to be taken to the life boat. Under the man's arms another rope was passed, both ends of this being held by the other mate on the wreck. By means of this loop the man was lowered to the water, the rope drawn back on board, and the man with only the trip about him was dragged to the life boat.

"The injured seamen and engineer were given the first chance. Capt. Lermond, the mates and two seamen were left on the wreck until daylight when all were taken to the main land.

"The crew were then brought to the office of the United States shipping commissioner and the injured taken to the Marine hospital.

"Captain Lermond arrived in the city with his son and was placed under the care of a physician. He was suffering with severe bruises and excruciating pains developed. He had had no sleep for four nights."

About the only item that stands out as missing from this account is specific mention of how Captain Lermond's daughter was saved. I can extrapolate, however, from the list of survivors and other information that is located elsewhere in the article. Captain Lermond's daughter was listed as being 22 years old and married. The cook's name was given as W.A. Tabbut, of Addison, aged 22. The first mate's name was given as E.H. Tabbut, of Addison, aged 54. The apprentice was given as "Rollin S. Tabbut, of Addison, age 17, son of the first mate."

From this information I can safely infer that the cook was the first mate's second wife. Her brother was listed as being 16 years of age.

The *Washington B. Thomas* sailed as a true family affair. It is tragic that she was lost so early in her career, under such dire circumstances, and that the captain lost not only his ship but his young wife as well.

The reason that volunteers assisted in the rescue was that lifesaving stations were closed during the summer months, when storms were few and far apart. Some of the men who were employed as lifesavers lived nearby. Volunteers were needed to replace those lifesavers who did not happen to be on hand at the time of the event.

Shortly after the survivors were rescued, the schooner was torn apart by the savagery of the sea. The stern portion was dragged away. Other wreckage washed ashore for days, scattered by wind and waves.

The *Washington B. Thomas* has broken in two. (From the collection of Dave Clancy.)

W. G. BUTMAN

Built: 1896
Previous names: None
Gross tonnage: 43
Type of vessel: Inland passenger vessel
Builder: East Boothbay, Maine
Owner: W. G. Butman, master
Port of registry: East Boothbay, Maine
Cause of sinking: Foundered
Location: West Penobscot Bay

Sunk: May 27, 1915
Depth: Unknown
Dimensions: 53' x 15' x 6'
Power: Coal-fired steam

The *W. G. Butman* was one of many inland vessels that carried people, supplies, and mail from the mainland to various islands off the coast. She was named after her owner, W. G. Butman, who had the vessel built to his specifications in 1896. He and she provided reliable delivery service for nearly two decades.

This is not to say that they did not have a few mishaps. In the first year of operation, the *W. G. Butman* was towing a small boat and a raft of timber near Rockland when they broke free and went adrift. The keeper of the White Head Life Saving Station recovered them with the station boat and returned them to Butman.

In 1899, the White Head Life Saving Station again came to Butman's rescue. This time the little steamer "Stranded at high water on a ledge in Long Cove, 3 miles NW. of station. Surfmen boarded her and transported her cargo to the Long Cove wharf. They then ran hawsers to shore and hauled them well taut. At high water the next afternoon, with the assistance of a tug, they released her without damage."

In 1906, "In spite of the fog and rain the steamer *W. G. Butman* took nearly sixty persons – ministers, church members, and friends – to Matinicus Wednesday to assists in the dedication of the first church building which the beautiful island has ever enjoyed."

In 1907, "Steamer *W. G. Butman*, W. G. Butman, master and pilot, broke shaft while attempting to make landing at Black Island, Me. Both anchors let go, but steamer was so near shore that it was impossible to prevent grounding. She was floated on next tide, with very little damage to hull, and towed to Rockland for repairs. Damage estimated at $150."

These incidents were but normal events in the career of an inland passenger vessel among the islands off the coast of Maine. In 1911, Charles Smalley was called upon to describe the conditions and business activity at Criehaven Island, near Matinicus [sic] Island, which at that time was a small but thriving community with a school, grocery store, and post office. Smalley "interviewed Capt. W. G. Butman, who operates the steamboat line to Matinicus and Criehaven, and he informs me that he carried 2,200 passengers to the latter place during the year 1911. He estimates 1,000 were conveyed by all other boats. During the same period he transported to Criehaven from Rockland and Matinicus 500 tons of merchandise, consisting principally of coal, lumber, and foodstuffs. He believes another 100 tons were conveyed by private boats during the year."

Nowadays, Criehaven is called Ragged Island and is bereft of full-time residents. A dozen or so summer homes enjoy part-time occupancy.

The end of the *W. G. Butman* – but not the end of W. G. Butman – came on May 27, 1915. According to a contemporary account, "The mail and passenger steamer *W. G. Butman* went to the bottom while on her regular run between Metinicus and Rockland late yesterday. In a rough sea, the ten passengers and the crew of four took to the ship's two small boats and after a hard row of seven miles reached Metinicus Island, wet to the skin.

"Although the steamer sank quickly, the crew managed to save the mail which they brought to the mainland last night in a motorboat. The passengers were able to bring off their hand baggage.

"It is believed that the sinking of the *Butman* was due to the fact that one of the deadlights was not securely closed. The steamer, which was of forty-three tons burden, was owned by her commander, Captain W. G. Butman."

In her original registration, the gross tonnage of the *W.G. Butman* was given as 25 tons. The tonnage was increased to 43 tons during her career. Tonnage is not a calculation of a vessel's weight, but of her carrying capacity. The increase in registered tonnage implies that the vessel's deck house was either enlarged or enclosed, in which case the formula for calculating gross tonnage would account for the higher registered tonnage.

A postcard picture of the *W. G. Butman* filled with passengers.

CAMILLA MAY PAGE

Built: 1905
Previous names: None
Gross tonnage: 688
Type of vessel: Wooden-hulled four-masted schooner
Builder: James W. Hawley, Bath, Maine
Owner: E.M. Baird, master
Port of registry: New York, NY
Cause of sinking: Ran aground
Location: Off Odiorne's Point (or Jaffrey Point) in Portsmouth Harbor

Sunk: November 18, 1928
Depth: 15 feet
Dimensions: 175' x 36' x 14'
Power: sail

The *Camilla May Page* had an atypical beginning. According to the *Coal Trade Journal*, "The vessel was christened with flowers instead of wine by Miss Marion Drisko, the daughter of Captain Drisko. The name of the schooner is *Camilla May Page*, named for the daughter of Albert Page, of Fairfield, a member of the lumber firm of Lawrence, Newhall, Page Co. The capacity of the new schooner is 1,200 tons of coal."

After several years in service as a collier, the *Camilla May Page* became a tramp. I do not mean this in a derogatory way. In shipping terminology, a tramp is a vessel (usually a freighter) that travels to any port that has a cargo, and transports that cargo to its destination, where it picks up another cargo for some other port. In this manner the vessel tramps around the world from one port to another, carrying cargoes of all kinds. The *Camilla May Page* worked in this manner for a couple of decades – until she was purchased by the Putman Lumber Company, of Jacksonville, Florida, for which she transported lumber (obviously).

In May of 1922, the *Camilla May Page* rescued the crew of the four-masted schooner *Josephine*. All the masts of the latter vessel were snapped off in the midst of a fierce northeaster. Her men clung to the top of the main cabin: the only portion of the vessel that was not submerged. The *Camilla May Page* appeared providentially after the storm blew itself out, and took the men off the drifting hulk. The *Josephine* might have sunk, and all her men would likely have drowned, had not her holds been filled with lumber.

Ironically, five years later the crew of the *Camilla May Page* met a similar but more disastrous fate on or about February 20, 1927. That was the date on which her abandoned hull was discovered off Asbury Park (or Little Egg Harbor; accounts differ), New Jersey. The crew – variously given as eight, nine, or ten – was missing. The only occupants were a cat and a dog – either pets or mascots – who had sheltered from the wind by staying below deck. Although the masts were battered and the sails were torn to shreds, as if the vessel had been beaten by a terrible tempest, the cargo of lumber was intact.

In fact, a number of vessels were lost in the storm that swept along the eastern seaboard at that time. One unidentified schooner was found adrift and ablaze, with no survivors anywhere in sight.

On February 22, the body of Captain Warren Grace, master of the *Camilla May Page*, was found on the beach at Atlantic City, New Jersey. None of the other crewmembers was ever found.

On February 23, the *Camilla May Page* was towed up the Hudson River by the *Standard Oil Barge No. 4*: the vessel that had found the abandoned schooner at sea, and that had searched the area unsuccessfully for survivors. Although they were saddened by the loss of their brethren sailors, the six crewmembers were otherwise jubilant because they could claim a salvage award for the schooner and her cargo. The lumber was estimated to be worth some $100,000.

According to a different account, the *Camilla May Page* "was driven ashore and grounded on the Brigantine shoal off the New Jersey coast in a howling snow storm. The crew endeavored to leave the ship in the ship's lifeboat. The boat capsized in the breakers and all hands drowned. The grounded vessel survived the storm with the only loss the ship's spanker top mast. Exactly how it happened was never revealed."

The Brigantine shoals are located a mile or two off the beach at Brigantine, New Jersey. If the above account is true, it is possible that after the storm abated, the abandoned schooner floated off the shoal at high tide and drifted out to sea, where she was spotted by the *Standard Oil Barge No. 4*.

Ultimate disaster struck the *Camilla May Page* on November 18, 1928. The schooner had been missing for several weeks, and was thought to have come to grief at sea: lost with a cargo of coal that was consigned to the Pierce and Hartung Coal Company at Boothbay Harbor, Maine.

Adverse seas forced Captain E.M. Baird, master and owner, to turn back from his intended destination and weather the storm until conditions moderated. Then, as the schooner approached land after dark in a fog, she crashed on the rocks at "Odiorne's Point, 300 yards from Little Harbor breakwater." She lay-to all night long until her plight was discovered in the morning by the Portsmouth Harbor Coast Guard. Captain and crew were alive and well, but the holds were taking on water after grinding all night on the rocks.

A week later, the schooner was still pinned to the rocks like a moth in a shadow box. There was no hope that she could be extricated from her plight. The hull and cargo were sold to Baker & Hudson, of Portland, Maine. Salvage operations commenced on November 28.

On December 10, it was reported, "The heavy seas during the storm yesterday caused considerable added damage to the wreck of the schooner *Camilla May Page* which went on a ledge at Jaffrey Point, New Castle on Nov. 18. The stern of the vessel together with two masts broke away from the remainder of the vessel and now it is feared that the remaining 960 tons of soft coal are a total loss."

Meanwhile, the *Camilla May Page* instigated trouble of a different nature. So many people flocked to the scene of the catastrophe, in order to catch a view of the stranded schooner, that the residents of Wild Rose Lane stretched a rope across the road, claiming that the lane was not a public thoroughfare but a private highway. Residents went as far as to post a constable to keep away the throngs. Wild Rose Lane was the only route that led to the viewing point.

Salvage operations were secured on December 13. "The lighter which came on from Portland to take charge of the salvage work on the wrecked *Camilla May Page* has all the equipment which was saved from the foundered schooner stowed away and is making ready to leave for her home port when the weather is favorable."

By that time there was little left to see: "Now only a small part of the bow of the four master remains intact. Drift wood is scattered along the beaches in this vicinity."

Today, only the bottom of the hull remains to mark the spot of the long-ago calamity.

Two views of the *Camilla May Page* on the rocks.
Right: from the collection of Paul Sherman.
Bottom: from the collection of Bill Quinn.

MARY A. BROWN

Built: 1876
Previous names: None
Gross tonnage: 15
Type of vessel: Fishing schooner
Builder: Bath, Maine
Owner: Gloucester, Massachusetts
Port of registry: Gloucester (or Dennis), Massachusetts
Cause of sinking: Ran aground
Location: Hampton Beach

Sunk: December 5, 1900
Depth: On land
Dimensions: 41' x 13' x 5'
Power: Sail

For the first two decades of her career, the *Mary A. Brown* appears to have been operated safely and efficiently by a number of owners. In 1897 she was registered in Bath, Maine, and all was quiet on the wide, wide sea. Then, the following year, her registry was changed to Gloucester, Massachusetts, and under the owner at this location the small fishing schooner suffered a number of misadventures.

On January 14, 1898, she ran aground outside the harbor at New Shoreham, Rhode Island. Attentive lifesavers found the stranded schooner, kedged her off her perch by running out her anchor and heaving, then helped her to get under way.

On October 26 of the same year, she stranded on Block Island, Rhode Island. A lifesaver on shore discovered her distress, and ignited a Coston flare so the people on board would know that their situation was known to authorities. "The master sent a boat ashore for him to go on board and aid in floating the vessel. As the tide was rising they succeeded in floating her uninjured."

On August 30, 1900, the much beleaguered vessel struck a sandbar on Negro Island, Maine. "Surfmen boarded her, bent on a masthead tackle, and as soon as the tide came in she floated without apparent injury. Keeper piloted her clear of dangers."

Three times may be a charm but the fourth time proved to be her undoing. A southern gale struck the New England coast on December 5, 1900. Vessels were imperiled from Maine to Massachusetts. Then the Canadian Maritimes took the blunt of the storm; casualties occurred in Nova Scotia and Newfoundland. Vessels were blown ashore all along the northeastern seaboard. Yet the only stranding that resulted in fatalities was the *Mary A. Brown*.

Patrolman Merritt from the Hampton Beach Lifesaving Station was making his rounds in the dark at 3 o'clock in the morning when he discovered wreckage washing ashore some three miles south of the station. After spotting the schooner in the breakers, he raced to the station and sounded the alarm. Captain Smart, the Keeper of the station, led his crew to the site of the wreck through six inches of snow.

Strong winds and pounding seas were hammering the schooner to pieces. "In less than an hour after the ill-fated vessel struck she was a mass of kindling wood and the beach was strewn with wreckage. Several articles that came ashore had 'Mary A. Brown' inscribed on them. By this means the wreck was identified as the Gloucester fishing schooner of that name."

The crew of the *Mary A. Brown* numbered five, six, or seven (accounts differ). Four bodies washed ashore over the next three days: Captain Arthur Eldredge, master of the schooner; Charles Green; Abraham Perry; and Henry Penry (the cook).

The *Mary A. Brown* would likely not be remembered at all today had it not been for a fortuitous circumstance. After the storm abated, the hull washed ashore where receding tides left it high and dry. It was such a picture perfect image that it became a tourist attraction that was photographed, drawn, and painted again and again for the next ten years or more, until it rotted away. Picture postcards have kept the fishing schooner alive to the present time.

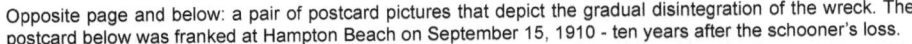

Opposite page and below: a pair of postcard pictures that depict the gradual disintegration of the wreck. The postcard below was franked at Hampton Beach on September 15, 1910 - ten years after the schooner's loss.

NEW ENGLAND

Built: 1833
Previous names: None
Gross tonnage: 300
Type of vessel: Wooden-hulled passenger vessel
Builder: Henry Eckford, New York, NY
Owner: Gardiner, Maine
Port of registry: Unknown
Cause of sinking: Collision with schooner *Curlew*
Location: Approximately 8 miles southeast of Isles of Shoals

Sunk: May 31, 1838
Depth: Unknown
Dimensions: 163' x 23' x 8'
Power: Cross-head engine

In the early days of steam navigation the biggest problem was boiler explosion. Materials studies were in their infancy, the forces of high-pressure mechanics were poorly understood, and trained engineers were often cavalier or not well trained about their duties. So many injuries and fatalities were caused by boiler explosions – both on steamboats and on locomotives – that Congress dealt with the problem on nearly a full-time basis: by ordering investigations to determine the cause of explosions, and by passing legislation to increase safety measures.

The evolution of steam containment was long and painful as passengers and crewmembers were scalded to death with great abandon.

One way to mitigate fatalities from boiler explosions on inland waterways was to put passengers on barges that were towed by steamboats. That way only the crew was put at risk, while passengers were towed at a safe distance astern.

Benjamin Silliman proposed an alternative method. Instead of locating the boilers under the deck, where the explosive force of a burst boiler escaped upward through the saloon and passengers' quarters, he suggested placing the boilers above deck and outside the hull, where the explosive force would escape outboard. This innovative design was incorporated into the construction of the *New England*. Furthermore, the boilers were made of copper instead of iron, as a way to avoid the corrosive effects that saltwater had on iron.

In 1833, the *New England* was put in passenger service on Long Island Sound. She ran between New York City and Hartford, Connecticut. On October 9 of that year, after one month in service, she was proceeding up the Connecticut River toward Hartford when she paused at Essex. The time was three o'clock in the morning.

"Her engine was stopped, the small boat was let down to land a passenger, and had just reached the shore, when both the boilers exploded, almost simultaneously, with a noise like heavy cannon. The shock was dreadful; and the scene which followed is represented, by those who were present, as awful and heart-rending beyond description. The morning was excessively dark; the rain poured in torrents; the lights on deck and in the cabin were suddenly extinguished, and all was desolation and horror on board. Those only who witnessed the havoc which was made, and heard the shrieks and groans of the wounded and dying, can form an adequate conception of the scene.

"There were upward of seventy passengers on board; the boat hands numbered about twenty, - making, in all, nearly one hundred persons. Most of the passengers were

From *Early American Steamers*, by Erik Heyl.

fortunately in their berths. Those who were in the gentlemen's cabin, escaped without serious injury. The most destructive effects of the explosion were felt on the deck, and in the ladies' cabin. The ladies were in their berths, and remained there, we believe were not much injured; but those who were on cots opposite the cabin doors, and others, who, on the first alarm, sprang from their berths, were more or less scalded. All who were on deck abaft the boilers, were either killed or wounded. Had the accident occurred in the day-time, when the passengers are generally scattered about the deck and promenade, the destruction of lives would, in all probability, have been much greater.

"Captain Waterman was on the wheel-house, at the time of the explosion, attending to the landing of passengers from the small boat. He noticed a movement over the boilers, and immediately jumped, or was thrown, upon the forward-deck. He was somewhat bruised, but not seriously injured."

Thirteen people were killed outright by the blast, or succumbed afterward from scalding and injuries: eight passengers and five boat hands. Another ten people were injured but survived.

"The cause of this dreadful explosion may be traced to the negligence or presumption of the engineer, in permitting the steam to accumulate beyond what the strength of the boilers could sustain. From the best information we could obtain, the steam was not blown off while the boat lay at Saybrook, nor during her stoppings at Essex. Mr. Potter, the engineer, who, for many years, had been in the employment of the proprietors, was not on board during this trip; his place was supplied by Mr. Marshall, from the West Point Foundry, who had the reputation of skill in his profession. He declared there were only eight or ten inches of steam on, at the time of the explosion; but, besides the improbability on the face of this statement, there was the strongest testimony of a very different character. The boilers were rent asunder and thrown into the river – the guards on which they rested were broken off – the promenade-deck, from the captain's office to the ladies' cabin, a distance of about thirty feet, was lifted from its place, and fell, in part, upon the main deck, and the ladies' cabin, and all the upper works of the boat were completely shattered.

It was crucial to the safe operation of a steamboat that excess steam be blown or valved off when that steam was not being exhausted by movement of the engine. Otherwise, steam kept building in the boilers until the pressure exceeded the strength of the sidewalls.

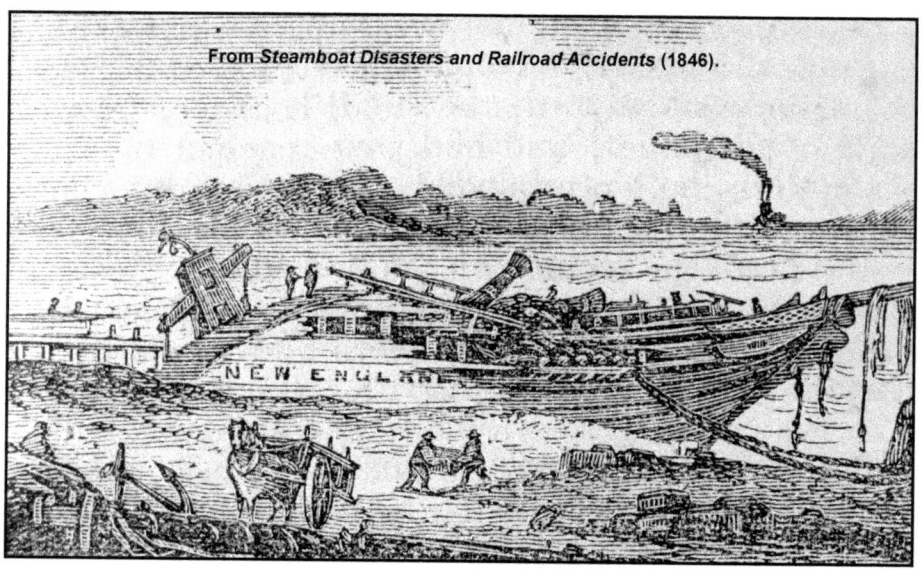

From *Steamboat Disasters and Railroad Accidents* (1846).

A coroner's jury found that the victims died "in consequence of the bursting of the boilers," but offered no recommendation as to how those boilers burst.

The Connecticut River Steam Boat Company, owner of the *New England*, conducted a "scientific" investigation into the cause of the boilers bursting. Committee members whitewashed the accident by finding that "we do not feel it necessary to attach any high degree of blame to those who were in charge of the boat and engine at the time of the accident; and they may be justly exonerated from any charge of voluntary or willful misconduct."

Furthermore, "The board of examiners are fully and unanimously of the opinion, that in the construction and management of this boat, the steamboat company, used their best endeavors, for the accommodation of the public, and committed the navigation of it to persons of established reputation for prudence and skill in their profession."

The majority consensus of blame for the catastrophe was cast upon the makers of the boiler for fabricating a substandard product. This was a copout, for in those days a substandard boiler referred to any boiler that exploded at normal steam pressure. To be sure, there were others who saw through this obvious tautology, but their minority voices were shouted down by the press of higher decibels.

Some saw through the charade and brought attention to the unlikely twist of fate of both boilers exploding simultaneously. Charles Hinson made note of this perceived fluke of happenstance: "If there was a sufficiency of water, and the steam was gradually increased to a point beyond what the boilers were capable of bearing, why did not the mercury take French leave of the gauge. And why is it that the steam could not find some weak point in the shell, flues, or legs, to escape, and relieve the boilers? Is it because there was not one foot or inch of surface of either of the boilers, but that was equal in strength to the remainder? If so, then her boilers were constructed by something more than human, or it was one of the most remarkable coincidences that has ever taken place."

Hinson did not leave his question unanswered: "The truth is, there was not a sufficiency of water; the engineer was deceived; the water foamed badly, as is generally the case in new boilers; and the water, when foaming, will deceive the engineer, unless he has had a good deal of experience on board of a steamboat; and the tendency of the water to rise when the engine is in motion, so as to take the appearance of solid water on the gauge-cock, would deceive the engineer unless he was an experienced one. The engineer for the *New England*, for that trip, was not experienced; he came from an engine establishment, where he had assisted in putting up steam-engines for years; still he was inexperienced, it being his first trip as engineer of a boat. The true cause of the explosion, there was want of water. The water had so far decreased as to leave the tops of the return-flues bare after the engine was stopped at the landing; that, while lying there, they were exposed to a hot fire, and would, in ten minutes, become red with heat; that, immediately after opening the cylinder-receiving-valves, millions of fine particles of water followed the first rush of steam, and, coming in contact with the hot metal, were made into steam instantly; and the pressure no man can calculate. We can only judge of the pressure by its effects: we can safely say that it is not possible to burst two boilers on board the same ship, at the instant, under a gradually-increased pressure of steam with a sufficiency of water; but where there is a want of water, and the steam is generated in the manner described above, no man on board such a boat is safe, even if the boiler were a half foot thick."

The hulk of the *New England* was towed to New York City, where she was repaired at a cost of more than $17,000. She recommenced service the following spring.

In 1835, the *New England* was purchased by a group of people in Gardiner, Maine. For three years she ran regular service between Bath, Maine and Boston, Massachusetts.

Her end came on May 31, 1838. She was on her southern passage when she collided with the schooner *Curlew* at one o'clock in the morning.

"The schooner was standing to leeward of the boat, and when a short distance from her, luffed up with the intention of passing her bow. Before this could be effected, she struck the larboard [port] bow of the steamer, and, after getting clear, passed on.

Captain Kimball, master of the *New England*, quickly ascertained that the damage to his vessel was severe, and hailed the schooner to lend assistance. The *Curlew* hove to while the steamer maneuvered. "The passengers, about seventy in number, among them fifteen ladies, were by this time on deck, and when the [steam]boat reached the *Curlew*, a general rush was made to board her. In their eagerness, several of them jumped too soon, and fell overboard, but they were all picked up, unharmed, with the exception of Mr. Standish, of Providence, who was crushed to death between the two vessels."

Many of the passengers were scantily dressed in night clothes. Some fifteen miles from port, the steamer *Portsmouth* took the *Curlew* in tow to Boston, where the survivors were treated favorably.

The location of the collision was given as "fifteen miles south of Boon Island." This puts the collision site about eight miles southeast of Isles of Shoals. However, when last seen, the *New England* had "sunk as low as the promenade-deck, in which situation she remained." How long the steamer stayed in this semi-submerged condition, and how far she drifted with the tide, is anyone's guess.

NUMBER 3666

Built: 1913
Previous names: None
Approximate tonnage: 125
Type of vehicle: Locomotive 4-6-2
Builder: American Locomotive Company, Schenectady, New York
Owner: Boston & Maine Railroad
Cause of sinking: Bridge collapse
Location: Piscataqua River, near the Sarah Mildred Long Bridge

Sunk: September 10, 1939
Depth: 50 feet
Approximate length (with tender): 80'
Power: coal-fired steam

GPS: 43-05.160 / 70-45.748

It is uncommon if not exceedingly rare for a train to sink. So seldom do they have the opportunity to crash into water. Yet locomotive *Number 3666* did just that: an unfortunate circumstance that caused the death of the engineer and fireman. It happened like this . . .

On September 10, 1939, *Number 3666* was on the track from North Berwick, Maine to Boston, Massachusetts. As the train approached the trestle over the Piscataqua River, in Portsmouth, New Hampshire, engineer John Beatie reduced speed to 3 miles per hour, as per standing orders from Boston & Maine Railroad officials, because of the dilapidated condition of the bridge. The heavy locomotive was inching across the span when its weight proved to be more than the wooden beams could support. When the bridge collapsed, the locomotive, the tender, and the empty car behind it fell into the river. The time was 8:12 p.m.

Beatie was trapped inside the cab, and drowned. Fireman Charles Towle leaped off the rear of the cab and managed to avoid being struck by the following two cars. The incoming tide dragged him upstream, where he drowned before help could arrive to pull him out of the water.

When the empty car behind the tender broke free of the coupling that connected it to the three occupied cars next in line, the automatic brakes of those cars engaged, and brought them to a halt before they plummeted into the water. All twelve passengers were alive and well, although they may have been unnerved by their near escape from death.

"The women and children were carried from the scene to the drawtender's shack by a handcar because some of the planking along the bridge catwalk had rotted away and other sections were made slippery by rain."

Afterward, the passengers were taken to their various destinations by bus.

The next day, a diver descended to the bottom of the river to search the cab of the locomotive for the engineer's body. The body was not found. The locomotive lay on its side, seemingly undamaged.

That afternoon, company officials were quick to report that the strength of the bridge was not the cause of the accident. According to the official statement, "Investigation during the early daylight hours indicated that the supports of one of the 80-foot spans of the bridge was displaced by the movement of the caisson which was being sunk nearby.

"The condition of the piles at the easterly end of the span indicate that they were pulled out of place before the train came on to the bridge.

"Perfect working of the air brakes on the train when the engine and first car, which was being deadheaded to Boston, were precipitated into the water, saved the other cars in the train from disaster. There is no indication of structural failure, and the disaster was caused by forces having no connection with the bridge itself.

"There was no evidence of derailment prior to the plunge of the equipment into the river.

"While there has been a bridge at this point for 100 years, this structure has been entirely rebuilt several times, and all parts have been renewed repeatedly."

Their first conclusion was that blasting activity for the new bridge some sixty feet downstream was responsible for weakening the structure of the old bridge. The company filed a lawsuit in the amount of $150,000 "against Frederick Snare Corporation of New York, contractors on the sub structure of the new bridge now being constructed across the Piscataqua River . . . seeking to recover loss and damage sustained by the railroad in the displacement of a section of the Portsmouth-Kittery railroad bridge. . . . The railroad contends . . . that a large caisson used by the Snare Corporation in the construction of a new bridge for the Maine-New Hampshire Interstate Bridge authority, broke loose and cables attached on the caisson pulled some of the pilings supporting the railroad bridge out of place. This caused a part of the bridge to give away when the local train started to cross it a short time afterwards."

Maybe. Maybe not. It seems to me that the railroad folks already knew that their bridge was defective, else why did they have standing orders for trains not to cross the span at a speed above 3 miles per hour.

The situation with regard to the caisson for the new bridge may have been reversed. "After the wreck the caisson was found to have moved from its location." The question this begs was: Did the caisson damage the railroad bridge, or did the collapsing bridge damage the caisson? This question seems never to have been settled.

The Frederick Snare Corporation carried liability insurance for the bridge building job. Yet the issues at hand appear to have been settled without resorting to suits and countersuits.

I bought this picture from eBay after searching for a generic 4-6-2 locomotive. Imagine my surprise when I received the item and discovered that it was *Number 3666*.

First, on September 27, "Derrick lighters of the Frederick Snare corporation today cleared away some of the sunken wreckage of the wooden railroad bridge across the Piscataqua river where three front units of the train plunged through into 80 feet of water, carrying the engineer and fireman to their death. Some of the heavy spans, splintered and twisted, were carried to a barge tied up at the Consolidation wharf."

Second, the Frederick Snare Corporation received additional compensation from the Bridge Authority because it failed to disclose the proximity of the railroad bridge when it sought a bid from the corporation. The proximity of the railroad bridge required "the hiring of extra tugs from Boston" to maneuver the floating caissons before they could be placed in the proper location to be sunk for the piers. This proved to be a "delicate and difficult job."

Third, the broken railroad drawbridge was never repaired or replaced. Instead, train service was rerouted for a year until completion of the Interstate bridge, by which time the tracks were relocated so that rail service could be resumed . . . on the lower level of the new Interstate bridge.

As for the three train units that lay on the bottom of the river, still connected, initial recovery contemplations yielded to calculations of expense and feasibility of salvage. They were abandoned in place.

In 1966, the Army Corps of Engineers commenced a multi-decade project to widen and deepen the Piscataqua River to a width of 400 feet and a depth of 35 feet throughout its six mile length. Sharp turning points were widened to 700 feet. In this dredging process the COE dragged the train out of the middle of the channel, where it was already comfortably deep enough not to pose a hazard to navigation, and left it lying at a depth of about 50 feet.

There has been talk of raising the locomotive as a museum piece, but so far nothing has come of the proposal.

Readers who are not railroad buffs should note that *Number 3666* was a 4-6-2 steam locomotive. According to the Whyte classification, the numeration system refers to the number of trucks and the number of wheels on each truck. On locomotives, a truck is a carriage or suspension that supports the weight of the locomotive while providing axles for a pair or a group of same-sized wheels.

Thus the leading truck on *Number 3666* held four wheels on two axles; the middle truck held six wheels on three axles; and the trailing truck held two wheels on one axle. All these wheels helped to spread the weight of the locomotive evenly. Only the axles on the center truck held drive wheels; the fore and aft trucks just distributed weight.

Hanging pennants and ice on the water make it appear that this picture of the *O-9* was taken on launch day (not to be confused with commissioning day six months later): January 27, 1918. (Courtesy of the Naval Photographic Center.)

O-9

Built: 1918
Previous names: None
Displacement tonnage: 560 (surfaced), 629 (submerged) Dimensions: 172' x 18' x 14'
Type of vessel: Submarine Power: twin diesel engines, twin electric motors
Builder: Fore River Shipbuilding Company, Quincy, Massachusetts
Owner: U.S. Navy Official designation: SS-70
Cause of sinking: Unknown
Lat/Lon: 42° 59' 48" North / 70° 20' 27" West

Sunk: June 20, 1941
Depth: 450 feet

Although no one knew it yet, World War One was nearly over by the time the submarine *O-9* was commissioned, on July 27, 1918. At that time German U-boats were sinking vessels left and right on the American eastern seaboard. The *O-9* was immediately placed on coast patrol but saw no action. She was dispatched to England in November, but before she reached the British Isles the Armistice was signed, so she was recalled without ever touching land on the other side of the Atlantic Ocean.

In peacetime she spent most of her working career as a training sub. Her longest trip took her as far as Colon, Panama, where the U.S. Navy maintained a submarine base and air station called Coco Solo. She stayed there for a year. Her subsequent duty stations were located at various New England bases. She was decommissioned at the Philadelphia Navy Yard on June 25, 1931.

In anticipation of American involvement in World War Two, the *O-9* was recommissioned on April 14, 1941. Ten years in mothballs left her in need of a major overhaul. After maintenance and repairs put her shipshape, she proceeded to New London, Connecticut along with other O-class submarines "for a 5 week period of post-recommissioning trials and training."

Over the course of two weeks, *O-9* made a series of shallow water dives to less than 150 feet. The number of dives was not recorded, but was estimated to have been between sixteen and twenty. According to the Court of Inquiry that was held aboard the USS *Vixen*, "The Commanding Officer reported the existence of minor leaks during initial dives. This leakage has been usual in recommissioned submarines. In fact, leaks usually exist in any submarine after an extensive overhaul. They are of no significance. In the case of the *O-9* it is understood that leakage was restored to normal (there are always a few trickles around periscopes and shafting) during the shallow water diving trials."

On June 20, 1941, she and two other O-class submarines (*O-6* and *O-10*) went to sea for deep submergence trials off the Isles of Shoals. *O-6* and *O-10* dived and surfaced as planned.

O-9 never surfaced. Onboard at the time were Lieutenant Howard Abbott (in command), Ensign Marks Wangsness, and thirty-one enlisted men.

The location of the last dive was somewhat in doubt because the submarines "had been operating on dead reckoning for some hours in hazy weather."

When the *O-9* did not surface on time, the *O-10* started calling her "by oscillator." (An oscillator was an instrument that emitted a sharp high-pitched tone; it was generally

A postcard picture of the *O-9* transiting the Panama Canal. Compare the size of the submarine with that of the freighter.

used to send submarine fog signals.) When no answering ping was received, search and rescue operations were initiated.

The probable location of the sunken submarine was made by observation of "a 'boiling' patch of air and oil and a quantity of wreckage on the surface. The wreckage consisted of pieces of cork of the sort used for interior sheathing of submarines, and three pieces of wood decking, one marked with a brass plate inscribed 'O-9 P-7'. These pieces, matched with the decking of another O-class submarine, fitted a section on the port side over the forward end of the after battery compartment. The ends of these battens had been broken off, indicating that they had been subjected to heavy stresses. Two grapnels, dragged in opposite directions, had caught in some object, probably O-9. The depth of water was 440 feet. . . .

"No sound had been heard from the submarine, and there was no other indication of life within the hull. *O-9* had an oscillator, but neither the oscillator nor hull taps were heard during the constant sound watch maintained until the area was abandoned. *O-9* had no marker buoys, due to the fact that the manufacturer had failed to make delivery.

"The available evidence indicated that at least one compartment of the submarine was open to the sea sufficiently to allow cork sheathing to float out, that at least part of the wood deck was damaged, that one or more fuel tanks were leaking, and air had ceased by the time I arrived." The "I" was Rear Admiral Richard Edwards, who conducted the Court of Inquiry.

Submarine salvage vessel *Falcon* rushed to the scene from the Portsmouth Navy Yard, in New Hampshire. "Her rescue chamber was not on board, having been left at New London with *Chewink*, the chamber assigned to *Chewink* being unfit for use because of errors in manufacture. Officers, men and equipment of the Experimental Diving Unit were on board *Falcon*, having been sent by plane from Washington [DC]."

Chewink arrived on the scene the morning after the accident. She deployed four mooring anchors so the *Falcon* could secure a four-point moor over the wreck site. Diving operations commenced that afternoon.

G.F.J. Crocker was the first diver in the water. He was breathing a mix of 20% oxygen and 80% helium. "Pressure in the diving hose was limited to 250 pounds, which is the specified maximum pressure for diving hose." He reached a depth of 370 feet in seven minutes, at which time he reported – through the communication line that was married to the hose that delivered the breathing gas – that the gas supply was inadequate. He was hauled up to the surface. The total time of his dive and subsequent decompression (in a recompression chamber) was two hours and thirty-five minutes.

"Meanwhile the Secretary of the Navy visited the area."

Next in the water was L. Zampiglione. By this time it was nearly 8:30 at night. The breathing gas was remixed so that it contained 10% oxygen and 90% helium, and the pressure on the hose was increased to 300 pounds. He reached a depth of 380 feet in ten minutes, then reported that his arms were becoming tired. He was brought to the surface and put into the chamber for decompression.

"Trouble was found to be that descending line was not exactly vertical, so that diver, when nearing the bottom, had to pull himself along a slanting line instead of sliding down a vertical line." Note that the diving dress – including bronze helmet, bronze breastplate, lead weight belt, and lead shoes – weighed more than 150 pounds.

"Decided to discontinue night diving in view of the difficulty of dealing with possible accidents in the dark and the fact that there was by this time virtually no chance of gaining access to the submarine soon enough to save life."

The *Falcon* shifted position so as to plumb the descent line.

At 7:19 on the morning of June 22 – more than forty-six hours after the *O-9* had submerged – hard-hat diver R.L. Metzger left the surface. Nine minutes later he was "on the bottom" at a depth of 440 feet. He remained there for forty-five seconds. During that time he directed his diving lamp in various directions.

"Contrary to expectations, the diving lamp did not crush at 440 feet. As he swung around he saw, first what he described as a vertical white line, and then, a white 'half moon' in 2 o'clock position. He saw this 'half moon' again, but it seemed to have turned around to about a 5 o'clock position. There was nothing conclusive in this, though he might have had a dim view of the figure '70' which was painted on both sides of the conning tower and on the bows of *O-9*. Metzger was unable to give any clear estimate of the visibility, but it was apparently very low. He saw nothing but the above described white objects, which he was unable to touch without leaving the descending line. He had been cautioned not to leave his line. Metzger suffered no discomfort, except cold, and was in good condition after the dive. He has the distinction of being the first man to go to 440 feet on a 'working dive'."

At 9:55, June 22, C. Conger started his descent. He touched bottom nine minutes later. He stated "that he could see the loom of a large dark object." Visibility was poor. "It was decided from divers' descriptions that visibility was such that work would have to be done by feel rather than by sight. Conger's dive was terminated."

It should be emphasized that Metzger and Conger held the deep diving record for a number of years.

Diving operations were secured. There was no possibility that the submarine's crewmembers could still be alive. The pressure put on the divers' breathing hose exceeded its breaking strength, which could have resulted in the sidewall bursting and killing the diver.

"The old-type telephone in use (the only type now available) made it difficult to

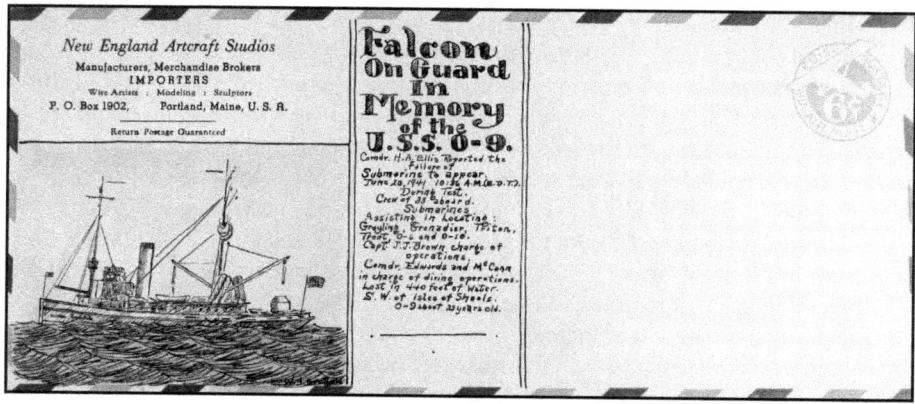

understand the divers' reports." With a helium concentration of 90%, the divers must have sounded like high-pitched Munchkins.

"There was no doubt that by shifting the *Falcon* a diver eventually could be landed on the submarine to work by feel, but, in view of the evidence that the submarine's wood deck had been damaged, this was a dangerous proceeding. If a diver became entangled below, it would have been a task of insuperable difficulty for a relief diver to go down to free him."

Edwards concluded that information gleaned from further investigation was not worth the risk. "The effort would require for a long period the services of ship, men and officers urgently needed to further preparations for war. Salvage was certainly hazardous and probably impossible to accomplish."

Memorial services were held at 5 o'clock on the afternoon of June 22 "on board the *Triton*, lying-to above the *O-9*. The Secretary of the Navy [Frank Knox] took personal charge of the ceremony."

In summation, "The nature and cause of the accident to *O-9* are not known. The present condition of the vessel is not known, but it may be inferred that her wooden deck is damaged, that at least one compartment is open to the sea, and that at least one fuel tank is ruptured."

Recommendations and repercussions followed the catastrophe.

Admiral H.R. Stark wrote that it was "remarkable . . . to conduct deep-dive tests in a swept area some 400 feet deep . . . for new boats built for 300 feet" and "for older boats built for 200 feet. It is my opinion that this needs change forthwith so that there are swept areas available in which the depth of water is not more than 50 feet greater than the depth for which boats are built."

From this opinion it can be inferred that the design depth of the *O-9* was 200 feet, and that during the submergence test she must have lost depth control and, before control could be regained, she had gone deeper than her crush depth.

Stark also noted, "It seems clear to me that the telephone buoy should be retained – when proceeding on active operations it should not be removed but will then have to be so secured as not to jar loose in case of being depth-charged – and so reveal location of boat!"

From this statement it can be inferred that the telephone buoy was removed from the *O-9* prior to the submergence test . . . not that it would have made any difference with regard to saving the lives of the crewmembers.

Admiral Ernest J. King agreed wholeheartedly: "The depth of her test dive was 200 feet and that to make it, she was in 400 feet of water. The question immediately pops up – wouldn't it be better on such test dives to make them in water where if anything happened, she would be in depths which her hull pressure could be expected to stand if she hit bottom, for example, in a depth of water of say not over 250 feet."

Notwithstanding these reasoned observations, the media pandered to the public with such phrases as "crushed like an eggshell," "crushed to pieces," and "folded like an accordion." The media claimed, "The primary consideration in building a submarine is weight and not safety. The media also claimed that the O-class submarines were old and obsolete.

It should be noted that deep submergence tests of seven other O-class submarines were conducted satisfactorily. This implies that there was nothing inherently wrong with the hull design, and that age was not a factor in the loss of the *O-9*.

Skip to 1997, when Glen Ream asked Garry Kozak – side-scan sonar specialist for Klein Associates – to search for the resting place of *O-9* with Klein's latest model. Kozak readily agreed. This was no easy chore, for the Navy's location had been obtained by the age-old method of sextant and chronometer along with stellar observations and a table of logarithms. After two days of dragging the towfish, they found a target that approximated the size and shape of the lost submarine, but the state of the sea introduced distortions in the image by yanking the tow rope. To be certain, they returned a couple of weeks later when the ocean was calm. The resulting side-scan image left no doubt that the target was indeed the *O-9*.

Opposite top: A commemorative envelope that summarizes the basic facts about the *O-9* catastrophe and the subsequent rescue attempt. The envelope is not postmarked, but the airmail imprint is contemporary with the year of the submarine's loss.

Below: Something is hokey about this commemorative envelope. Although the stamp was issued in 1940, and was still in use for several years afterward, it was postmarked on the same morning as the *O-9's* loss. This is a physical impossibility, as no one knew at that time that the submarine was lost.

PYTHIAN

Built: 1894
Previous names: None
Gross tonnage: 69
Type of vessel: Fishing schooner
Builder: Essex, Massachusetts
Owner: Benjamin A. Smith
Port of registry: Gloucester, Massachusetts
Cause of sinking: Driven ashore off Fort McClarey, Kittery Point

Sunk: February 1, 1908
Depth: Unknown
Dimensions: 79' x 21' x 8'
Power: sail

There is not much to say about this two-masted fishing schooner except that the vessel was typical of those that plied the nearby ocean to catch fish for the standard market. Despite her small size, she was known to have brought in as many as 3,000 haddock per voyage. Commercial fishing was a rugged way to earn a living, and one that was seldom if ever appreciated by those who ate the catch.

"The Gloucester fishing schooner was torn from her anchorage in the harbor tonight by the southeast gale and driven onto the rocks off Fort McClarey, Kittery Point. Ten members of the crew were saved by men on shore, while three others trusted themselves to a dory and rowed for another vessel lying near by. The weather was so thick that their fate could not be learned.

"When the *Pythian* was forced well up toward shore, giving the men a desperate chance of jumping overboard and being hauled to safety by the people on shore, each of the ten men saved watched his opportunity and took the risk. They were pulled out half conscious."

This is not a picture of the *Pythian*, but the caption reads "A Gloucester Fishing Schooner." The postcard was franked in 1904, so the image is contemporary and undoubtedly typical of fishing schooners like the *Pythian*.

SAMUEL J. GOUCHER

Built: 1904
Previous names: None
Gross tonnage: 2,547
Type of vessel: Wooden-hulled five-masted schooner
Builder: H.M. & R.L. Bean Company, Camden, Maine
Owner: Coastwise Transportation Company (John G. Crowley, manager) Boston, MA
Port of registry: Boston, Massachusetts
Cause of sinking: Ran aground
Location: None

Sunk: November 11, 1911
Depth: Unknown
Dimensions: 281' x 48' x 23'
Power: Sail

This majestic tall ship was the type that gave vent to the descriptive phrase "majestic tall ship." The spread of her canvas on five tall masts must surely have looked the part. Unfortunately, "majestic" is a cognomen that was invented and ascribed by modern-day tall-ship enthusiasts, not by the sailors who worked onboard. In reality, these tall ships were little more than the equivalent of today's eighteen-wheelers: freight transporters whose crewmembers looked upon sailing as nothing more than back-breaking work.

Yesteryear's labor is today's glamor.

The *Samuel J. Goucher* was carrying coal from Newport News, Virginia to Portland, Maine when she encountered thick fog on the lee of White Island. Captain Hart, master, wisely anchored his vessel until the sun rose and the fog dissipated. Captain Hart was slightly off in his calculations of his whereabouts. When he realized his true position, he altered course in order to avoid shoal water. Unlike steamships, the navigation of schooners is dictated by the wind. He was unable to clear the ledges that projected under water from Duck Island.

"It was high water when the schooner struck, and she stove a bad hole in her hull, and began to take water rapidly, and as the tide fell the big schooner apparently broke in two between the main and mizzen mast."

A broken back spells the end of any vessel: wood or iron, sailer or steamer. The date of the stranding was November 11, 1911.

"The wreck was discovered by the patrolmen of the Isles of Shoals life saving station and Captain Staples and his crew at once went to the rescue. The Captain and crew of 12 men were in no immediate danger, but they were taken off, and Captain Staples at once telephoned Supt. Harding of this city [Portsmouth], and asked that tugs and lighters be sent out to strip the wreck. At the same time the owners of the schooner, the Crowley brothers, were notified in Boston."

The schooner was then treated the way a crashed tractor-trailer is treated today, when it is blocking traffic on a crowded highway and its contents are spread across the macadam.

"The tugs *Portsmouth* and the *Mitchell Davis*, with one of the Piscataqua Navigation barges were sent out to the wreck, and when they arrived they found that the schooner would be a total wreck. The sea for some distance about the schooner was black with coal dust, showing that there was a large hole stove in her bottom and from

This portrait of the *Samuel J. Goucher* was painted by contemporary artist Solon Badger (alias Samuel Badger).

the shakey condition of the stern, it was evident that she was broken in two.

"There was a good sea running and work was at once started in stripping the schooner of all of her rigging. Her sails and all running rigging, and stores and all of the effects of the crew were taken off by hand. Owing to the sea the lighter could not get in near enough to take off her anchors, spars and hoisting engine.

"Saturday afternoon [of November 11] the Tug, *Confidence* with wrecking lighter from the Boston wrecking company, arrived and assisted in taking off some of the rigging. Sunday the tugs and wrecking lighter stood by to take off her anchors, and if possible remove the spars, but there was a strong southerly wind blowing and it kicked up such a sea that it was impossible to get near the wreck, and later in the day the tugs and lighters came into this city.

"When they left the schooner was still standing, but the seas were breaking across her stern and she is expected to go to pieces any minute.

"Captain Hart and the crew remained at the island to assist in the salvage of the equipment still on the schooner should the sea fall.

"The schooner had a cargo of 4,300 tons of coal consigned to the Maine Central Railroad.

"This is the first wreck that has occurred at the Isles of Shoals since the establishment of the Isles of Shoals life saving station and the timely assistance rendered by Captain Staples and his crew, show the wisdom of the United States government in establishing a station at the island. The value of the Isles of Shoals cable was also shown as word was telephoned to the mainland for the assistance of the tugs."

The Howe Wrecking Company purchased the hull and cargo with an eye toward salvaging the coal for profit. After three weeks of work – which was interrupted periodically by rough seas and foul weather – the salvage outfit had succeeded in recovering only 180 tons of coal. The only coal that was accessible to the digging buckets of the lighters was that which was stowed under the hatchways. The chunks of coal were cemented together by the water that filled the holds.

On December 19, it was reported that the *Samuel J. Goucher* "moved near two miles from her former position. The coal had evidently dropped out through the bottom and the deck forward was well out of water. The stern however, had been entirely washed out by the heavy sea of the past few days. There are about nine fathoms of water where the vessel lay, and what holds her in her present position is the subject of much discussion among sea-faring men."

The floating derelict was now a hazard to navigation, bouncing back and forth with the changing tides like a billiard ball in perpetual motion. The hull bobbed too deep in the water to get it to a wharf, and could not be anchored because the anchors had been removed. The two wrecking tugs and the revenue cutter *Androscoggin* towed the peripatetic hulk out of the shipping lanes and grounded it in Portsmouth Harbor on the flats off Kittery Point. A line was run from ship to shore to keep the hulk in place.

The job of demolition fell to the Army Corps of Engineers: "N.H.—The *Samuel J. Goucher* was a large five-masted wooden schooner. Loaded with 4,400 tons of bituminous coal, the vessel went ashore at Isles of Shoals November 10, 1911. The vessel was stripped and wrecked, but December 18, 1911, went adrift and was towed into Portsmouth Harbor by a revenue cutter. Allotments amounting to $2,500 were made for breaking up the wreck, which was completed in February, 1912. The total cost was $2,500. Some old timber and scrap sold for $379."

In the 1980's, archaeologists from Cornell University conducted an underwater survey of a wooden wreck that they found near Duck Island. They tentatively identified it as the *Samuel J. Goucher* because that was where she originally stranded. Not a bit of coal did they find on the site. They never ascertained the wreck's true identity, but it definitely was not the *Samuel J. Goucher*.

Why not?

According to records of the T.A. Scott Company, a long-time and respected commercial salvage outfit, the company kept "a list of materials salvaged from the schooner *Samuel J. Goucher* of Boston, MA, which was stranded on Isle of Shoals, NH, Nov. 12, 1911. Owners, Coastwise Transportation Company, Boston, MA, and manager, John G. Crowley, sold her and her cargo at auction in Boston, MA, Nov. 25, to Charles N. Rowe, Portland, ME. After most of her cargo was removed or washed out, she floated and was towed to Boston, presumably to be blown up."

At first glance the T.A. Scott Company information appears to conflict with the statement of the Army Corps of Engineers. Perhaps not. A close reading can infer that the two statements are complementary, with neither one referring to the actions that are stated in the other, so that both statements could be correct as far as they go. And neither one got the accepted stranding date correct.

In any case, I included this locally well-known shipwreck story so that future generations will not waste time and effort in searching for a wreck that no longer exists. This now begs the question: What wreck did the university archaeologists survey?

WILD CAT

Built: 1918
Previous names: *SC-222*
Displacement tonnage: 75
Type of vessel: Submarine chaser
Builder: Newcomb Lifeboat Company, Hampton, Virginia
Owner: Alexander Johnson, Lee, New Hampshire
Port of registry: Unknown
Cause of sinking: Foundered in the Piscataqua River

Sunk: November 14, 1935
Depth: 50 feet
Dimensions: 110' x 14' x 5'
Power: gasoline engines

GPS: 43-07.704 / 70-51.429

    Despite the assassination of Archduke Ferdinand, and the resulting conflict among European nations, America stayed out of the war as long as possible. Part of the reason was that the government did not know whose side to take. Anti-German sentiment ran rampant in the majority, but minority voters disliked the British policy of blockading German ports against neutral merchant vessels. Some Americans still wanted to trade with the Central Powers.

    The deciding factor that turned America against Germany was its illegal policy of unrestricted submarine warfare. According to the Hague Convention of 1907, warships of belligerent nations were duty bound not to attack merchant vessels on the high seas until the passengers and crew were given time to abandon ship in lifeboats; and that those lifeboats were close enough to shore to reach a position of safety. Germany violated this treaty when its submarines started to torpedo merchant vessels unannounced, with disdain and disregard for human life.

    As the American tide swung toward support of the Allies, the Navy geared for war against German U-boats by designing and constructing a fleet of submarine chasers that could be mass produced cheaply and rapidly. Thus was born the so-called mosquito fleet of SC-class warships (or warboats). More than four hundred submarine chasers were built by dozens of companies on both coasts and in the Great Lakes: companies that normally built fishing boats and private yachts.

    They were built out of wood on a keel of yellow pine, framed in white oak, planked with yellow pine, and decked with Oregon pine. They were propelled by three 6-cylinder gasoline engines, each turning its own shaft and propeller, and could attain a maximum speed of 17 knots (although cruising speed was 12 knots, which allowed a range of 1,000 miles).

    Armament consisted of one 3-inch deck gun, two machine guns, and either a depth-charge rack or a Y-gun (which could throw two depth charges: one to either side).

    Most of the two hundred thirty-five sub chasers that crossed the Atlantic Ocean did so under their own power. A few were towed. Those that did not serve in the European theater protected home waters from U-boats when they marauded the eastern seaboard in 1918. *SC-222* was deployed to Plymouth, England.

    After the Great War, the Navy had more sub chasers in its inventory than it needed in peacetime. Some were kept in active service, some were laid up in mothballs, some were transferred to other services, and some were sold to private interests. In 1921, the *SC-222* was sold private and renamed *Wild Cat*.

Sister ship of the *SC-222*.   Courtesy of the Naval Photographic Center

A postcard picture of another sub chaser that was converted to a fishing vessel. Joe Cushing told me that divers can reach the wreck from shore: "Enter the water at the old Cedar Point boat ramp at the end of Cedar Point Road and keep to your left as you work your way down to 50 feet. The remains of the old bridge will be seen on the way out to the wreck approximately 200 yards from shore."

Of those that were sold private, many saw service as excursion vessels or head boats. The *Wild Cat* was utilized in the transport service. It was common practice to remove the center engine, shaft, and propeller: both as a measure of economy and to create more space below deck.

On October 26, 1935, the *Portsmouth Herald* started a series of frivolous mentions of the *Wild Cat* under the heading "The Herald Hears," to wit: "That the former submarine chaser that went up the river a few days ago with a load of coal for Durham started quite a bit of excitement on the water front. That the small craft was taken for a coast guard repair boat, a rum runner, coast guard rum chaser and survey boat."

On November 15, 1935, under the headline "Boat Sinks Near Durham," the *Portsmouth Herald* published a single sentence factual account concerning the ultimate fate of the *Wild Cat*: "The former submarine chaser 'Wild Cat,' which is owned by Capt. Alexander Johnson of Lee, and has been used to carry coal to Durham, broke away from its moorings at a wharf near Ackroyd's Point, Durham, last night and is reported to have sunk."

Not content to let the facts speak for themselves and let the matter drop, the *Portsmouth Herald* continued its October harangue with a series of fictional follow-ups that ridiculed either Alexander Johnson or the *Wild Cat*, or both.

November 23, under the heading "We're Wondering," "If the home port of that former submarine chaser known as the 'Wild Cat' has been changed. If her mystery cruise from Durham, minus a crew, has terminated. If the Coast Guard ever got a line on her since the night she started so much alarm among B. & M. officials. Why she wasn't drydocked at Frankfort Island off Eliot. If the 'Wild Cat' didn't give the boys a wild chase."

"We're Wondering" of November 30: "If any reward will be offered for the former navy sub chaser, now known as the 'Wild Cat' which was reported recently cruising in Great Bay minus a crew."

It seems to me that this derisive attempt at humor was given in poor taste. After all, the owner of the *Wild Cat* lost a valuable commodity that was probably uninsured. He was now out of work. I cannot fathom why the newspaper proceeded to kick the man after he was down.

CHEROKEE

Built: 1925
Previous names: None
Gross tonnage: 5,896
Type of vessel: Passenger liner
Builder: Newport News Ship Building & Dry Dock Company, Newport News, VA
Owner: Clyde-Mallory Lines, Inc., New York, NY
Port of registry: New York, NY
Cause of sinking: Torpedoed by *U-87* (Kapitanleutnant Joachim Berger)
Lat/lon (attack position): 42° 25' North / 69° 10' West

Sunk: June 15, 1942
Depth: Unknown
Dimensions: 387' x 54' x 20'
Power: 2 oil-fired steam turbines

The *Cherokee* was one of four sister ships that were built for service along the eastern seaboard. All were named after Indian tribes, the others being *Algonquin, Mohawk*, and *Seminole*. Their primary function was to transport passengers between New York City and Jacksonville, Florida, although on occasion they might stop at other ports. They could also carry a fair amount of freight.

According to company brochures, the passenger capacity was 446 persons. Cargo capacity was 272,500 cubic feet. Two steam turbines were coupled to a single shaft whose propeller could drive the vessel at a speed of sixteen knots for 7,000 miles without refueling. Her fuel capacity was 6,180 barrels of oil.

Except for inspections and minor repairs and maintenance, the *Cherokee* stayed in continuous service between New York and Jacksonville until the end of 1941. After the commencement of war, she was taken off her usual route in order to serve as a troop ship. At that time she was transferred to the Agwilines, which operated the *Cherokee* under bare-boat charter to the War Shipping Administration. Captain Twiggs Brown was in command.

Mid-June found the *Cherokee* proceeding westward across the Atlantic Ocean. She ran with a fast convoy because of her high rate of speed. Then, "for no apparent reason," she was detached to Halifax. There she joined Convoy XB-25 for Boston, Massachusetts. This 8-knot convoy consisted of six merchantmen and five escorts.

On board the *Cherokee* were 169 people: 112 crewmembers, 11 armed guards to man the deck gun, and 46 passengers. The passengers consisted of 41 Army enlisted men, four Russian naval officers, and a coast pilot.

Shortly before midnight, the convoy was attacked by German U-boat *U-87*. Both the *Port Nicholson* and the *Cherokee* were torpedoed. The *Cherokee* sank within ten minutes with the loss of 86 lives.

Captain Brown survived the attack. He was interrogated "before the 'C' Marine Investigation Board of Boston, Massachusetts" concerning the loss of his vessel. According to Brown, at the time of the attack "our time was a little past 11:20." By that he meant forty minutes before midnight.

He was in the chart room abaft the wheelhouse "when I heard an explosion out on the port bow, and I knew it was either a torpedo or a depth charge some escort had dropped, which depth charges in convoys are very frequent things, (You hear them any time day or night) but our junior third officer was in the wheel house; he was on watch;

Postcard advertisement.

he opened the door and told me a ship had been torpedoed and he said, "I think it is the COMMODORE.'"

By "commodore" he meant the person in charge of the convoy, not a vessel by that name. The commodore was aboard the *Port Nicholson* (which see).

Captain Brown: "We threw in the alarm. In fact, he threw in the alarm for the gun crew, and I in turn threw in the general alarm for the crew and passengers, but I don't think they worked. After we had been hit, when I heard the first explosion I went hard right, and we had swung 50° by the compass when we were hit. The quartermaster was calling out the degrees. . .

"Then we were hit by the first torpedo under, or near, the port wing of the bridge, and that is when we put in the alarms, and it was a matter of a few seconds until the next torpedo struck us, and we have been wondering ever since whether it was one torpedo or two that struck together, because the explosion – the force of it – noise and everything else – and jarring of the ship was much more than the first one, so we have been commenting on that, whether it was two that hit us together in place of one. . . .

"As soon as we were hit the gun crew alarm had been put in already. Then I threw in the other alarms, but I didn't hear them ring. There is an alarm bell just down the stairway from the chart room, and I didn't hear that bell ring, but I was told later by this young officer in here that someone told him he did hear the alarm bells going, and I sent him and the quartermaster at the wheel to their stations. The first torpedo that struck us buckled the floor in the wheel house, and the port wing of the bridge was practically gone. The steering wheel was laying over almost 45°, and the foremast was back over the top of the wheel house, and the lights all went out. I tried the loud speaker; that was gone; it wouldn't even light; you couldn't do anything with it; get nothing out of it. I tried the whistle; it wouldn't work. In the convoy we had a whistle signal in case you were torpedoed; we tried that, and that wouldn't work. This young officer tried it before I did. After he left the wheel house (I sent him and the quartermaster away) I was there alone. In the meantime I had sent for the first officer; (He is here now) as soon as the first ship was torpedoed and I heard the explosion, I sent this young officer from the bridge down to his room, which was about 50', to call him. It wouldn't be more than 50' he would have to walk, but he never got to the bridge. The time the second torpedo hit even the doors and everything else……. [sic] The radio room back of the chart room, that just about fell apart, and there was a radio operator that was picked up with us. He was not on watch at the time; he told me he tried to get in the door below, near his room, which led up to the radio room, and the door was jammed and twisted; and I tried the door near the chart room, and I couldn't get that open. The ship began listing with the first explosion, and she never stopped. . . .

"She went right over to port, and she never stopped. We had a large battery box on top of the radio room. That was for emergency batteries, direction finder, etc. She listed so that that box and all went over. I tried to get out of the starboard side of the bridge, and that whole thing was wrecked too. The whole wheel house was a wreck. I got as far as the door and slipped and landed out on the port wing of the bridge, and I couldn't get word; I couldn't talk with anybody; there was nobody there you could talk to. There were men around, of course. When I seen the ship was going, there wasn't a thing in the world I could do, or anybody else could do. She had listed then until the top of her house, that is where the bridge was, was under water. That is where I was standing. The port wing of the bridge submerged, and she had almost gone 90° then. Her stack was just about laying in the water, and then I jumped."

Brown treaded water for half an hour until, despite utter darkness, he managed to find a life raft and climb aboard. This raft already had twelve to fifteen survivors onboard. At seven o'clock in the morning they spotted a vessel in the distance. They fired a distress signal, and all were soon rescued by the Canadian corvette *Halifax*.

Because the *Cherokee* sank in less than ten minutes, the casualty rate was high: 86 people lost their lives in this Nazi bid for world domination.

Meanwhile, other vessels were helping to rescue survivors who were floating in the water. The Coast Guard cutter *Escanaba* launched a surfboat, which plucked eleven men from building seas. Eleven more men were saved when the *Escanaba* drifted down onto life rafts so that the survivors could tie up to the cutter's stern and clamber aboard.

The most heroic rescue involved the merchantman *Norlago*. According to Able Seaman Richard Dion's service medal, "While proceeding in convoy from Halifax to Boston, the SS *Norlago*, in which he was serving, was placed in serious jeopardy when the vessel directly ahead and the one on her starboard beam were torpedoed and sunk within short intervals. Nevertheless the Master ordered the ship to circle the area for survivors. During the ensuing maneuvers Dion volunteered to go overboard to rescue a seaman clinging to a piece of wreckage, and reached him just as the weakened man's head slumped forward into the water. Despite the fact that Dion weighed but 115 pounds compared to the unconscious seaman's 230 pounds, he secured a line to his arm, held his head above water and assisted in getting him alongside the ship from whence he was hoisted on board. His courage and utter disregard of personal safety in going to the aid of one in peril will be a lasting inspiration to all seamen of the United States Merchant Marine."

Existing records do not state how the rest of the survivors were rescued.

The *U-87* was sunk on March 4, 1943 by the HMCS *Shediac* and the HMCS *St. Croix*. There were no survivors.

Readers should note that the *Cherokee*'s sister ship *Mohawk* sank in 80 feet of water off the New Jersey coast in 1935. The wreck is one of the – if not *the* – most popular dive sites off the State. See *Shipwrecks of New Jersey: Central* for particulars.

In March of 2013, the National Oceanic and Atmospheric Administration published a 43-page boilerplate pamphlet with the highfalutin name of Screening Level Risk Assessment Package, which was aimed at addressing the potential threat that the *Cherokee* posed to the local environment from a catastrophic release of petroleum products. According to NOAA's findings:

"The *Cherokee* is classified as High Risk because the bunker oil is heavy fuel oil, a Group IV oil type," and "The *Cherokee* is classified as High Risk because there was no report of fire at the time of casualty," and "The oil volume risk classifications refer to the volume of the most-likely Worst Case Discharge from the vessel and are based on the amount of oil believed or confirmed to be on the vessel. The *Cherokee* is ranked as High Volume because it is thought to have a potential for up to 10,000 bbl [barrels] (based on original approximations of bunker capacity of the vessel's gross tonnage, it was recently discovered that the vessel actually had a bunker capacity of 7,519 bbl), although some of that was lost at the time of the casualty due to the explosions and breakup of the vessel."

NOAA's scare tactics were invalidated in 1967, when the U.S. Coast Guard conducted the Submerged Tanker Project, in which they actually dived on a number of tankers that had been torpedoed by German U-boats in World War Two. They found that no tank compartments contained cargo because the product had long since escaped a drop at a time through pinholes in the rusted steel bulkheads. Now, 46 years later, NOAA is claiming that the *Cherokee* – which was a passenger vessel and not a tanker, and therefore carried oil only for propulsion requirements – posed a high pollution risk to Maine residents.

If no substantial quantities of oil were found in 1967, what could possibly make NOAA believe that 46 years of continuous deterioration would increase that risk?

In order to justify the wasted expenditure of the public's hard-earned dollars on producing a pointless and repetitive "study," NOAA published pages and pages of tables and graphs that showed what might happen along the coast of Maine should the *Cherokee* suddenly release the huge quantity of oil that it never had in the first place. In fact, NOAA did not conduct any bona fide field studies. It relied on secondary Internet sources for information about the *Cherokee*.

Consider this travesty of rabble-rousing: "Ecological resources at risk from a catastrophic release of oil from the *Cherokee* (Table 3-1) include numerous guilds of birds that use shorelines and coastal waters. The islands of coastal Maine support an incredible diversity and abundance of nesting seabirds, migrating shorebirds and passerines and overwintering waterfowl. Shorelines in this region are important haul-out and pupping sites for seals. Coastal waters are summer foraging habitat for several species of large whales. Nearshore regions also support productive commercial fisheries for fish and invertebrate species.

"Socio-economic resources in the areas potentially affected by a release from the *Cherokee* include very highly utilized recreational beaches from Cape Cod and Nantucket, Massachusetts, up to northern Maine during summer, but also during spring and fall for shore fishing. fishing, [sic] and wildlife viewing. A national seashore and national park would also potentially be impacted."

The pamphlet harped upon "socio-economic" risks literally dozens or scores of times throughout the text, stressing a condition that did not and could never exist with respect to the *Cherokee*.

Worse yet, NOAA scientists continually confused the words "ecology" and "ecological" with "environment" and "environmental." Time and again the pamphlet used the word "ecological" when the meaning was "environmental." (For example, see the quote three paragraphs above.)

Ecology is the study of the environment. One would think that NOAA scientists should know better. There are "environmental resources," but there is no such thing as an "ecological resource."

GULF STREAM

Built: 1963
Previous names: None
Gross tonnage: 43
Type of vessel: Steel-hulled oil-drilling support vessel
Builder: ?
Owner: Nova University Oceanographic Center, Fort Lauderdale, Florida
Port of registry: Fort Lauderdale, Florida
Cause of sinking: Foundered
Location: In the Gulf of Maine

Sunk: January 1975
Depth: Unknown
Dimensions: 48' x 13' x 7'
Power: Twin diesel engines

When a vessel goes missing and all hands are lost, the incident falls into that unfulfilling category in which questions can never be answered, and the mystery of her disappearance can never be solved. The *Gulf Stream* vanished under circumstances that left her fate undefined.

All that is known is that five men perished without having time to call for help on the radio. These men were Captain William Campbell; mate Jack Spornraft; William Richardson (director of oceanography); James Riddle (research technician); and John Hill (assistant development engineer).

The *Gulf Stream* was designed and built as an oil-drilling support vessel: one that transported workers and supplies to the oil rigs and drilling platforms in the Gulf of Mexico. After she was purchased by Nova University, she was modified and registered as a research vessel. In addition to her scientific apparatus, she was equipped with modern safety appliances such as radios, fire extinguishers, flare kit, life rings, life vests, and two 5-person life rafts.

At the time of her loss, the *Gulf Stream* was conducting scientific studies "to perfect a heavy weather buoy testing program." Richardson designed drifting buoys with transmitters that could be tracked by satellite or aircraft. Their drift patterns could be used to determine current speed and direction, and to measure "surface marine and atmospheric characteristics."

Most vessels that founder at sea do so as a result of structural failure or adverse weather conditions. The weather during the time of the *Gulf Stream's* final cruise was mild, with moderate winds and waves that rose to a height of four feet or less. She departed from the Bigelow Laboratory in Boothbay Harbor at ten o'clock on the morning of January 4, her planned four-day mission being to recover eight buoys that were located some forty miles southward. That was the last time that she was positively identified.

A lobsterman saw a vessel on January 6 that reminded him of the *Gulf Stream*, but he could not be certain of her identity. During the intervening time, the research vessel had made no radio calls, despite the fact that it was her routine to check in every night that she was away from her working port at Boothbay Harbor. This makes it seem unlikely that the boat that the lobsterman saw was the *Gulf Stream*.

Yet two other witnesses spotted what they were certain was the *Gulf Stream* at the same time and place: ten o'clock in the morning, proceeding south past Squirrels Island.

If they did in fact spot the *Gulf Stream*, it still leaves unanswered the question of why she did not check in by radio the previous evenings. The research vessel was equipped with two radios.

Squirrels Island was located only four miles from the *Gulf Stream's* dock.

Another witness in the Coast Guard investigation testified that on January 6 he recognized the voice of William Campbell when he intercepted a radio transmission that was *not* a distress call.

Testimony from the Coast Guard was even more confusing. At the precise time at which the *Gulf Stream* departed from Boothbay Harbor on January 4, the Coast Guard intercepted the following transmission: "Coast Guard, this is the R/V *Gulf Stream*. Over." The Coast Guard radio operator replied, "This is Coast Guard Boothbay. Can we be of assistance?" The next transmission was given in a normal if somewhat nervous voice: "Coast Guard, this is the *Gulf*..." After the interrupted transmission, the Coast Guard was unable to re-establish contact with the calling vessel.

Three days later, on January 7, the Coast Guard intercepted the following message in a normal voice: "U.S. Coast Guard Boothbay, this is the R/V *Gulf Stream*. Over." Further contact was not established. Later that day, a fishing vessel overheard radio traffic in which a voice claimed to be calling from the *Gulf Stream*.

The Coast Guard initiated a search for the missing research vessel. But that night – January 7 – the weather turned nasty. The 95-foot cutter *Cape Horn* was forced back to port by twelve-foot seas. A Coast Guard aircraft reported 40-knot winds and low visibility, with seas increasing to twenty feet; it, too, was forced to terminate its search.

Search operations were recommenced after the worst of the storm passed. Search efforts were still handicapped by high winds. As the seas lay down, the search for the vessel and its crew intensified. Participating in the search were five Coast Guard cutters and "numerous small craft.... Aircraft are being launched as weather permits."

Called into the search were two 210-foot Coast Guard cutters: *Active* and *Decisive*. The *Cape Horn* returned to sea. Also assisting was the 210-foot research vessel *Atlantis II*, which operated out of the Woods Hole Research Institute. Two helicopters from as far away as the Cape Cod Air Station at Otis Air Force Base, in Massachusetts, assisted in the aerial search.

Despite the fancy description, this magazine picture of the *Gulf Stream* shows a vessel that looks more like an ordinary fishing boat than most people's perception of an "oil-drilling support vessel."

On January 9, the Coast Guard cutter *Duane* found the body of James Riddle some twenty-five miles south of Portland, Maine. A life vest had kept the body afloat. The Cumberland County medical examiner found that the cause of death was exposure.

Using the body as a drift indicator, "The primary search area is along the coast from Newburyport, Mass, to Boothbay Harbor, Maine, and extends fifty miles offshore."

A Coast Guard helicopter "recovered a life ring bearing the name *Gulf Stream* from the water 48 miles southeast of Portsmouth, New Hampshire."

Also retrieved from the sea was a wooden drawer that belonged "well inside the vessel."

Ultimately, "Coast Guard units with the assistance of the Navy and civilian authorities have searched over 77,000 square miles despite weather conditions which hampered operations during the seven day period. . . . Three life rings and one life jacket, positively identified as equipment from *Gulf Stream* were also recovered in an area between Cape Elizabeth Maine and Cape Ann Massachusetts. Further search efforts produced nothing of significance. Routine Coast Guard patrols in the Maine Gulf will continue to be on the lookout for any sign of the *Gulf Stream* and her crew."

Lacking firm indications as to the cause of the catastrophe, Coast Guard investigators concluded, "There is no evidence that any act of misconduct, inattention to duty, negligence, or willful violation of law or regulation on the part of licensed or certified personnel contributed to the casualty. There is no evidence of any mayday or distress being sent from the R/V *Gulf Stream* at any time."

The case was closed on such a note of uncertainty.

The best eulogy that can be made for the men of the *Gulf Stream* is that they died in the cause of science.

In 1998, John Perry Fish, side-scan sonar expert who co-owned American Underwater Search and Survey with Arnie Carr, found a sonar target that closely matched the dimensions of the *Gulf Stream*. The wreck was located 36 miles southeast of Cape Porpoise, in 600 feet of water.

The dedicated search for the *Gulf Stream* was funded by the Scripps Institute of Oceanography, the Woods Hole Oceanographic Institute, the Office of Naval Research, and the National Oceanic and Atmospheric Administration. The search area was defined by WHOI scientist Richard Limeburner. "Using debris found from the vessel," he "used wind, current and tide information to calculate what could have been the vessel's last position."

According to the *Boothbay Register*, Fish planned to return to the site "with remote controlled underwater cameras to examine the wreck." I have been unable to determine if the follow-up examination was ever conducted.

MARINE MERCHANT

Built: 1944
Previous names: *Joseph-Augustin Chevalier*
Gross tonnage: 6,639
Type of vessel: Bulk carrier
Builder: New England Ship Building Corp., South Portland, Maine
Owner: Marine Navigation Company, New York, NY
Port of registry: Wilmington, Delaware
Cause of sinking: Broke in two
Lat/lon: 42° 49' North / 69° 46' West

Sunk: April 14, 1961
Depth: 690 feet
Dimensions: 441' x 57' x 37'
Power: oil-fired steam

The *Joseph-Augustin Chevalier* was a Liberty ship that was built for the Emergency Fleet during World War Two. As in all Liberty ships, her single screw was propelled by a triple-expansion reciprocating steam engine that could propel the vessel at a speed of 11 knots.

In 1947, the vessel was converted to a bulk carrier, and renamed *Marine Merchant*. The conversion reduced her available tonnage capacity from the standard 7,177 tons to 6,639 tons. Extra safety equipment was installed due to the flammability of her intended cargo, which was sulfur.

On February 5, 1952, fire broke out in Hold No. 2 when the vessel was being unloaded by means of a huge bucket scoop, in Charleston, South Carolina. Flames and poisonous fumes overwhelmed nearby stevedores, blinding and choking them. Suffering from smoke inhalation and serious lung burns, the victims were rushed to the hospital. The fire in the scoop was extinguished before the dock or the vessel came to harm.

The Marine Navigation Company, which owned the vessel, declined to pay the injured longshoremen for the injuries that they sustained in the accident, so the victims filed a lawsuit against the company. The victims lost the suit by the slenderest of margins: what might almost be called a matter of semantics.

According to Coast Guard regulations (ellipses refer to outline numbers), "In loading or unloading of sulphur in bulk the following conditions shall be complied with: . . . When sulphur in bulk is loaded in a deep hold with general cargo in the Tween Deck hold above the sulphur a dust proof wooden bulkhead inclosure shall be built in the hatchways from the over deck of the lower deck to the weather deck forming a tight enclosure to prevent dust entering the Tween Decks during loading. . . . Holds shall be cleaned of all debris. . . . Ceiling shall be made tight to prevent sulphur dust finding its way into the bilges; any chinking necessary in the way of tank tops or bilges shall be with noncombustible material. . . . In order to minimize the movement of fine sulphur dust during the loading, cowl ventilators serving the hold into which the sulphur is being loaded shall be blanked off to prevent circulation of air. . . . No smoking signs shall be conspicuously displayed, and the officer in charge shall see that they are observed. . . . An oxygen breathing apparatus, or proper gas mask, shall be made readily available. . . . A fire hose, supplied with fresh water from a shore supply source, shall be available at each hatch through which the sulphur is being loaded. . . . Upon completion of loading, the sulphur shall be leveled off and the sulphur dust deposited during

The *Marine Merchant* before she broke completely apart. (Courtesy of the U.S. Coast Guard.)

the process of loading, being extremely inflammable, shall be cared for by sweeping or washing it down. This applies to the decks and to the overhead structure within the holds. . . . After unloading, all residue of sulphur shall be thoroughly cleaned out of cargo holds before loading other cargo therein. . . . When sulphur is loaded by metal chute method, provision shall be made for proper grounding of the chute, using flexible cable to prevent static discharge."

This sounds pretty clear-cut – and it is; but it is *too* clear-cut, or perhaps more specific than it should be.

Here are some quotes from the court: "In the first line of the Regulation are the words 'loading or unloading of sulphur.' Then follow ten sub-sections. . . . Some of these sub-sections apply only to loading; others clearly affect only unloading. . . . the draftsmen of the Regulations clearly recognized the difference between the loading and unloading of Sulphur and for these two operations they prescribed different precautions. . . . It is of little use to argue that the fire hose is just as necessary in unloading as in loading, that flash fires, such as the one involved here, are just as apt to break out in unloading as in loading. We are here concerned not with what the Regulation *should* have required, but rather with what it *did* require." [Italics mine.]

After this accident, the Coast Guard realized its mistake in wording the regulations, and changed the wording so that all subsections applied to unloading as well as to loading. Specifically, "A fire hose, preferably supplied with fresh water from a shore supply source, shall be available at each hatch through which sulphur is being worked." In other words, literally, the Coast Guard changed the word "loaded" to "worked," so that the regulation also applied when sulfur was being unloaded.

But the correction of the oversight was made too late to apply to the present case. Law has no provision for retroactive application. On the basis of a single word, the company avoided paying compensation to the victims.

In 1961, an incident of an entirely different nature occurred on the *Marine Merchant*. She was on a passage from Port Sulphur, Louisiana to Portland, Maine with a cargo of 8,125 long tons of sulphur when she encountered adverse weather off the Nantucket Shoals. As the storm intensified, high seas started breaking over the main deck. Captain Robert Ruse, master, operated his vessel in a cautious manner.

According to the Marine Board of Investigations, "Speed was gradually reduced to prevent pounding. The storm reached gale proportions at about noon and the vessel was rolling heavily in an easterly swell. At about 1700 the vessel hove to in an effort to ease the force of breaking seas and shaft revolution were maintained at the minimum necessary to hold the desired headings. By 2000 on 13 April major storm conditions prevailed. Seas had become extremely adverse; the wind was logged at force 10 and was accompanied by rain, snow, sleet and fog.

"At about 2230, while the vessel was still hove to approximately 40 miles southeast of *Portland* Lightship, with the engine turning 32 RPM, a loud report was heard followed by an appreciable settling of the vessel amidships. Realizing that the vessel had suffered a major structural failure the engine was stopped, the general alarm was sounded, the radio officer was instructed to send an SOS and the crew was directed to prepare and swing out the boats. The sending of the SOS was delayed when it was learned that the sagging condition of the vessel had caused the antenna to slacken and ground out on the radar scanner. After rigging an emergency antenna, an auto-alarm signal was transmitted on the distress frequency. The Coast Guard Radio Station, Boston, Mass, and several merchant vessels responded but closest vessel was at least 5 or 6 hours away. In the meantime it was determined that the vessel had sustained a complete fracture of the sides and underbody just forward of the forward part of number 3 hatch coaming at about frame 73. The two halves were joined solely by the main deck plating which, though working with the seas, appeared to be holding. Due to the severe weather and sea conditions then prevailing the master elected to delay abandonment of the vessel as long as possible with the hope the halves would remain joined until daylight.

"With the coming of daylight wind and sea conditions moderated somewhat. At about 0430, 14 April, the SS *Daru* and the SS *Esso Raleigh* were in the area and since the vessel's sagging condition had increased dangerously during the previous hour the master ordered the vessel abandoned. Fires to the boilers were secured. Life nets, Jacob's ladders and mattresses had previously been rigged over the side and since the vessel was nearly on an even keel no difficulty was encountered in lowering away the

Survivors steering for the rescue vessel. (Courtesy of the U.S. Coast Guard.)

two lifeboats. Number 2 boat was on the lee side and was lowered away first and held alongside with 8 or 10 men aboard. The number 1 boat was then lowered with 9 men aboard but because she was on the weather side she had to be cast off to keep from being stove in. The remaining crew then disembarked into number 2 boat. Before departing the vessel, the Radio Operator locked the radio transmitter key in the 'on' position on the distress frequency.

"The crew members in the number 1 boat were picked up by the SS *Daru* and those in number 2 were picked up by the *Esso Raleigh*.

"At 0910, 14 April, the vessel sank in 115 fathoms of water."

The nine crewmembers who were rescued by the *Daru* were taken to Portland, Maine. The twenty-six crewmembers who were picked up by the *Esso Raleigh* were taken to Boston, Massachusetts. None of the thirty-five crewmembers was injured. Captain Ruse got a dunking when he leaped from the life net, but was picked up immediately by lifeboat number 2. He must have felt cold because the water temperature was 42°; air temperature was 38°.

The Coast Guard took particular notice of Fireman/Watertender Jose Aragao for "courage and unselfish regard for others . . . who, because he had no dependents, remained on watch in the engineering spaces from the time the vessel fractured until ordered abandoned rather than let some other crew member risk his life." The Coast Guard further recommended that the Maritime Administration give Aragao an award for "commendatory conduct."

Absent the vessel to examine, it was difficult for the Coast Guard to determine the exact cause of hull plate separation. Mitigating factors were, obviously, rough seas; stresses upon the bending moment imparted by the distribution of the cargo; and possibly four prior grounding incidents: October 6, 1950 at Antwerp, Belgium; November 13, 1951 in the Savannah River; September 24, 1953 in Tampa Bay, Florida; and September 3, 1959 (location not given). Damaged plates and brackets were repaired or replaced after every grounding incident.

The *Marine Merchant* had five cargo holds. The fore and aft holds (numbers 1 and 5) were empty. All the sulfur was carried in the three center holds (numbers 2, 3, and 4). Coast Guard investigators speculated that the concentration of weight in the midbody of the vessel contributed to the hull failure. They noted "the inherent weakness incident to structural notch sensitivity common to welded vessels of this class."

However, investigators also noted that this "sensitivity" had long been acknowledged as a design flaw in the original construction of Liberty ships, and that structural strengthening measures had been applied to the *Marine Merchant* at the time of her conversion to a bulk carrier in 1947, to wit: hatch reinforcements, deck crack arrester straps, gunwale arrester straps, and bilge keel alterations.

Despite these reinforcements, Coast Guard investigators speculated that the bottom hull must have fractured first, the sides of the hull then split, the midbody sagged, and the top deck held the two sections of the vessel together like a hinge.

"The stern section of the *Marine Merchant* sank beneath the surface causing the bow section to assume a vertical position after which it, too, passed beneath the surface."

Crewmembers could be thankful for the gunwale arrestor straps, for the Coast Guard credited them with preventing the two sections of the hull from separating, thus enabling the hull to remain afloat until the seas moderated and rescue vessels arrived.

NOVADOC

Built: 1924
Previous names: *Northton*
Gross tonnage: 2,227
Type of vessel: Bulk carrier
Builder: Swan, Hunter & Wigham Richardson, Newcastle-on-Tyne, England
Owner: Paterson Steamships, Fort William, Ontario
Port of registry: Fort William, Ontario
Cause of sinking: Vanished
Location: Unknown

Sunk: March 3, 1947
Depth: Unknown
Dimensions: 248' x 43' x 25'
Power: coal-fired steam

There is not much to write about a vessel that disappeared with all hands, and a wreck that has never been found.

The *Novadoc* was on a passage from Bigby, Nova Scotia to Boston, Massachusetts with a cargo of gypsum when, somewhere off the coast of Maine, she sent a radio message stating that "she was shipping water, had a hatch stove in and was running before the wind." This message was intercepted in the same terrible storm that dragged the *Portland* lightship five miles off her station in thirty-foot seas, and that broke in two the collier *Oakey L. Alexander* (which see).

Twenty-four or twenty-five crewmembers were onboard when the *Novadoc* went missing. (Sources differ.) The skipper was Allen (or Allan) Vallis.

Coast Guard aircraft searched more than 6,000 square miles of ocean between Portland and Boston. They found not a trace of flotsam.

If the *Novadoc* is remembered at all today, it is largely thanks to Blain Henshaw, who wrote a commemorative song entitled "All Hands Lost." Hail to the missing!

From the collection of Dave Clancy.

PORT NICHOLSON

Built: 1919
Previous names: None
Gross tonnage: 8,402
Type of vessel: twin-screw refrigerated freighter
Builder: Hawthorne, Leslie & Company, Newcastle, England
Owner: Port Line, London, England
Port of registry: London, England
Cause of sinking: Torpedoed by *U-87* (Kapitanleutnant Joachim Berger)
Lat/lon (attack position): 42° 11' N / 69° 25' W (German); 42° 20' / 69° 11' (American)

Sunk: June 16, 1942
Depth: 700 feet
Dimensions: 481' x 62' x 33'
Power: 4 coal-fired steam turbines

AWOIS (Low): 42-09-00.38 / 69-22-28.04

The *Port Nicholson* was technologically advanced for the period in which she was built: 1919. Her power train consisted of four steam turbines that were separated into pairs so that two inline turbines turned each propeller shaft. She was fitted with refrigeration equipment whose four compressors chilled eight insulated storage chambers that had a combined capacity of 328,598 cubic feet.

Her primary trade route stretched between England and Australia plus New Zealand.

Between World Wars, the *Port Nicholson* met with several maritime misfortunes that brought her into unwelcome prominence in the newspapers: stranding in 1924, fire in 1928, another conflagration in 1937, and collision in 1938 (in which the tugboat *Ocean Cock* was sunk). She survived these peacetime accidents only to fall prey to Nazi aggression.

June 15, 1942 found the *Port Nicholson* in convoy XB-25: Halifax, Nova Scotia to Boston, Massachusetts. Lurking under water offshore of Cape Cod was the *U-87*. It launched a spread of torpedoes that struck the *Port Nicholson* first and the *Cherokee* second (although the *Cherokee* sank first) (See the *Cherokee* chapter for details).

By that time in the prosecution of the war, a virtual news blackout had been enforced by Secretary of the Navy Frank Knox. Elaborate accounts of U-boat attacks were no longer published in the papers, except on rare occasions. Definitely not permissible was any mention of attacked vessels' names, tonnages, and nationality. Survivors were sworn to secrecy. The ban on facts led to much confusion and misinformation that historians are still trying to unravel, especially in light of the dearth of official military memoranda and written records that have been archived. If survivors were interrogated and written records were generated, some of the paperwork has been lost or misfiled.

The War Diary of the Eastern Sea Frontier had only this cryptic entry: "PORT NICHOLSON – June 15, at 2225, in 42-20N/69-11W, struck by two torpedoes on starboard side. Distress calls, flares. Ship was abandoned, but stayed afloat. Escort vessels circled around her. In the morning, the captain and chief officer returned to get the ship's papers. While aboard, the vessel's bulkheads 'started to pop' in quick succession. She sank quickly, taking both men down with her. Flares from the PORT NICHOLSON lit up all the vessels in the convoy."

The newspaper version was muddled like this: "According to a United Press report

From the author's collection.

from a New England port, eighty-three crewmen and three passengers were rescued from the British ship, which was sunk off the New England coast on June 15. [Note that the *Port Nicholson* was torpedoed before midnight on the fifteenth, but did not sink until after the following dawn. Also note that the number of rescued crewmembers was mixed with those from the *Cherokee*.]

"One of the victims from the rescue vessel was an officer. Two engine-room men, trapped in the British freighter when the first torpedo struck without warning, also were lost, bringing the total death toll to six.

"The skipper of the freighter, Captain H. E. Jeffry of London, decided to return and determine if he could save his vessel, according to 3d officer Paul Stansbury.

" 'Then he got into a lifeboat with six men and an officer from the rescue ship and rowed to his slowly sinking vessel,' Stansbury said.

" 'Shortly after that the ship settled quickly at the stern. I guess they weren't able to pull away in the lifeboat, for the men and the boat were dragged under as the ship sank."

Only in retrospect can this account be attributed to the *Port Nicholson*, because her skipper was named Harold Charles Jeffrey (not Jeffry).

This might have been all the facts available with regard to the loss of the *Port Nicholson* if it were not for modern methods of locating and preserving living sources of information. First there was oral history: recording dictation of veterans before their eventual decease. Now these recordings and other verbal recollections are being published on the Internet: a new mechanism of tapping primary sources: people who were actually on site when events occurred. This is the kind of information that is seldom documented in archives because it is considered to be anecdotal rather than official. It is valuable information nonetheless, despite inaccuracies due to fading memories of incidents long past.

One of the two known significant memoirs in this regard is that of Kenneth Eugene Cowan, a Canadian sailor who was serving on the convoy escort vessel *Nanaimo* at the time the *Port Nicholson* and *Cherokee* were torpedoed. He was a Coder whose "duties were to code and decode wireless messages."

According to Cowan (verbatim, including typos), "June 14 1942 found us in convoy outbound from the port of Halifax Nova Scotia, Canada. We were joined with a group of six merchant ships on their first leg of their journey headed south for Boston. The ships were arranged in two columns of three. One column was led by the merchant ship S.S. *Cathart*, with S.S. *Port Nicholson* and *Pan York* behind. The other column of merchant ships was led by S.S. *Malcrest*, with *Norlago* and *Cherokee* behind.

"*Port Nicholson* was carrying war supplies and trucks bound for the Pacific. The *Cherokee* was a fast freighter just down from Iceland carrying 41 army enlisted men, 4 Russian naval officers, and an army air force pilot, all headed for the US.

"The convoy had a large escort with a Destroyer in the lead and four Corvettes. *Nanaimo* was positioned on the starboard side of the convoy.

"Torpedoed!

"We were frequently called to practice action stations during the day. Around midnight on June 15 we were again called to action stations. My station is on the aft anti-aircraft gun. I grumble as I rise to answer the call and the thought of another practice. Only this time things are different. Our main 4-inch deck gun is firing Star shells into the center of the Merchant convoy. The other escorts are doing the same. The scene is as light as day. I'm very scared. We search the seas desperately for a sign of a U-Boat. Two torpedoes have hit the S.S. *Port Nicholson* and she is firing flares.

"The *Nanaimo* is on the starboard side of the convoy and we turn to cross the convoy to search for the U-Boat. As I look astern I spot the troopship S.S. *Cherokee* passing 500 yards astern. Suddenly a load [sic, read "loud"] boom followed by two huge explosions can be seen on the troopship. Two torpedoes have hit her. The color of the explosions is a brilliant red and blue light as the torpedoes hit. The trooper ship sinks almost immediately taking half of her ships crew and the soldiers down with her. The *Nicholson* remains afloat and her crew abandons ship using the Jacob ladders and lifeboats. It is all a very eerie sight 100 miles out and backlight by the lights of Boston.

"We were detailed to stay and pick up survivors from the *Nicholson*. The rest of the convoy was ordered to sail on. We rescued her whole crew, including the ship's captain and the convoy's commodore. The rest of the convoy was ordered to sail on. The next morning found the *Nicholson* still afloat. It was decided to send a boarding party over to see if she could be salvaged. Included in the boarding party were our 1st Lieutenant, 1st Petty officer seaman, a regular seaman and our 2nd signalman. From the crew of the merchantman we sent the ship's chief engineer and the convoy commodore. The *Nicholson* was easy to board as the Jacobs ladders were still over the side of the ship. We were signaled to radio for a tug to take the *Nicholson* in tow. We could see the boarding party walking the open decks of the *Nicholson*.

"At about the same time the wind came up and whipped up the seas. The rough seas proved too much for her weakened bulkheads and she suddenly took the death plunge for the bottom. The boarding party rushed for the ladders and got into the lifeboat. We close in tight to rescue the boarding party. The suction of the *Nicholson* going under overturned the lifeboat. We lost our first Lieutenant and two members of the merchant ship. Our signalman (from Truro Nova Scotia) went down with the ship when his legs got caught in the rigging.

"Fortunately he was wearing rubbers boots and these were blown off him when the ships boilers exploded. He struggled to the surface and was saved. I'll never forget the death rattle of a ship when it goes down. We auctioned off our first lieutenants' kit a few days latter, as was the custom. We landed all of *Nicholson's* survivors in Boston the next day.

"About two weeks later we retraced our route over that same track. A US navy blimp was dropping flares and there were bodies floating in the water. They were bloated bodies of uniformed US soldiers wearing life jackets, some partially eaten. We didn't any pick up. Such were the casualties of the war at sea."

Another memoir was assembled by Lorne Norman, whose father was a crewmember on the *Nanaimo* at the time of the double casualty: his name was Lewis Charles Norman. Lorne Norman wrote, "Two ships in the convoy were torpedoed. One was the *Port Nicholson*, a freighter, and the other was the U.S. troop ship *Cherokee*. There were eighty-three survivors from *Port Nicholson* and twelve from *Cherokee*. *Nanaimo* picked up seventy-nine of the eighty-three survivors from *Port Nicholson*. As she did not sink immediately, *Nanaimo* remained with the ship throughout the night.

"The next day a sea boat was sent from the *Nanaimo* with two of the freighter's officers and five crewmen from *Nanaimo*, one officer and four ratings. These men were Lieutenant Wakely, Leading Seaman; Aubrey Pickles, Signalman; Jack Tedford, Able Seaman; Leslie (Buzz) Horne and an A.S.D.I.C. operator named Pat Ginevin. They went to see if the ship could be salvaged.

"The sea boat made its way to *Port Nicholson* and tied up near her bow. The boat's crew and the two officers from *Port Nicholson* had to climb about fifteen feet to gain the deck. After the boarding part was aboard the *Port Nicholson* the boat's party went below decks near the bows of the ship leaving only Jack Tedford above decks. Jack was standing at the ship's side where the sea boat had been secured. *Nanaimo* signaled, by light, that the ship was sinking by the stern. Jack commented that he had not noticed it as she was going down very gradually. Jack then ran to the hatch and yelled to the others. He commented that some of them got up and some of them did not. The after bulkhead gave-way and the ship went down by her stern very quickly.

"The rest of the story will be told in Jack's own words as he described them to this writer almost fifty years later.

" 'The boat came right up. It was maybe fifteen or twenty feet to climb on to the ship but when we went to get into the boat it was right at our feet. As a matter of fact it swamped and went under. I know I got my feet caught in the falls from one of the ship's boats. I kicked my rubber boots off and when I came up I looked around and there was Pickles on a Carley Float, a life raft, that had fallen down off the foc'sle of the *Port Nicholson*. He hollered at me and said, "Over here, come on over here, Ted". I had a life jacket on so I swam over.'

"Jack went on to say that the A.S.D.I.C. rating Pat Ginevin was also picked up with Pickles and himself. The two officers from *Port Nicholson*, her skipper and executive officer did not even get above decks before she went down. Lt. Wakely and Buzz were able to get above decks, but they were unable to get clear when the sinking ship struck and swamped the sea-boat. As a result they were lost."

Lorne Norman added another tidbit, this one from *Nanaimo* crewmember Puffy Summerfeldt: "We laid right in the middle of where she'd gone down there. Her boilers blew and she covered us from stem to stern with soot!"

In his history of the *Nanaimo*, Lorne Norman included a photograph of the *Port Nicholson's* final plunge, with her bow nearly vertical in the air.

In summation, six lives were lost as a result of torpedoing the *Port Nicholson*: two unnamed engine room personnel who were killed by the explosion (one of whom may have been fireman Thomas William Blundell; records are unclear); Captain Jeffrey and Chief Officer Philip Arthur Munday, both of the *Port Nicholson*; and *Nanaimo* crewmembers Lieutenant Wakely and Leslie (Buzz) Horne).

From the author's collection.

On March 4, 1943, the *U-87* was sunk by the HMCS *Shediac* and the HMCS *St. Croix*. There were no survivors.

Skip to 2008. Enter long-time treasure salvor Greg Brooks and his salvage outfit Sub Sea Research (alias Sea Hunters). Brooks wanted to find the *Port Nicholson* because two archival documents that he later showed on videotape purported to list the freighter's cargo as platinum, 1,600 tons of automobile parts, and 4,000 tons of military stores. The only reason I used the word "purported" is because the two documents were shown separately: one named the vessel, tonnage, and attack location; the other listed the cargo. Both documents were heavily redacted so that lines of text above and below the visible entry were blacked out. The viewer is left to assume that the two documents were connected, but the connection is only implied, not demonstrated.

Not to nitpick, but the top line of the entry on the second document shows four columns that are separated by vertical lines. Written in the columns are (1) cargo, (2) general inc. [in which inc. is likely the abbreviation for "including,"] (3) 1,707,000 ozs. [abbreviation for ounces], and (4) 49,000,000.00 [with no dollar sign but with "US" typed underneath, on the second line in which the word "platinum" appears in the first column. This may be a simple typing oddity, but I thought that I should indicate that the weight in ounces is not typed on the same line as the word "platinum."

The second document (which lists the cargo) bears a declassification stamp that is dated April 23, 1987. I mention these peculiarities only because of the controversy that later raged about the validity of platinum being part of the cargo. See below.

According to court documents:

> Brooks heard about the *Port Nicholson* from Terry Kelley of Australia in approximately 2006-07. *Id.* ¶ 7. He then contacted Edward Michaud, a researcher with whom he had previously worked, and paid for Kelley and Michaud to come to Maine and meet. *Id.* ¶ 8. That meeting led to Brooks' efforts to find the *Port Nicholson*. *Id.* ¶ 9. In 2007 and 2008, these efforts were based upon limited and sketchy information suggesting approximate location and possible valuable cargo, not upon any certainty as to the location or con-

tents of the wreck. *Id.* ¶ 10. With initial financing of $125,000 from Brooks and his long-time partner John Hardy, since deceased, Brooks and Hardy looked over a large area of ocean floor off of the coast of Maine and Massachusetts. Plaintiff's Additional SMF ¶ 11; Brooks Aff. ¶ 9. Using data from multiple sources, they made dozens of trips to the area of the reported sinking of the *Port Nicholson* and searched an area of approximately 125 square miles of ocean. Plaintiff's Additional SMF ¶ 12; Brooks Aff. ¶ 9. They eventually identified the remains of a vessel that was the approximate size of the lost *Port Nicholson*, reported the finding to this court, and commenced this action. Plaintiff's Additional SMF ¶ 13; Intervenor's Reply SMF ¶ 13.

With only limited information, Sea Hunters undertook to raise funds for initial attempts to survey and, to the extent possible, recover items from the identified wreck site. Plaintiff's Additional SMF ¶ 14; Brooks Aff. ¶ 10. Efforts during this initial period included raising approximately $5 million from a substantial number of investors in 2008 and 2009. Plaintiff's Additional SMF ¶ 15; Intervenor's Reply SMF ¶ 15. These investors were warned of the risks involved in the salvage venture. Plaintiff's Additional SMF ¶ 16; Brooks Aff. ¶ 11 & Exh. A (ECF No. 264-6) to Plaintiff's SMFs.43

Sea Hunters assembled a skilled crew and hired other independent contractors such as researchers. Plaintiff's Additional SMF ¶ 17; Brooks Aff. ¶ 12. As is typical in the industry, Sea Hunters' contracts with crew members and other contractors called for them to receive a portion of any eventual recovery as a significant part of their compensation. Plaintiff's Additional SMF ¶ 18; Brooks Aff. ¶ 12.

The vessel that was eventually named "Sea Hunter" was acquired in 2008 and was substantially renovated, refurbished, and improved, including extensive work on equipment throughout the vessel, such as winches, motors, and electrical equipment. Plaintiff's Additional SMF ¶ 19; Intervenor's Reply SMF ¶ 19. The initial acquisition and refurbishing cost eventually exceeded $2 million of the $5 million acquired from investors. Plaintiff's Additional SMF ¶ 20; Brooks Aff. ¶ 13. Many of the repairs and upgrades were done by Sea Hunters' crew. Plaintiff's Additional SMF ¶ 21; Brooks Aff. ¶ 13. The purpose of the upgrades was to provide a platform for salvage, including a large-scale grapple, and anchors and winches for ROV operations. Plaintiff's Additional SMF ¶ 22; Brooks Aff. ¶ 13. Fuel-carrying capacity was increased, and hydraulics were substantially upgraded. *Id.* The Sea Hunter was to be the primary platform from which Sea Hunters would seek to survey and eventually bring up artifacts from the wreck. Plaintiff's Additional SMF ¶ 23; Intervenor's Reply SMF ¶ 23.44

While Brooks had a small ROV (the Hy Ball) for several years, Sea Hunters purchased a new "Mark V" ROV for close to $400,000 for the primary purpose of observing and possibly recovering small items from the vessel with a "grabber." Plaintiff's Additional SMF ¶ 25; Brooks Aff. ¶ 14.

The depth of the suspect shipwreck was 700 feet.

Brooks recovered "six metal items" which he transported to Gorham, Maine, "within the jurisdiction of this court." On August 19, Brooks filed an Admiralty claim under the corporate name Sea Hunters (a subsidiary of Sub Sea Research).

According to court records, "The court granted Sea Hunters motions to execute a warrant for the arrest of the defendant vessel and to appoint Sea Hunters as substitute custodian to preserve and maintain all artifacts, cargo, and property recovered in its salvage of the vessel and to inventory and account for the same to the court."

On December 31, 2008, the court granted protection to Sea Hunters "against all persons, entities, or parties with claims against the vessel who had failed to plead or otherwise defend their claim."

As is customary in shipwreck salvage cases in which treasure is found or suspected to exist, opportunists lurked on the sidelines waiting to pounce on salvors who spent their own time and their investors' money in searching for wrecks and recovering cargoes. These treasure leeches learned long ago that there is more money to be made by letting someone else take the risk and do the work, and then pirating the treasure by means of litigation, than there is in honest endeavor. This case was no different.

The machinator in this instance was the British government which, in accordance with the War Risk Insurance Act, reimbursed maritime underwriters for insurance claims that resulted from enemy action during World War Two. Even though the British government had abandoned the *Port Nicholson*, and had never searched for it in the subsequent sixty-six years, it now sought to reassert title in the hope of profiteering off the salvor's efforts.

On August 11, 2009, the British government filed a "restricted appearance" with the Admiralty court. The British government did not wish to stake a claim at that time, it merely wanted to put on record that, if the wreck was positively identified as the *Port Nicholson*, it wanted the salvor to understand that the consent of the British government was required before the salvor could proceed with recovery operations; and that if the salvor recovered any treasure, that treasure was the property of the British government.

Meanwhile, Sea Hunters (Greg Brooks) conducted videographic surveys of the wreck site by mounting a camera on a remotely operated vehicle. After Brooks submitted the resultant footage to the court, representatives for the British government complained that they were "unable to discern the name of the vessel from the video footage."

British reps must have been blind or illiterate. I viewed the footage after Sub Sea Research posted it on the Internet. When the ROV camera panned the upper bow of the starboard hull (the wreck lies on its port side), it clearly – and I emphasize *clearly* – showed the letters that spelled out the name. Despite the growth of marine fouling organisms, the words were perfectly legible.

British reps played hardball by refusing to accede to Brooks' request for discovery with regard to the government's claim of ownership. He asked for documents "between the government of the United Kingdom and any insurance company regarding the loss of the *Port Nicholson*" that supported the government's "claim of ownership of any of the cargo onboard the *Port Nicholson* at the time of its loss," and "showing any efforts by the government of the United Kingdom to attempt to locate the wreck site of the *Port Nicholson* or attempt to salvage the vessel or any of her cargo."

Without such evidence, the wreck fell into the public domain by dint of neglect and lack of performance on the part of the British government.

The British government offered specious arguments about why it did not feel beholden to provide such documentation. In short, the British government did not wish to *prove* that it owned the *Port Nicholson*; instead, it wanted Brooks, the court, and the world to *believe* that it owned the hull and cargo simply because the government said it was so.

American courts do not work that way. After two years of wrangling, and submitting briefs and motions and cross motions, on April 13, 2013 the judge ORDERED (in capital letters) the British government to produce documentary evidence of ownership within thirty days. In other words, put up or shut up. I have been unable to ascertain if the British government ever complied with the court order of production. The British government's case will be severely prejudiced if it continues to ignore American court protocols. So far, the British government's claim to ownership has not been adjudicated. Therefore, British ownership is based purely on assumption (or presumption).

On several occasions throughout 2011, when weather permitted, Brooks conducted additional videographic surveys of the firmly identified *Port Nicholson*. The ROV roved over the wreck from stem to stern, and investigated the debris field where the superstructure had collapsed into a complex pile of wreckage. Near the stern, objects that the video camera focused on proved to be wooden crates that measured approximately eighteen inches in length and seven inches in height (as given by the narrator), and some ten to twelve inches in width (by my estimate).

The narrator stated that these crates looked very much like ammo boxes, and indeed that is what they looked like to me. The significance of ammo boxes was that it was known that Russia shipped gold ingots in ammo boxes aboard the *Edinburgh*: a fact that was proven when those gold ingots and ammo boxes were recovered in the early 1980's. It was also well established that Russia paid for lend-lease cargoes with gold and platinum.

The wooden crates were too heavy for the ROV to pluck off the bottom. The ROV was barely strong enough to lift the edge of a crate with its manipulator arm, and flip it upward. The narrator conjectured that the heavy weight might be due to gold or platinum ingots.

I cannot help but mention that the narrator's speculation may have been driven by wishful thinking: proposing what he hoped would be stored inside the crates. On the other hand, these crates were found near the stern of the wreck where the deck gun was emplaced. In that case the ammo boxes may have contained . . . ammo. I mention the obvious only as information, not as an aspersion.

Be that as it may, at the time of publication of the present volume, although a small box of hatchets was recovered, not one of the aforementioned crates has been recovered because, despite an infusion of more than $8 million from investors, Sea Hunters pleaded that it had run out of money and could not afford to hire the kind of outfit that possessed the heavy-duty equipment to do the job. Which starts another chapter in this unending saga . . .

Also spotted in the debris near the crates was a brick-shaped, brick-sized object that looked like, well, quite frankly, like a brick. Specifically, a boiler brick.

The boiler room of a steamship is insulated with heat-reflective bricks that increase the efficiency of the boiler (or boilers) by containing and reflecting heat that escapes through the boiler casing, and by shielding the boiler from external cold, much like insulating blankets around household water heaters. As a shipwreck collapses, these boiler bricks break away from the mortar and tumble into piles – especially when a wreck is lying on its side. These bricks are a common sight to wreck-divers.

The video narrator stated that the object in question was trapezoidal in shape, implying that it more closely resembled an ingot than a brick. The footage was not clear enough for me to make that distinction, but what I noticed right away was that the exposed surfaces of the object appeared "fuzzy" and pale brown in color, as if the sides were coated with marine fouling organisms: typical of brick, wood, and metal objects except for those that consisted of precious metals such as gold and platinum: elements that are poisonous to sessile organisms that need a solid substrate on which to cling. Gold displays a gold-colored sheen; platinum gleams like silver. Just my perception . . .

In January 2012, Brooks started issuing press releases in which he claimed that the *Port Nicholson* held more than seventy tons of platinum worth some three *billion* dollars at current market prices. This announcement garnered much media attention, and brought a slew of skeptics out of the woodworks.

Long-time archaeologist and treasure salvor Robert Marx stated that "both an American company and an English Company previously went after the contents of the ship years ago and surely retrieved at least a portion." This contention seems unlikely, and has so far not been substantiated.

Others found fault with the cargo list, claiming that auto parts and military stores should have been transported in the opposite direction: *to* England instead of away from it. This seems to make sense until the scenario is reasoned out. While Russia's bullion was always delivered to New York, the *Port Nicholson's* ultimate destination was Wellington, New Zealand. ANZACS were fighting on the Pacific front against the Japanese, so it requires no stretch of the imagination to infer that England was supporting their efforts in the war, especially as Australia and New Zealand were shipping food to the beleaguered British homeland.

Yet others noted that Brooks had been in the treasure hunting business for thirty years without making a significant find. The word "significant" is somewhat subjective. And anyway, one could have made a similar criticism about Mel Fisher after fifteen years as a treasure hunter. But he struck a bonanza in his sixteenth year when he found the mother lode of the *Atocha*.

Treasure hunting is a high-risk venture in which no return on investment is guaranteed. For every treasure hunter who makes it big, a thousand others search hopefully without ever making a major strike. That is the nature of the business.

One pundit proclaimed, "The real winners will be the lawyers." This is because lawyers generally get paid whether they win, lose, or draw.

Although Brooks' 214-foot-long salvage vessel *Sea Hunter* was sitting idle at the dock, Brooks himself was not sitting idle. He was trying to obtain backing from underwater robotics firms who, he hoped, would provide their services on a contingency basis. He was also trying to interest more investors to underwrite the actual recovery operation.

Brooks told reporters, "We know that this stuff is on board and it's frustrating not to be able to go down and just grab it."

Then in February, with propitious timing, there erupted the biggest news of all: Brooks' researcher produced a consignment sheet that listed the Russian payment in platinum and gold, to be delivered by the *Port Nicholson*!

The document was not a cargo manifest or bill of lading, but a notification from the Procurement Division of the U.S. Treasury Department, which stated that the *Port Nicholson* was carrying a shipment from the Soviet Purchasing Commission for delivery to Chase National Bank in care of Guaranty National Bank in New York, in the quantity of 741 platinum bars in 149 boxes, and 1,889 bars of gold in 977 boxes.

Proof positive! Or was it?

Naysayers registered disbelief at the fortuitous discovery. First to deny the credibility of the document was the British government, which insisted that the *Port Nicholson* carried only automobile parts and military stores at the time of her loss. Brooks made a valid point when he wondered aloud that, if the British government truly believed the guff that it was peddling, why was it trying so hard to claim ownership to a pile of rusted iron that was essentially worthless?

Precious metal on the bottom of the sea is not the same as money in the bank. The gold and platinum might lie only a block and a half under the *Sea Hunter's* keel, but that distance was straight down where the ambient pressure was crushing. Only sophisticated and expensive machinery could operate at that depth without imploding.

Investors did not come flocking to Brooks' door or hatch. Just the opposite: one group of investors sued Brooks for not proceeding fast enough – or at all – with recovery operations.

Daniel Stochel was the manager of a New York City investment firm known as Equitron Capital Management. In 2011, Stochel and Equitron customers invested money in Sea Hunters. As the years dragged on, and Brooks appeared to be dragging his feet, they ran out of patience.

On March 12, 2013, Stochel formed a corporation called Mission Recovery "for the express purpose of salvaging the *Port Nicholson* and recovering Stochel's personal investment and the investment of Equitron (together totaling $600,000)." Stochel's portion was $200,000.

According to Stochel, on May 3, 2013, Brooks informed him that "Sub Sea Research was out of funds and was intending to shut down operations."

On June 21, 2013, Mission Recovery filed a motion to intervene in Sea Hunters' Admiralty claim, citing that investors had grown "disillusioned with the lack of progress of Sub Sea Research and its related entities in attempting to salvage the *Port Nicholson*."

According to the motion to intervene (with cites replaced by ellipses), "Stochel avers that on May 5, 2013, Mission Recovery entered into an exclusive agreement with Swire Seabed AS, an experienced international salvage company based in Norway, to effect the salvage of the *Port Nicholson*. . . . On May 21, 2013, Stochel traveled to Gorham, Maine, with transactional counsel to meet with Brooks and other principals of Sub Sea Research to propose a joint venture between Mission Recovery and Sub Sea Research/Sea Hunters. . . . On May 31, 2013, Brooks sent Stochel an email rejecting the proposal and providing no alternative proposal."

The court noted that, under Admiralty law, a court appointed custodian must exercise due diligence in the performance of his duty; and that appointing a substitute custodian was not out of order. Mission Recovery was permitted to intervene so that it could show just cause for its allegations.

Mission Recovery stated that "it has obtained $15 million in financing commitments to complete the salvage of the *Port Nicholson*." A financing commitment on paper is not the same as money in the bank.

Here is the picture of Sea Hunters' salvage efforts that subsequent court documents painted:

The vessel that was eventually named "Sea Hunter" was acquired in 2008 and was substantially renovated, refurbished, and improved, including extensive work on equipment throughout the vessel, such as winches, motors, and electrical equipment. Plaintiff's Additional SMF ¶ 19; Intervenor's Reply SMF ¶ 19. The initial acquisition and refurbishing cost eventually exceeded $2 million of the $5 million acquired from investors. Plaintiff's Additional SMF ¶ 20; Brooks Aff. ¶ 13. Many of the repairs and upgrades were done by Sea Hunters' crew. Plaintiff's Additional SMF ¶ 21; Brooks Aff. ¶ 13. The purpose of the upgrades was to provide a platform for salvage, including a large-scale grapple, and anchors and winches for ROV operations. Plaintiff's Additional SMF ¶ 22; Brooks Aff. ¶ 13. Fuel-carrying capacity was increased, and hydraulics were substantially upgraded. *Id.* The Sea Hunter was to be the primary platform from which Sea Hunters would seek to survey and eventually bring up artifacts from the wreck. Plaintiff's Additional SMF ¶ 23; Intervenor's Reply SMF ¶ 23.44

The Sea Hunter was ready to go in mid-summer 2009, and initial efforts commenced. Plaintiff's Additional SMF ¶ 26; Intervenor's Opposing SMF ¶ 26. The Sea Hunter has been physically at the wreck site during July 20-29, 2009, August 2-19, 2009, September 5-8, 2009, September 19-21, 2009, October 26-27, 2009, July 15-17, 2010, July 30-August 2, 2010, August 10-12, 2010, August 21-22, 2010, September 11-14, 2010, October 11-13, 2010, April 7-9, 2011, May 3, 2011, June 3-9, 2011, July 1-6, 2011, July 26-August 5, 2011, August 16-19, 2011, October 10-12, 2011, October 22-23, 2011, April 29-May 2, 2012, May 11-13, 2012, May 22-26, 2012, June 8-14, 2012, August 8-17, 2012, September 23-30, 2012, March 28-31, 2013, and August 29-31, 2013. *Id.* ¶ 76. In addition, another vessel used by Sea Hunters, the Son Worshipper, went to the wreck site a few times in 2009 to help set the anchors and moorings. *Id.* Her last trip to the site was April 24, 2012, to do a side scan survey. *Id.*

There followed long descriptions of the trials and tribulations that Sea Hunters encountered on each of the various trips to the wreck site.

Sea Hunters had very substantial operating expenses, including costs of crew, fuel, insurance, and equipment acquisition, rental, and repairs. Plaintiff's Additional SMF ¶ 31; Brooks Aff. ¶ 18. For example, fuel alone costs hundreds of thousands of dollars. *Id.* By 2011, the initial funding had all but run out, and an additional round of financing raised approximately $1 million for continued operations. Plaintiff's Additional SMF ¶ 32; Brooks Aff. ¶ 18. . . .

Total funding by the end of 2011 approached $8 million, more than $2 million of which had been spent on the acquisition and refurbishment of the Sea Hunter vessel. Plaintiff's Additional SMF ¶ 38; Brooks Aff. ¶ 22.48 . . .

In the spring of 2013 Sea Hunters faced a difficult choice: it could initiate another round of financing now that the vessel and likely presence of valuable cargo were more clearly known or, under its agreements with prior investors, enter into a joint venture with third parties providing funding, technology, and know-how in exchange for a percentage of the gross salvor share of the recovery. Plaintiff's Additional SMF ¶ 49; Brooks Aff. ¶ 28.51 Three different joint venture agreements were considered, the first being the proposal of Stochel, in a brief document presented in May 2013. Plaintiff's Additional SMF ¶ 50; Brooks Aff. ¶ 29.

The Stochel proposal was problematic for a number of reasons. Plaintiff's Additional SMF ¶ 51; Brooks Aff. ¶ 29. First, he requested a 75 percent share of all salvor monies. *Id.* Second, there was no assured source of funding. *Id.* The commitments that Stochel allegedly had received were predicated on the ability to bring up one sample of gold (or the equivalent). *Id.* Next, an actual operational plan was something that was to be negotiated over some unknown period of time with unspecified participation by Swire, a Norwegian firm. *Id.*52 Although Sea Hunters' manager carefully considers any potential source of funding, the Stochel proposal did not look promising and was not accepted. Plaintiff's Additional SMF ¶ 52; Intervenor's Reply SMF ¶ 52.

In the fall of 2013, Sea Hunters received a joint venture proposal from individuals who had previously invested with Sea Hunters. Plaintiff's Additional SMF ¶ 53; Brooks Aff. ¶ 30 & Exh. C (ECF No. 264-7) thereto. This resulted in the signing of a joint venture agreement with potential to raise up to $10 million. *Id.*53 The joint venture was premised on the funding partners receiving 39 percent of the gross salvor share. *Id.* After the agreement was signed, the joint venturers ceased to perform, acknowledging in writing in December 2013 that they were not going forward with the joint venture. Plaintiff's Additional SMF ¶ 54; Brooks Aff. ¶ 31. They gave several reasons, but the primary one was their lack of confidence in the documentation of the cargo. *Id.*

The third joint venture proposal came through Tony Dyakowski of Vancouver, British Columbia, on behalf of a very experienced salvor, Donald Rodocker, and his son Jesse Rodocker.

As opposed to this wealth of salvage experience, court documents noted:

Stochel, Mission Recovery's sole member, has never owned a boat or operated salvage equipment. Plaintiff's Additional SMF ¶ 88; Intervenor's Reply SMF ¶ 88. He had no prior experience with adventures involving undersea salvage. *Id.* ¶ 90. Stochel is the sole employee of Mission Recovery. *Id.* ¶ 94. Under Mission Recovery's proposal, all recovery and salvage work on the Port Nicholson would be done by Swire. Plaintiff's Additional SMF ¶ 95; Second Stochel Aff. ¶ 9.63 Mission Recovery currently has no binding contract with Swire for Swire to do anything. Plaintiff's Additional SMF ¶ 96; Stochel Dep. at 109.64 Neither Mission Recovery nor Swire has a written salvage plan for the *Port Nicholson*. Plaintiff's Additional SMF ¶ 100; Stochel Dep., Exh. A (ECF No. 264-3) to Affidavit of Marshall J. Tinkle (ECF No. 264-2), attached to Plaintiff's SMFs, at 104.65

Sea Hunters' other investors oppose Mission Recovery's attempt to replace Sea Hunters on the ground that, were the attempt to succeed, they would be irreparably harmed in that they would lose the benefit of their bargain with Sea Hunters and would lose all or a substantial portion of the sums they have invested. Plaintiff's Additional SMF ¶ 103; Shugars Aff. ¶ 3; Lanfer Aff. ¶ 3.

Finally, the court determined:

> 1. Sea Hunters has been duly diligent, having persisted in an unusually challenging salvage effort, grappled with such hurdles as poor and even dangerous weather, equipment failure and loss, and dwindling capital reserves, and made trips to the wreck site during each year's short salvage season since 2009.
> 2. Sea Hunters' salvage efforts are ongoing, as demonstrated not only by its past operations but also by its plans, in conjunction with PNSC, to complete an AUV side-scan sonar survey and then attempt to pierce the Port Nicholson's hull to gain access to any valuable cargo using grab technology and/or saturation divers.
> 3. Despite Sea Hunters' failure after six salvage seasons to retrieve a single item of valuable cargo, or for that matter virtually any artifacts, its efforts are clothed with some prospect of success. It is poised to draw not only upon the knowledge and insights gained from its own long-running attempts to salvage the Port Nicholson but also upon the extensive experience, savvy, and financial resources of PNSC's principals.
>
> In any event, Mission Recovery adduces virtually no cognizable evidence regarding its own bid to be appointed salvor-in-possession. This, in itself, is insufficient as a matter of law to demonstrate on summary judgment that it is better qualified than Sea Hunters to effectuate the Port Nicholson's salvage.

The court's findings made it clear that Brooks had done and was doing everything in his power – within his financial constraints – to obtain the proper equipment and personnel for the eventual salvage of the treasure from the *Port Nicholson*.

Not everyone agreed with the court's assessment of Brooks' dedication and capability, or in the existence of treasure on the *Port Nicholson*.

Michael Kaplan, attorney for the British government, informed the media that the U.S. Geological Survey estimated that the annual world production of platinum in the 1940's averaged 15.5 tons. This made it seem unlikely that the *Port Nicholson* could have carried nearly five times that amount. Notwithstanding this declaration, the British government did not opt to bow out of the case.

Another broadside was fired by Kevin LaChance, who had worked for Sea Hunters' *Port Nicholson* project as an ROV pilot. He alleged that Brooks purchased a fake gold bar online, and intended to deposit it on the wreck, then film the ROV recovering it from the seabed as a way to pique the interest of new investors. Under oath, he testified in a deposition that he had actually held the fake gold bar in his hands.

Brooks laughed off LaChance's allegation by asserting his suspicion that someone in his employ was leaking imagery and information to the American lawyers whom the British government hired to prosecute its case. He staged the story and presence of the fake gold bar in order to trap the informer, and the disgruntled ex-employee LaChance took the bait that was offered.

But the final bombshell came from Brooks himself. On November 25, 2014, he submitted to the court the following affidavit (#1 is salutation; other deleted parts refer to the British government):

2. I have never personally conducted archival research and cannot claim to have any particular expertise in that area. Accordingly, Sea Hunters farmed out all tasks involving archival research relating to the S.S. PORT NICHOLSON to an independent contractor, Edward Michaud of Massachusetts, doing business as Trident Research. A copy of the Independent Contractor Agreement between Mr. Michaud and Sea Hunters' general partner, Sub Sea Research LLC, is attached hereto as Exhibit A. I had worked with Mr. Michaud in the past and have never known him to be untrustworthy. Sea Hunters has relied entirely on Mr. Michaud with respect to the retrieval of historical documents pertaining to the S.S. PORT NICHOLSON. . . .

6. Early in the week of November 16, 2014, I received a phone call from Mr. Michaud. He indicated that he had been contacted by federal investigators concerning the archival documents, copies of which had been attached to the Joint Status Report filed with the Court on June 19, 2012. Mr. Michaud had represented that these documents came from the National Archives, yet subsequent searches of the archives failed to locate them. He asked me what he should do, and I told him to just tell the truth. I had always believed his explanations concerning the documents and did not think he had anything to hide.

7. On November 22, Mr. Michaud contacted me and indicated that it was urgent that he see me. I met with him in Maine the following day, November 23. During that meeting, he disclosed to me for the first time that he had fabricated the two documents in question. I was stunned and extremely dismayed. He had previously told me that he had obtained the documents from a well-connected contact of his named Jack MacCann, formerly of the Office of Naval Intelligence. I asked him, "what about Jack MacCann?" He replied, "I made him up."

8. Prior to that time, Mr. Michaud had never indicated or even hinted that any of the copies of documents furnished to Sea Hunters had been altered or falsified in any way. I certainly did not ask Mr. Michaud to furnish altered or falsified documents; and I would never consent to file with the Court any documents that I did not believe were genuine.

The only knowledge that I have of Michaud relates to a German U-boat that he claimed to have discovered in 1993: one that lay partially buried in shallow water on the Nantucket Shoals. His announcement made a big media splash. According to Michaud (both in writing and on video), he explored the wreck the following year, entered the hull, and identified it as a Type XIB. He has never recanted his story, has never returned to the wreck site, and still insists that it is there. No one else has ever found the wreck, nor confirmed its existence through historical documentation.

Because of my extensive research experience in the National Archives, I can offer some insights about the document in question. For my readers to make sense of my interpretations, I must provide some background information about copying protocols in the National Archives. Please bear with me.

Researchers are not allowed to bring their own photocopy machines into the building. Self-service photocopiers are provided in the Central Research Room, where researchers review documents after they are pulled from the stacks. Most documents in file folders are loose. Sometimes several sheets are stapled or clipped together. Most of these documents may be photocopied, but there is a precise procedure that must be followed in doing so.

Researchers must obtain photocopy approval from an attendant at the central desk. Relevant to the instant case are documents that were originally stamped or typewritten with words such as Confidential, Secret, or Top Secret. These documents may be photocopied under certain conditions: (1) the information is no longer classified (such as World War Two material, which was universally declassified by Congress in 1976); or (2) the document bears a declassification stamp or sticker. If the document does not bear a declassification notice, the attendant will provide one (assuming that the document is no longer classified).

Nowadays this is done by means of a clear plastic sticker on which is printed a standard declassification notation, on which the attendant writes the source information taken from the label on the file box, the current date, and his or her initials. A length of clear tape is stuck to the back of the clear plastic sticker, which is then placed face down on the glass of the photocopier so that it is copied when the document is copied.

The photocopier lid must be closed when making a copy, in order to prevent toner wastage. If a copy is made when the lid is open, the photocopied sheet will be surrounded by a black mask of toner, wherever the glass was not covered by the document. Attendants watch the photocopiers and prevent researchers from keeping the lid open.

If several documents are stapled together, the desk attendant may either remove the staple for you, or let you fold the pages back from the staple while making photocopies.

These photocopiers print in black. A color photocopier is available but the cost is many times per copy of black and white photocopies.

All photocopies are examined by a guard when the researcher leaves the building. If a photocopy of a classified document does not bear a declassification sticker, that sheet is taken from the researcher; or all photocopies are taken from the researcher.

Alternatively, researchers may photo*graph* documents. For this reason I always select a seat by a widow. Strobes and flash units are not allowed. Otherwise, there are no restrictions on photographs because a document's fragility is not compromised by flipping it upside down on the copier bed, is not exposed to intense light, and does not generate paper that must be inspected by a guard on the way out of the building. Digital pictures are less expensive than photocopies, and *far* less expensive than color photocopies.

Now let us examine the document that Brooks swore was provided to him by Michaud. Although the copy printed here is black and white, on the original scan the words "Confidential" and "June 17 1942" are red. Confidentiality warnings were commonly stamped in red; dates that were added at a later time were sometimes typed in red. The words "File Copy" appear to be typed in blue. None of this is unusual.

Originally the document was stacked in a top two-hole binder. It has been removed (possibly by personnel of the National Archives for regrouping in different subject-matter folders when the document was accessioned). Now it is stapled with other documents. These other documents have been lifted out of the way in order to expose the pertinent document. Again, this is not unusual; I have done this hundreds of times.

The absence of a crease in the upper left corner implies that the document was not photocopied, in which case the sheets would have been pressed flat by the photocopier

OFFSHORE

LTO-5/EF61
June 17 1942

UNITED STATES TREASURY DEPARTMENT

Mr. J.S. Baylis
Port Control
Manhattan District
New York, New York
Area 3
Area A
Chase National Bank, New York
C/O Guaranty National Bank, New York
SA/B
OP-TS-B-2

Procurement Division

Washington

DA-TPS- SOV.F...CON.
REQ. AMTORG
ODT BLOCK PERMIT 41-00-12
NO. QMR.NO.
P-D RELEASE NO. 26477-01

CONFIDENTIAL

Gentlemen:

Following are shipping instructions for the material xxx
equipmentxready for shipment against the above noted contract:

Consign to: Soviet Purchasing Commission C/O W. Hulman, CAF-5,
Upon arrival at New York. Transfer materials to
Guaranty Bank C/O bank agent.
"IN - TRANSIT" - On Board SS Port Nicholson

Route: LIVERPOOL - WELLINGTON via HALIFAX and NEW YORK

Material: 741 Krast. refined Platinum bars in 149 boxes.

4,889 Narodny Bank bars gold in 977 boxes.

Bills of Lading From 621310 To K/001 - K/149
N/001 - N/977

CONFIDENTIAL

LL-109 Revised

Above: The document that Michaud gave to Brooks.
Below: The British government relied on this entry in *Lloyd's War Losses*.

| 16 | PORT NICHOLSON (2.15 a.m. G.M.T.) | Br | 8402 | Avonmouth, Barry & Halifax for New York & Wellington. | 1600 tons automobile parts & 4000 tons military stores. | 42 11 N., 69 25 W. | S. | Crew 87, 4 lost. | Master & 3 of crew & 6 men from corvette reboarded vessel to attempt salvage. All but 4 from corvette lost when vessel sank. |

lid, and the surrounding white space would have been black from toner. Furthermore, in order to make inspection of photocopies easy for the guards, the National Archives uses *only* 11 x 14 inch paper in the photocopiers, not 11 x 8-1/2. Therefore the document must have been photo*graphed*.

The declassification notation at the bottom of the photocopy is dated 2/10/12: February 12, 2012. Yet the presence of a declassification notation is not required on a photograph, and is never employed. Guards cannot see pictures on film cameras, and they do not examine pictures on digital cameras. This obviates the declassification process, but that is another story . . .

What I see is not a document that was photocopied on a color copier, in which case a declassification sticker was required; but a document that was photo*graphed*, in which case a sticker was *not* required, was not necessary, and was superfluous. In my opinion, it is possible that some other document was used to obtain the sticker, and the sticker was then used on a doctored document, or on a document that was later doctored, faked, or forged.

In other words, it appears to me that the declassification sticker may have been used to legitimize a doctored document. This theory is bolstered by the fact that the original document can no longer be located in the file box to which it was ascribed.

Theft of original documents from the National Archives is an ongoing concern. Many documents are stolen because they bear the signature of a famous person. More recently, witness the case of Sandy Berger, which received a great deal of media attention. Therefore, theft of the document that is under consideration is an ever-present possibility – but one that seems to lack motive in this case because it deprives the document of its provenance.

I must also allow that my theory could be totally wrong, and that other circumstances might account for the hybridization of photocopy and photograph protocols. Furthermore, I must admit that, at first blush, and without preconceived notions, the

document appears to be genuine.

Michaud might be able to account for the disparities that I have noted, but at the time I wrote the explanation above, he appeared to have gone missing. His phone number was no longer in service, and emails were returned as undeliverable. His whereabouts were unknown to authorities who wanted to question him. But see his reappearance below.

Brooks' potential backers have backed out of the *Port Nicholson* project. Treasure salvage operations have been terminated. The *Sea Hunter* has been put up for sale.

Brooks is facing serious charges of fraud from the Maine Office of Securities.

At the risk of appearing to take sides, or sounding like an apologist for Brooks, I have simply tried to make a balanced report of events which are confusing, misunderstood, misinterpreted, or otherwise mysterious.

The possibilities of outcome are endless.

Meanwhile, now that there is no one to defend ownership of or salvage rights to the *Port Nicholson*, without opposition the British government has expanded its "restricted appearance" by insisting that the U.S. Marshal Service should take charge of the items that Brooks recovered from the wreck – six metal objects, hatchets, a boiler brick, and a compass – and turn them over to the British government. The British government's American attorney Timothy Shusta said, "There are one or two things that might make good souvenirs in the case."

Such souvenirs hardly seem to be worth the money that the British government must pay in attorney's fees in order to collect them. This insistence on artifact recovery (or theft) by continued litigation has incensed British taxpayers and other British factions over what they view as a waste of good money for worthless objects for the inane purpose of making a point of no value.

If the British government is so insistent about its ownership of abandoned British vessels, it should also be held accountable for the damage that those vessels have inflicted upon the American people. The U.S. government has spent millions of dollars in cleaning up the mess that the British freighter *Empire Knight* (which see) has caused as a result of a cargo of mercury that has contaminated local waters. Yet, when the U.S. Coast Guard organized the recovery of the unbroken canisters of mercury, the British government was manifestly silent.

The British government did not offer to pay for the cost of salvage operations, and did not offer compensation for the damage that the contamination caused. In consideration of the attitude of the British government with regard to abandoned British vessels, the U.S. government should force the British government to pay for the cleanup and decontamination of the *Empire Knight*, and to disburse reparations to the commercial fishing industry for ongoing restrictions with regard to contamination containment.

The British government should not be allowed to reap unjust rewards at the same time it dodges legitimate responsibilities that result from the same mindset and nebulous train of logic.

As this book was going to press, official documents have been released and made available to the public. They either clarify or confuse the issue at hand, depending upon how the reader interprets the information when it is compared to Brooks' prior statements. It sheds an alternative light on the allegation of fraud. Who do you believe?

One document is an application for a search warrant. It is dated December 3, 2014. The "Affidavit in Support of a Search and Seizure Warrant" was ascribed to William

Johnson, of "the National Archives and Records Administration (NARA), Office of the Inspector General (OIG)."

According to this document, "On or about June 19, 2013, your affiant [Johnson] learned that Archival Specialist Richard Peuser, NARA, received an electronic report through the internet entitled '*Confidential Documents Relative to the S.S. Port Nicholson*' from Godfrey Bradman of the United Kingdom. Your affiant reviewed this report and found that the Port Nicholson Cargo Documents were attached to the report and which indicated that the vessel's cargo included bullion, platinum, and gold. The report was signed and submitted electronically to Bradman by Edward Michaud ("Michaud"), a Primary Archival Researcher/Analyst at Trident Research. . . .

"Trident Research contracted a private archival researcher to review NARA records. . . . The researcher conducted extensive research and electronically sent photographs of various historical and ship history records involving the Port Nicholson to Trident Research and Michaud.

"Your affiant reviewed the photographs sent from the NARA researcher to Trident Research and consulted with NARA experts about the report submitted by Michaud to Bradman which referenced NARA documents involving the Port Nicholson. Your affiant found original records within NARA holdings that showed that documents submitted by Trident Research were not authentic and had been altered and were fraudulent.

"On or about June 12, 2014, Brooks, on behalf of Sea Hunters, filed a supplemental affidavit in United States District Court for the District of Maine, Portland Division. Your affiant reviewed the affidavit and believes that Brooks intentionally made false statements to the Court regarding his knowledge of the altered ship documents involving the Port Nicholson's bullion, platinum, and gold cargo. Brooks claimed in his court filing that NARA lost the original records of the Port Nicholson that verified its precious cargo of bullion, platinum, and gold."

At this point I must interrupt in order to annotate personal knowledge of three examples of records being lost or misplaced within the National Archives, so that my readers can understand that such instances do occur.

In the mid-1970's, I viewed deck plans of the U.S. armored cruiser *San Diego* in the cartographic and architectural room of the National Archives. A dozen or so plans were rolled together; some of them were eight to ten feet in length. After viewing them, I submitted a purchase order for the entire set, and paid for reproductions on the premises. The plans were duplicated in-house and sent to me by mail. The originals never left the building. Subsequent researchers informed me that they were unable to locate one of the plans when they viewed the set. To date, that missing plan has yet to be found. I may have the only copy whose existence and location are known.

I have always speculated that the *San Diego* plans were duplicated at the same time that plans of another vessel were duplicated, and that the missing plan was accidentally rolled up with the plans of the other vessel. In other words, the plan was misfiled. This error will not be discovered until another researcher views the plans of that other vessel, and informs an archivist of the discrepancy.

In the 1980's, Joe Milligan and I were each researching separately a New Jersey shipwreck (whose name I have forgotten). At the National Archives, I asked the research assistant to pull every bit of information that was available about the ship. Several months later, Joe visited the National Archives and asked for all documents that related to the ship. Afterward, we shared the results of our research. I was shocked to see that he had copies of documents that I had not been given, and I had copies of documents that he had not been given.

The only difference between our research approaches was the research assistant who was assigned to help us. My assistant did not know about files that Joe's assistant knew about, and vice versa. From this incident I learned to duplicate my research on subsequent visits whenever a different research assistant was assigned to help me. I confirmed on other occasions that I could obtain additional documentation by duplicating my research through different research assistants.

Throughout the 1970's, 1980's, and early 1990's, a full set of the *Annual Report of the United States Life Saving Service* was kept on a shelf in the room that was occupied by Navy and Maritime research assistants. While I was there to have them pull records for me, I could take each volume off the shelf and photocopy pages that were relevant to my research.

When Archives II opened in 1994, the Navy and Maritime Team was moved to College Park, and the annual reports were boxed and put in the stacks. From then on I had to fill out a call slip in order to access the books. In the early 2000's, I duly submitted a call slip for the annual reports. A few hours later, a research assistant tracked me down in the central research room and told me that he could not locate the books, that I must have made a mistake, and that the National Archives did not possess such a set.

Had this been the first time I ever asked for the books, I would have believed him, and innocently left without seeing them. But I knew that they were filed in the stacks because I had had them pulled on numerous occasions. I told him so. When he protested, I told him to ask Barry Zerby, a research assistant I had worked with for more than twenty years. Zerby knew where they were located. But Zerby was not in work that day. I insisted that I had called for the books before. The research assistant promised to continue looking for them.

A few hours later, the research assistant tracked me down again and escorted me to the offices where he and two other research assistants were all trying to locate the reports. I explained to all of them that I had accessed them only a few months ago, and described them as occupying five file boxes. They believed me and promised to keep looking.

Near the end of the day the research assistant proudly informed me that they had located the file boxes. They did so by tracking down my name on the sign-in sheets, obtaining the date of my previous visit, then searching the call slips in my name for that day. For future reference, I made a note of the Record Group, the Stack Area, the Row, the Compartment, and the Shelf on which the set of reports was located. That information was supposed to be on record, but somehow it was not.

My point in all of this is that records do go missing in the National Archives, and not every research assistant knows how to find every record in the stacks, which rivals in size the warehouse in which the lost Ark was stored. Records can also be stolen, the way Sandy Berger stuffed documents inside his clothing.

Again, I do not mean to sound like an apologist for Brooks and Michaud, but I must inform my readers of the reality of the situation. Also, before you read the quote in the next paragraph, understand that this information was not released until six months after I wrote my opinion about the unusual characteristics of the copy of the *Port*

Nicholson's cargo manifest.

Back to the affidavit. "On or about November 14, 2014, your affiant interviewed Michaud at his place of business in Framingham, Massachusetts. Michaud admitted to a scheme to defraud investors by fraudulently altering photographs of NARA ship's records that he received from a private researcher hired by his company, Trident Research. Michaud provided details and correspondence between his company and Brooks/Sea Hunters outlining the transmission and submission of the fraudulent and altered ship records involving the Port Nicholson. Michaud admitted that Brooks pressured him to alter the documents based on pressure that Sea Hunters was facing with potential investors who were interested in the Port Nicholson. Michaud agreed to cooperate with NARA OIG by providing email correspondence between Michaud and Brooks regarding the altered and fraudulent documents.

"Your affiant learned through Michaud's cooperation that he traveled from Massachusetts to Archives II in College Park, MD on or about June 23, 2014 for the express purpose of furthering the criminal scheme by fraudulently obtaining certifications from NARA that the falsified documents were original NARA records. Specifically, Michaud advised that he took the altered documents falsely representing that the Port Nicholson cargo contained bullion, platinum, and gold to NARA and had them stamped with a NARA seal for the purpose of falsely representing them to be 'original NARA records.' Your affiant learned that Michaud wrote 'RG 38' and 'Box No. 399' on the back of the fraudulent document in an effort to mislead potential investors and provide archival attribution to Brooks/Sea Hunters' claims in district court."

Let me intrude again to note that if Michaud had been really smart, he would have slipped a copy of the doctored document into the file box, in order to give the appearance of authenticity. Had he done so, investigators might never have noticed that the document was not original, and had been altered.

I should also like to mention that, in all the years since Michaud supposedly discovered a German U-boat on the Nantucket Shoals, he has never denied its existence. Yet in this instance he readily admitted to committing fraud. Obvious by their absence is what inducements might have inspired Michaud to confess to a criminal offense. Johnson makes it seem that Michaud voluntarily and of his own accord told him about his fraudulent activity. Did he willingly turn State's evidence? Or did he make a deal to implicate Brooks in return for immunity or leniency, such as a "Get Out of Jail Free" card? (For those of you who have ever played Monopoly.)

As speculation, perhaps Johnson was trying to make a case for an offense that was greater than the minor alteration of an archival document. Perhaps he was willing to let the small fry go free in order to make a bigger catch, even if the bigger catch had been duped and was innocent. Not to accuse Johnson of impropriety, but law enforcement officers get more brownie points and feathers in their caps for solving capital crimes than they do for detecting misdemeanors.

"Your affiant learned that Michaud and Brooks have been friends for over 16 years and worked extensively on several reclamation projects involving other unrelated vessels. Michaud admitted his role in the scheme which included his altering of ship records to show that the Port Nicholson contained precious cargo. In turn, Michaud transmitted the altered documents electronically to Brooks/Sea Hunters at his Subsea Research email address. Brooks, through Sea Hunters, utilized the fraudulent documents to solicit monies from potential investors. Michaud told your affiant that Brooks operates Sea Hunters from his residence located at 193 Gray Road, Gorham, Maine. Michaud has visited Brooks at his residence on at least three occasions to discuss the Port Nicholson scheme.

"Your affiant found numerous news articles depicting Sea Hunters, specifically Brooks, making claims about the value of the Port Nicholson cargo in an effort to solicit investors.

"On November 23, 2014, your affiant monitored a consensually recorded conversation between Michaud and Brooks at the Home Depot parking lot at 300 Clarks Park Parkway in South Portland, Maine." [This means that Michaud was wearing a wire.] "During the conversation, Michaud and Brooks discussed their scheme to alter documents and use the altered documents in subsequent court filings in the District Court of Maine, Portland Division. Brooks acknowledged that he never wanted the altered documents submitted in federal court and blamed his prior attorney for it. Brooks acknowledged that as a result of the scheme he is anticipating being '*charged*' by State of Maine, Office of Securities. Michaud acknowledged altering the documents on behalf of Brooks and stated several times during the conversation that he lied for Brooks in his (Michaud) deposition in US District Court. Brooks didn't challenge Michaud's frequent assertions that he (Michaud) altered the documents on his (Brooks') behalf."

Note that although Brooks did not challenge Michaud's assertions, neither did he acknowledge that he had asked or conspired with Michaud to alter the document on his behalf. Johnson chose to interpret Brooks' silence as an admission of guilt or complicity, whereas Brooks could simply have been so stunned by Michaud's tacit admission that he did not know how to respond. In other words, he could have been struck speechless. Once again, I am not acting as an apologist for Brooks; I am merely providing counterpoint to Johnson's self-serving interpretation. Johnson needed to color his suspicions as black as possible in order to show probable cause for obtaining the search warrant.

I should also point out that, although Michaud admitted to committing a crime, he did not use the fraudulent document to obtain money from investors. Brooks did. If Brooks knew that the document was fraudulent, then he could be indicted for bilking millions of dollars from unsuspecting investors. But if Brooks did *not* know that the document was fraudulent, then there was no case against him, and Johnson's expectation of making a big bust would go bust. For the good of his reputation, Johnson had a personal interest in proving Brooks' guilt. I don't mean this as an accusation, but as food for thought.

"Michaud discussed with Brooks a prior conversation they had regarding the need for concrete evidence and documentation showing that the Port Nicholson contained valuable cargo. Michaud discussed a saying they used during their initial scheme by stating: '*I lie and you swear to it.*' Brooks didn't dispute the statement during their conversation."

But neither did Brooks admit to making the statement; he was noncommittal.

"Michaud told Brooks that he '*tried to cover your ass as best I could*' to give you '*plausible deniability*' and Brooks did not respond to the statement."

Again, neither did Brooks admit to prior knowledge of the altered documents. Michaud seemed to be trying to draw Brooks into making admissions of culpability, which he never did.

"Michaud told Brooks that he (Michaud) is '*on the hook for the documents*' and

Brooks is '*on the hook for the money*' and [sic] which point Brooks replies '*Oh, I know.*' "
Now note that it was after this conversation that (on November 25, 2014) Brooks submitted an affidavit to the court (see above) in which he swore that he had only just recently learned that certain documents had been altered, and disavowed all knowledge of Michaud's wrongdoings.

Depending upon who you believe, Brooks' affidavit and Michaud's admission amount to a "he said, she said" finger-pointing argument in which each casts blame on the other.

Affiant Johnson summed up his warrant application thus: "In order to search for data that is capable of being read or interpreted by a computer, law enforcement personnel will need to seize and search the following items." He then listed all of Brooks computer equipment, processing equipment, modems, docking stations, monitors, printers, encryption devices, optical scanners, and any magnetic, electronic or optical storage devices including floppy disks, tapes, DC-ROM's, CD-RW's, DVD's, optical disks, printer or memory buffers, smart cards, memory calculators, electronic dialers, electronic notebooks, cellular telephones, and personal digital assistants; plus documentation, operating logs, reference manuals regarding the operation of the computer equipment, storage devices or software; any applications, utility programs, compilers, interpreters, and other software used to facilitate direct or indirect communication with the computer hardware, storage devices or date to be searched; any physical keys, encryption devices and similar physical items that are necessary to gain access to the computer equipment, storage devices or data; and any passwords, password files, test keys, encryption codes or other information necessary to access the computer equipment, storage devices or data.

The warrant was granted. A slew of law enforcement officers descended upon Brooks' house like a horde of hungry locusts attacking a ripe cornfield: members of Maine's state police computer crimes unit, the inspector general of the National Archives, and FBI agents. According to Brooks, they arrived with drawn rifles and pistols and held him at bay as they tore his house apart.

Brooks continues to proclaim his innocence. Michaud has admitted to altering sensitive documents, but claimed that he did so at Brooks' insistence. No one has yet been charged with a crime, but the latest document (dated September 4, 2015, regarding a Grand Jury indictment) enumerates the charges against Brooks, and seeks to force his lawyers to ignore the client-attorney privilege, and to produce documents that might be subject to the "crime-fraud exception," which stipulates that such privilege can be revoked if "the client sought or employed legal representation in order to commit or facilitate a crime or fraud."

In support of this contention, this document cites information that is either alleged by investigators or instigated by Michaud's testimony. The court noted that Michaud "is now a witness for the government." Generally speaking, paid witnesses are not the most credible.

The court summarized the case against Brooks thus: "In a June 19, 2012, status report filing in the admiralty case, S.H. [Sea Hunters] attached three altered documents: (1) altered document derived from *Lloyd's War Losses* labeled as a 'Copy of US Treasury Ledger-Listing Platinum as cargo' (the 'Treasury Ledger'); (2) a version of the Cargo Report purportedly from the P.N.'s [Port Nicholson's] final voyage that removed or completely obscured the 'FEB 6 1941' date-stamp; and (3) a third document, a purported copy of a 'US Treasury Department, Procurement Division' cargo listing (the 'Treasury Procurement') altered to show that the P.N. contained 741 platinum bars and 4,889 gold bullion bars. A September 10, 2012, amended complaint in the admiralty case referred to the '(o)fficial documents of the United States Customs Service and the United States Treasury Department' and were 'attached to the (June 19, 2012, status report).' According to E.M. [Edward Michaud], appellant 'pressured (E.M.) to alter the documents based on demands that (S.H.) was facing from potential investors who were interested in the (P.N.)"

Perhaps more damning to Sea Hunters were two other allegations. One was an interim summary which claimed "that a remote-operated vehicle had entered the ship and the 'bullion boxes (we)re then located.'"

According to the other, "And on December 22, 2014, a NARA [National Archives and Records Administration] agent interviewed the captain of the S.W. vessel (which was supposedly used by S.H. to recover the six metal pieces), who stated that no material was recovered from the P.N. while he was captain."

This is where the case stands as this book goes to print.

The author wishes to express his thanks to Paul Whittaker for his constant monitoring of the *Port Nicholson* situations as they unfolded over the course of two years, and for copying me with the efforts of his research.

Right: The final plunge of the *Port Nicholson*. (From the memoirs of Lewis Charles Norman.)

Bottom: From the author's collection.

ROBERT & RICHARD

Built: 1915
Previous names: None
Gross tonnage: 140
Type of vessel: Wooden-hulled fishing schooner
Builder: J.F. James & Son, Essex, Massachusetts
Owners: John Chisholm & Son (plus shares owned by Robert Wharton, master, and Robertson & Griffin), all of Gloucester, Massachusetts
Port of registry: Gloucester, Massachusetts
Cause of sinking: Bombed by *U-156* (Kapitanleutnant Richard Feldt)
Location: 100 miles offshore

Sunk: July 22, 1918
Depth: Unknown
Dimensions: 108' x 24' x 14'
Power: sail

Lat/lon: 42° 42' N / 68° 23' W

The reasons that I put both of these vessels in the same chapter, especially in light of the fact that the *Dornfontein* did not sink and therefore should not be included in this book at all, is because they are the only two vessels that were attacked by a German U-boat off the coast of Maine in World War One, and because together they demonstrate contemporary U-boat tactics. Furthermore, in order to make sense, their stories must be read in the sequence in which I have arranged them, instead of the other way around (alphabetically).

During the Great War, U-boats ravaged the North American continent from Canada to North Carolina. Of the seven U-boats that waged war against merchant shipping, the *U-156* was the most successful (in the eyes of the Central Powers), or the most deadly (in Allied eyes). It torpedoed, shelled, bombed, or mined thirty-six vessels, of which thirty-three sank and three were salvaged.

Robert & Richard under construction. (Photo by Henry Fisher.)

The largest vessel that fell prey to the *U-156* was the armored cruiser *San Diego*. The 13,680-ton American warship struck a mine off the south shore of Long Island, New York. She capsized and sank in twenty minutes. (For complete details, see *U.S.S. San Diego: the Last Armored Cruiser*.)

The U-boat then continued its path of destruction northward: to Cape Cod, Massachusetts; then offshore of Maine, then along the Nova Scotia coastline. Afterward, it turned south to Nantucket, Massachusetts; then north again to Nova Scotia; and finally to St. Pierre and Miquelon. The U-boat never made it home; it was lost with all hands in the North Sea Mine Barrage. (For full particulars, see *The Kaiser's U-boats in American Waters*.)

The *Robert & Richard* was a fishing schooner that habitually stayed at sea until her holds were filled to the brim. She departed from Wharf Street in Gloucester, Massachusetts on July 8, 1918. On board were twenty-two men and one boy, including plank owner Captain Robert Wharton. It took two days to reach the rich fishing grounds off LaHave Bank: east of the southern tip of Nova Scotia, and some 350 miles from Gloucester.

After more than a week of fishing from dories, the schooner's accumulated catch consisted of 30,000 pounds of halibut and 75,000 pounds of "fresh, mixed fish, such as cod, hake and cusk." The *Robert & Richard* departed for the long passage home on July 19. According to Captain Wharton, "The sea was smooth, the sky clear, just breaking away from a haze. It was foggy up to about two hours before."

The morning of July 22 found the schooner still a hundred miles from the American mainland. From a distance of two miles, the *U-156* fired a shell "across the bow of the schooner."

Wharton: "The entire crew and myself took to dories and made for sea, but I was personally called back by an officer (not the Commanding Officer.) Whereupon, I rowed up alongside the submarine and was questioned as follows:

"Did you see any vessels on your trip?

"What is the tonnage of your vessel?

"What kind and how many pounds of fish have you aboard?

"This was all he said, but the crew laughed while I was being questioned. Three men, one an officer, came aboard the dory with me and asked for the papers and flag which I turned over to them. At this time, one of the three men stated that he owned a house in the United States in which he had a similar flag. I asked him what he was going to do with us and he told me when I reached shore to state that they never harmed crews. They then instructed me to give them another pair of oars for their dory which was left behind and then instructed me to make for sea. While I was aboard [the *Robert & Richard*] they proceed [sic] to place a bomb, starting from the stern end of the ship and slinging it underneath with the help of a sounding lead, pulling it up to about midships. After this was accomplished, they fooled around the ship, while I was making a course shoreward, for fully a length of one-half hour and when I reached a distance of about a mile off, the ship was blown up."

The German submariners many never have harmed the crews of the vessels that sank, but they thought nothing of abandoning them to their fate on the open ocean a hundred miles from land: a case of passive harm if not active harm.

Wharton: "One of the Germans aboard the boat when going after the flag, stated upon looking at the picture of my two sons, that there was a young fellow apparently

This contemporary postcard picture is captioned "A Gloucester Fishing Schooner." It is a lookalike for the *Robert & Richard*. Note the dories towed astern.

that same age, which was six years, aboard a vessel which they sank a few nights ago and whom, he believed, could have never reached shore according to his statement of weather conditions."

Four dories managed to stay in close proximity to each other. The men who occupied these dories rowed northwesterly for the rest of the day and all that night. When they reached a position approximately 18 miles south-southwest of the *Portland* lightship, they were picked up by the steamship *Snug Harbor*, on route from Norfolk, Virginia to Portland, Maine. Wharton: "We arrived in Portland on this steamer about 10.30 P.M. on July 23, 1918."

Patrick Murphy was in a dory that got separated from the group of four: "We were in the dory for about thirty hours when we were picked up by the Standard Oil Boat, *Standard The Second*, at about twelve miles Southwest of Cape Elizabeth and transferred from the *Standard The Second* to a Coast Patrol Boat and landed at East Boston on Wednesday morning, July 24th about 4:30 A.M." (The vessel that Murphy called *Standard The Second* was the tugboat *Standard II*.)

Another dory with four men made it all the way to shore. They landed at Cape Porpoise, a mainland village near Kennebunkport, Maine.

Everyone survived. Partly this was due to their untiring exertions and their toned rowing muscles. But partly this was due to calm seas and favorable weather. Other victims of U-boat depredations were not so fortunate.

The U.S. Navy dispatched a small fleet of "seaplanes, submarine chasers and other craft" to supplement the regular coast patrol that was searching for the marauding U-boat, but it stayed well hidden for a week and a half, until . . .

DORNFONTEIN

Built: 1918
Previous names: None
Gross tonnage: 695
Type of vessel: Wooden-hulled four-masted lumber schooner
Builder: D.H. Sakar of Marine Construction Company, St. John, Newfoundland
Owner: Job Fishing Corporation, Montreal, Canada
Port of registry: Eastport, Maine
Cause of sinking: Set afire by *U-156* (Kapitanleutnant Richard Feldt)
Location: Mouth of the Bay of Fundy

Sunk: August 2, 1918
Depth: Salvaged
Dimensions: 186' x 40' x 17'
Power: sail

The *Dornfontein* was the first vessel to be built at the Marine Construction Company, at St. John, Newfoundland. The keel was laid down in 1917, and the hull was launched the following June. The construction methods were standard, but the launching mechanism was unusual for the time, for the schooner was launched sideways.

After the finishing touches were added, the schooner was loaded with 900,000 board feet of lumber that was consigned to South Africa. The crew of nine men packed a sufficient quantity of food to last them for the extraordinarily long passage across both Atlantic Oceans (North and South) to the southern tip of the continent. The *Dornfontein* departed on her maiden voyage only six weeks after her launching. Disaster struck on her third day at sea.

According to the statement of Captain Charles Dagwell, master, "It was about twelve o'clock noon on Friday when the submarine was first sighted; we thought at first that it was a tug but we soon found out that it was an enemy craft when a shell came screaming through the air and struck the water amidships of the *Dornfontein*, but short, doing no damage; then followed another shell which fell aft about thirty or forty feet, the submarine gradually coming nearer and nearer until they were able to order our crew to be brought to the submarine in our boats; this order was obeyed and we were taken aboard the submarine; the members of the crew, except myself, were taken into the depths of the U-Boat; . . .

"We were about five hours on the submarine during which time the crew of the U-Boat robbed us of all we had on board worth taking; then I was taken below and he [presumably the U-boat commander] performed his duties such as setting fire to my ship, then I, with the other members of my crew came on deck, and we [were] ordered to our boats and set out; as far as we could see the submarine remained in the same position as when we had left her; we were fourteen hours on the water. . . . The submarine never submerged; she sighed us at nine o'clock in the morning; they treated us all right and gave us food."

An interesting piece of information that the U-boat skipper divulged to Captain Dagwell was that he had sunk the U.S. cruiser *San Diego*.

The survivors rowed throughout the evening and night, landing safely on Grand Manan Island in the Bay of Fundy shortly after dawn the following day, August 3.

The Germans did a poor job on the *Dornfontein*. After torching the schooner and releasing her crew, the U-boat did not hang around to witness her sinking. Thus the

The *Dornfontein* still smoldering. Note the salvors onboard and the towline leading from the stem (to the left). (Courtesy of the Naval Photographic Center.)

Germans were unaware that they had failed in their mission to destroy the vessel. All they accomplished was the burning of the sails and upperworks. Furthermore, they failed to take into account the fact that wood floats, and that her cargo of lumber was therefore buoyant.

The *Dornfontein* in her new but short-lived guise. (From the author's collection.)

The day after the attack, people on land saw curls of smoke on the horizon. The smoldering hulk was still afloat. The remaining flames were soon extinguished, and the *Dornfontein* was then towed to port. The charred hull that had cost $110,000 to build, was sold for $5,500. Like the phoenix, she was rebuilt, by the Pushee Brothers of Dennyville, Maine. She was renamed *Netherton*, and lived again to sail the seven seas . . . but knot furlong.

Fire was her nemesis. On August 4, 1920, she caught fire and sank off the southwest coast of England. The eight sailors on board escaped with their lives.

U-156. (Courtesy of WZ Bilddienst.)

WILLIAM H. MACHEN

Built: 1916
Previous names: *Bristol*
Gross tonnage: 3,922
Type of vessel: Collier
Builder: New York Ship Building Corp., Camden, New Jersey
Owner: Pocahontas Steam Ship Company, New York, NY
Port of registry: New York, NY
Cause of sinking: Collision with SS *Maid of Stirling*
Lat/lon: 43° North / 70° West (Lloyd's of London);
 42° 57' 00" N / 70° 30' 48" W (Wreck Information List of 1945)

Sunk: July 7, 1942
Depth: Unknown
Dimensions: 360' x 49' x 30'
Power: coal-fired steam

I think of the *William H. Machen* as the Ghost Ship of New Hampshire. Practically nothing is known about her loss, and absolutely nothing is known about her actual location. For those reasons she is all the more intriguing.

I found only two mentions of her in primary sources. According to a newspaper account that was dated February 27, 1934, "The steamer *William H. Machen*, of New York, reported to the coast guard base here [Mobile, Alabama] yesterday by radio that it has sighted a wrecked seaplane floating in latitude 40.38, longitude 72.35. Officers said the description of the plane did not fit that of any service craft. Due to the position, belief was expressed that the plane might have been that of a prominent Jacksonville, Fla. Society woman who flew out to sea in a bizarre suicide several weeks ago."

The other mention appeared on March 26, 1942, in the "Executive Hearing Before the Committee on the Merchant Marine and Fisheries House of Representatives Seventy-Seventh Congress Second Session." With regard to safety at sea during the time of war and unrestricted U-boat attacks, one J. Bodge testified: "A good example of how economy prevails on Mystic ships is that on a ship like the Steamship *William Machen*, of the Pocahontas Co., this ship turns better than 80 revolutions per minute, while on some of the Mystic ships they only turn over about 60 to 66 revolutions per minute. On the *William Machen* they burn about 40 of tons in every 24 hours with two boilers that operate about the same plant that Mystic have. While on Mystic ships they use only about 21 tons of coal in the same 24 hours. The men sailing on these ships feel that the time for economy has passed and we also believe that the captains of these ships feel the same way about it, especially if a submarine were to chase them but office orders have to be carried out."

Above: From the author's collection. Opposite page bottom: An official U.S. Coast Guard photo that was taken only three weeks before the *William H. Machen* disappeared into the briny deep.

In essence, Bodge was saying that the *William H. Machen* was inefficient and uneconomical to operate. Bodge did not have to be concerned for very long, for three and a half months later the *William H. Machen* sank after a collision with the *Maid of Stirling*. To my knowledge, no additional information about this collision has come to light. Even the location is approximate.

Note that the two locations in the statistical sidebar are twenty-five miles apart. And both come from reliable sources. To that I must add that in *Dictionary of Disasters at Sea During the Age of Steam*, which was published by Lloyd's of London, the location is given as "about 50 miles E. of Boston."

Nor was there any mention of the fate of the collier's crew.

Secondary sources often give the location as "off the Isles of Shoals." The word "off" covers a broad area that could mean anything from northeast to southwest at any imaginable distance. I think that most people have interpreted "off" to mean "nearby," but that is an unwarranted assumption that might be based on the location that was posited by the Wreck Information List, which is five miles east of the Isles of Shoals.

Please note that fifty miles due east of Boston is also fifty miles southeast of the Isles of Shoals.

The truth is that so far no official documents are known to shed any light on where the collision occurred, or how long the collier stayed afloat and drifted before she took her final plunge, or precisely where she sank. In those days locations were calculated by means of sextant, sun or other star sightings, and chronometer, then by dead reckoning: a process that required time that officers generally did not have when their vessel was sinking.

My best guess is that the wreck lies in deep water, possibly within the triangle that is created by connecting the three approximated positions with lines . . . and possibly outside of the triangle. Time may tell.

Suggested Reading

Anonymous (1835) *The Mariners' Chronicle: Containing Narratives of the Most Remarkable Disasters at Sea, Such as Shipwrecks, Storms, Fires and Famines, also Naval Engagements, Piratical Adventures, Incidents of Discovery, and other Extraordinary and Interesting Occurrences*, George W. Gorton, New Haven, CT.

Bachelder, Peter Dow (1997) *Shipwrecks & Maritime Disasters of the Maine Coast*, The Provincial Press, Portland, ME.

Bavendam, Fred (1980) *Beneath Cold Waters: the Marine Life of New England*, Down East Books, Camden, ME.

Brockman, R. John (2005) *Twisted Rails, Sunken Ships: the Rhetoric of Nineteenth Century Steamboat and Railroad Accident Investigation Reports, 1833-1879*, Baywood Publishing Company, Amityville, NY.

Deane, John (1711) *A Narrative of the Sufferings, Preservation and Deliverance of Captain John Deane and Company, in the Nottingham galley of London . . .* , S. Popping, London, England.

Fish, John Perry (1989) *Unfinished Voyages: a Chronology of Shipwrecks: Maritime Disasters in the Northeast United States from 1606 to 1956*, Lower Cape Publishing, Orleans, MA.

Gentile, Gary (2006) *The Fuhrer's U-boats in American Waters*, Bellerophon Bookworks, Philadelphia, PA ($25).

Gentile, Gary (2010) *The Kaiser's U-boats in American Waters*, Bellerophon Bookworks, Philadelphia, PA ($25).

Gentile, Gary (1995) *The Nautical Cyclopedia*, GGP, Philadelphia, PA 18229 ($20).

Gimpel, Erich (2003) *Agent 146*, Thomas Dunne Books, New York, NY.

Grendon, Ingrid (2010) *Lost Maine Coal Schooners*, The History Press, Charleston, South Carolina.

Howland, S.A. (1846) *Steamboat Disasters and Railroad Accidents in the United States, to which are Appended Accounts of Recent Shipwrecks, Fires at Sea, Thrilling Incidents, etc.*, Warren Lazell, Worcester, MA.

Keatts, Henry (1988) *New England's Legacy of Shipwrecks*, American Merchant Marine Museum Press, Kings Point, NY.

Langman, Christopher (1711) *A True Account of the Voyage of the Nottingham-Galley of London, John Deane Commander . . .* , London, England.

Martinez, Andrew J. (1994) *Marine Life of the North Atlantic*, Aqua Quest Publications, Locust Valley, NY.

Miller, Robert A. (2013) *A True story of An American Nazi Spy*, Trafford Publishing.

Parker, Lt. W.J. Lewis (1948) *The Great Coal Schooners of New England: 1870-1909*, The Marine Historical Association.

Puleo, Stephen (2005) *Due to Enemy Action*, The Lyons Press, Guilford, CT.

Quinn, William P. (1983) *Shipwrecks Around Maine*, Lower Cape Publishing, Orleans, MA.

Roberts, Kenneth (1956) *Boon Island*, Doubleday & Company, Garden City, NY.

Rowe, William Hutchison (undated but circa 1948) *The Maritime History of Maine*, W.W. Norton, New York, NY.

Upton, Joe (1986) *Amaretto*, International Marine Publishing Company, Camden, Maine.

GPS CAVEATS

In previous volumes of the Popular Dive Guide Series, I obtained loran and GPS coordinates from dive boat skippers who had actually visited the sites. This is not always the case in the present volume. Wreck sites off Massachusetts are confirmed and accurate, but most of those off Maine and New Hampshire I cannot vouch for because they originated from secondary sources that I cannot verify.

Some numbers, such as those from the AWOIS list, may or may not be accurate. Accuracy depends on the "quality" of the originating source. What NOAA calls "GPQUALITY" is given in four grades: poor, low, medium, and high.

"Poor" refers to locations that were wildly approximated from unofficial sources such as land sightings from which a vessel was seen to sink; or from a dead-reckoning course that was based on the last sextant sighting and subsequent estimated speed and direction of the wind and current; or from calculated drift after a vessel lost motive power; and so on.

"Low" generally refers to locations that had an original position accuracy of "1 to 3 miles."

"Medium" generally refers to locations that had an original position accuracy of "within 1 mile."

"High" refers to locations that were examined by divers, or that were calculated from side-scan sonar tracks, or that were interpolated from a wire-drag survey where a "hang" was found. These sites were actually confirmed to exist in the location that was specified.

I have gone through Section 1 of the AWOIS list – the section that covers offshore Maine, New Hampshire, and northern Massachusetts – and integrated the most promising sites into the following list. Generally, for unnamed wreck sites, I copied only those coordinates in which the quality was graded "high." I included some that were named wreck sites, but where appropriate I noted that the quality was either "low" or "poor."

"Medium," "low," and "poor" quality grades will show you where to find approximate locations on a nautical chart, but they will *not* show you where to find the wreck under water. This is an important point to keep in mind when using the GPS and loran list.

Keep in mind that AWOIS is a font of misinformation. NOAA adds new entries in order to expand the list, but it never deletes old or incorrect entries; nor does it correct or otherwise revise invalid entries. A large percentage of the entries are leftover from World War Two or shortly thereafter. These entries give erroneous position data for wrecks that have long since been found or identified at other locations. There are also entries for named wrecks that do not exist. Some decades-old entries for shallow-water barges neglect to mention that the barge was later salvaged.

With regard to barges, understand that some of them might refer to turn-of-the-century schooner barges that are more interesting to explore than square-ended work barges of more recent vintage.

I included whatever loran numbers I have managed to obtain even though the government has switched off the loran system. I did this because some GPS receivers can

GPS Caveats

translate loran numbers to GPS numbers, although the accuracy of the translation leaves much to be desired.

For the Automated Wreck and Obstruction Information System, NOAA configures GPS coordinates in four pairs of digits, or eight numbers in all. Thus the "poor" location given for the *Washington B. Thomas* is 43-30-12.30 and 70-18-22.17.

Normal GPS numbers read this way: 43-07.640 and 70-24.900. These are right-on accurate numbers for the bow of the *Empire Knight* – although I must note in this instance that the wreck site is not a single contiguous hull section but a debris field that is spread out in all directions from the center point. Locations that are given in this seven-digit fashion originated from more reliable sources than the AWOIS list – although, again, I must reiterate that although those sites off the coast of Massachusetts are extremely accurate, those sites off the coasts of Maine and New Hampshire may be less accurate.

I suspect that some of the GPS numbers that I obtained from secondary published sources did not originate as GPS numbers. They may have originated as lat/lons (shorthand for latitude and longitude) which were translated to GPS. Thus numbers that have the appearance of pinpoint accuracy due to the number of decimal places that are carried out in the translation program, may not be accurate at all if they were based on a sextant sighting.

This kind of translation yields a number that is precise but inaccurate. Make sure you understand the difference between precision and accuracy. To word it another way, a very precise coordinate may be based on an inaccurate position.

Lat/lons in the sidebars that accompany chapter text will enable you to locate the approximate position of a wreck on a chart, but not to find the site in the water.

Name	Lat	Lon		
50/50 Barge	42-20.408	70-53.748		
Addie M. Anderson	41-27.104	71-24.923	14424.0	43989.9
Albany	43-55-39	69-01-40		
Albert Gallatin	42-33.897	70-44.865		
Alice E. Clark	44-21.022	68-51.299		
Alice Lawrence (bow)	41-24.334	70-13.004		
Alice Lawrence (stern)	41-24.309	70-12.991		
Alice M. Colburn	42-33.884	70-44.267		
Alice M. Colburn	42-33.819	70-44.186		
Alma E.A. Holmes	42-27.509	70-45.718		
Alva (bow)	41-33.332	69-54.268		
Alva (stern)	41-33.315	69-54.248		
Amaretto	44-05.590	68-59.881		
Andrea Doria (stern)	40-29.345	69-52.041	25148.5	43481.0
Angela	41-28.233	71-01.635		
Anne El (fishing vessel)	43-05-10	70-45-44		
Aransas	41-35.440	69-52.543	13837.0	43909.1
Arches	41-27.072	71-19.676	14291.4	43981.5
Ardandhu (AWOIS #)	41-25.066	70-49.968	14201.9	43929.1
Argo Merchant (bow)	41-00.700	69-27.200		
Argo Merchant (stern)	41-02.200	69-27.500		
Asa H. Purvere (false)	41-43.153	69-50.832		
Augusta W. Snow	42-27-42.35	70-34-46.14		
AWOIS 2047 (wreck)	42-18-57.35	70-51-34.06		
AWOIS 2957 (wooden barge)	44-35-21.46	68-51-52.12		
AWOIS 2959 (wreck)	44-33-59.76	68-47-42.21		
AWOIS 2963 (wreck)	44-27-52.77	68-52-35.71		
AWOIS 3010 (wreck debris)	44-21-00.47	68-51-25.59		
AWOIS 3015 (wood ribs)	44-15-04.18	68-55-15.61		
AWOIS 3029 (wooden deck/beams)	44-16-40.28	68-54-58.00		
AWOIS 7175 (wreck)	44-27-31.00	68-53-51.00		
AWOIS 7176 (110-foot wreck)	44-27-29.00	68-53-50.00		
AWOIS 7178 (140-foot steel hull)	44-27-13.97	68-46-59.10		
AWOIS 7191 (beams/cross pieces)	44-15-17.00	68-55-07.00		
AWOIS 7391 (hulk)	43-37-45.70	70-54-15.70		
AWOIS 8896 (wooden wreck)	44-11-28.52	68-26-33.55		
AWOIS 10041 (wooden ribs)	44-53-59.47	67-00-16.20		
AWOIS 10216 (wreck)	42-22-29.50	71-02-32.50		
AWOIS 10224 (wreck)	42-23-03.60	71-02-19.80		
AWOIS 10237 (barge)	42-23-37.60	71-00-57.50		
AWOIS 10238 (barge)	42-23-39.20	71-00-56.20		
AWOIS 10243 (wreck)	42-22-50.00	70-59-35.00		
AWOIS 10331 (125-foot wreckage)	42-14-55.86	70-58-21.17		
AWOIS 10332 (110-foot wreck)	42-15-22.76	70-58-50.57		
AWOIS 10333 (100-foot wreck)	42-15-23.36	70-58-48.17		
AWOIS 10334 (wreck)	42-15-23.36	70-58-46.17		
AWOIS 10337 (barge)	42-15-15.36	70-55-32.97		
AWOIS 10338 (wooden wreck)	42-17-56.36	71-00-10.18		
AWOIS 10342 (wreck)	42-17-54.76	70-56-07.97		
AWOIS 10348 (wreck)	42-18-54.15	71-00-52.38		
AWOIS 10364 (barge)	42-21-07.31	70-54-38.54		
AWOIS 10366 (giant barge)	42-20-06.36	70-53-44.17		
AWOIS 10369 (steel barge)	42-20-24.35	70-53-56.17		
AWOIS 10371 (270-foot barge)	42-20-19.36	70-53-09.17		
AWOIS 10372 (100-foot barge)	42-21-08.85	70-53-33.67		
AWOIS 10380 (barge)	42-17-10.60	71-02-17.40		
AWOIS 10381 (wreck)	42-17-07.76	71-02-15.18		
AWOIS 10382 (wreck)	42-17-08.76	71-02-08.18		

GPS / Loran Numbers - Alphabetical

Name	Lat	Lon	Loran 1	Loran 2
AWOIS 10383 (wreck)	42-17-14.56	71-02-01.78		
AWOIS 10426 (wreck)	43-38-38.06	70-09-48.90		
AWOIS 10561 (wreck)	43-40-08.62	70-13-08.20		
AWOIS 10726 (wreck)	44-26-17.91	68-54-03.08		
AWOIS 10753 (wreck in ruins)	43-04-54.32	70-43-07.19		
AWOIS 10754 (schooner keel)	43-04-53-12	70-43-07.19		
AWOIS 11122 (wooden barge)	43-44-12.46	70-08-18.00		
AWOIS 11126 (wooden barge)	43-40-07.22	70-13-14.87		
AWOIS 11127 (wreck with 2 masts)	43-43-29.29	70-11-39.08		
AWOIS 11129 (100-foot wood wr.)	43-43-22.26	70-11-08.31		
AWOIS 11130 (small wreck)	43-42-58.11	70-08-05.74		
AWOIS 11615 (wreck)	42-32-14.06	70-49-37.47		
AWOIS 11619 (wreck)	43-31-49.40	70-10-18.76		
Baleen	42-23.478	70-44.302		
Barge	41-26-06.20	71-04-45.53		
Barge (empty)	41-46.698	70-29.566		
Bay State	43-34-28	70-11-53		
Belleville	41-26.618	71-21.046	14401.7	43980.5
Bohemian	43-34-28	70-11-53		
Bone Wreck	42-19.560	70-39.354		
Brenton Reef Lightship	42-29.740	70-43.625		
Briry	41-29.236	69-55.941	13883.6	43875.5
Bump	42-03.166	70-32.820		
Cambridge	43-50.683	69-18.934		
Cannon Wreck	41-35.487	69-59.050		
Cape Fear	41-28.512	71-21.032	14394.7	43993.5
Castine	44-04-42	68-57-31		
Catherine Marie (FV)	41-49.327	70-23.403		
Charles	43-32-31	70-13-14		
Charles H. Trickey	43-21-20	70-25-36		
Charles S. Haight (engine)	42-40.685	70-34.985	13773.2	25813.7
Charles S. Haight (hawsepipe)	42-40.613	70-35.125		
Chelsea	42-38.892	70-34.211	13777.6	44319.8
Chester A. Poling (bow)	42-33.899	70-36.955		
Chester A. Poling (stern)	42-34.342	70-40.280	13840.9	44327.8
City of Portland (AWOIS poor)	44-02.932	69-02.998	44-02-27.29	69-02-25.14
City of Rockland	42-32.743	70-47.854		
City of Salisbury (bow)	42-22.419	70-51.604	13974.1	44283.3
City of Salisbury (stern)	42-22.367	70-51.605		
Coal Barge	42.22.571	70-42.699		
Coke Bottle Wreck	41-34.888	69-57.964	13870	43913
Colbrook	42-02.314	70-30.030		
Colburn	42-33.884	70-44.267		
Colonel William B. Cowin	41-28.258	70-58.336		
Cora F. Cressy	43-59.066	69-24.862		
Corbin	41-28.258	70-58.336		
Cormorant (FV)	42-02.010	70-10.266		
Cornwallis (AWOIS poor)	44-01-00.30	68-19-58.05		
Corvan	41-28.258	70-58.336		
Corvin	41-28.258	70-58.336		
Cowen	41-28.258	70-58.336		
Coyote	42-22.221	70-43.061	13920.8	44266.2
Crane and Barge	42-37.152	70-33.559		
Crane Barge	41-29.241	71-24.293		
Crane Wreck	42-37.152	70-33.559		
Cumberland	44-01.697	68-50.941		
Delaware	42-14.969	70-44.531	13965.5	25714.4
Dixie Sword	41-32.956	69-58.854		

Dragger	41-49.811	70-08.550		
D.T. Sheridan	43-45.369	69-19.308		
Dwight	41-24.270	70-52.978	25514.5	43922.3
Eagle 42	42-23.133	70-39.750		
Edmund Burke (Wenonah)	43-22.317	72-02.520		
Edna M. McKnight	43-51.112	69-37.911		
Edward E. Briry	41-29.236	69-55.941	13883.6	43875.5
Edward J. Lawrence	43-40.132	70-13.134		
Empire Knight (bow)	43-07.640	70-24.900	Joe Cushing	
Empire Knight (bow)	43-07.601	70-24.898	Don Stevens	
Empire Knight (stern)	43-06.239	70-26.966	Joe Cushing	
Empire Knight (stern)	43-06.200	70-27.100	Don Stevens	
Endicott (barge)	41-54.747	70-29.624	13967.7	44081.1
Explorer	41-25.908	71-18.102	14386.0	43970.8
F.C. Pendleton	44-19.630	68-54.498		
Fishing Boat (possible)	41-23.983	70-01.154		
Fishing Vessel 1 (Stellwagen)	42-18.737	70-17.824		
Fishing Vessel 2 (Stellwagen)	42-31.679	70-14.780		
Florence Nowell	41-31.542	69-55.886		
Flyer (FV)	42-01.858	70-10.432		
Formless Wreck	41-29-09.35	70-34-16.48		
Frank A. Palmer (bow)	42-29.030	70-16.000		
Frank A. Palmer (stern)	42-28.942	70-16.146		
Gallatin	42-33.897	70-44.865		
Gardiner G. Deering	44-22.916	68-46.476		
George Hudson	41-38.004	69-46.030		
Georgia	43-55-39	69-01-40		
GKB Dragger	41-49.630	70-22.283		
Gov. Endicott	43-33.202	71-27.672		
Granite State	42-34.228	70-44.783		
Granite Wreck (Stellwagen)	42-29.140	70-16.260		
Gypsum King	44-28-48	66-49-54		
Hada County	44-36.378	66-41.261		
Hartwelson (AWOIS low)	43-43-47	69-37-26	43-43-45.30	69-37-28.16
Helldiver	41-47.943	70-05.980		
Henry Endicott (barge)	41-54.747	70-29.624	13967.7	44081.1
Herbert	42-24.910	70-51.470	13961.2	44297.1
Herman Winter	41-21.118	70-50.380		
Hilda Garston	41-26.892	71-02.124	14284.0	43983.4
Holmes	42-27.509	70-45.718		
Horatio Hall	41-33.158	69-54.159	13856.2	43897.0
Howard W. Middleton	43-33.679	70-16.361		
Irvington	44-00.799	69-02.135		
James Longstreet	41-49.887	70-02.548		
James M. Hudson	42-22.573	70-42.742		
Jason	40-00.51'	70-01.23'	13772.1	44071.2
Jeff's Barge	42-20.890	70-40.990		
Jessica Ann	43-32.113	70-12.235		
John Dwight	41-24.270	70-52.978	14238.0	43922.3
John Paul (Schooner)	41-26-51.83	70-23-10.07	14050.3	43897.0
Josephine Marie	42-10.925	70-13.466		
Joseph S. Zeman	43-53.640	69-06.971		
Keith's Wreck	42-02.103	70-10.158		
Kenwood (near)	42-13.258	70-42.207		
Kershaw	41-28.756	70-32.977	14094.6	43922.1
Kiowa (cargo area)	42-19.246	70-51.683	13991.6	44265.5
L-8	41-23.196	71-22.501	14423.2	43959.2
Lackawanna (tug)	41-28.302	70-07.315	13952.5	43884.7

Lady of the Lake	43-35.285	71-23.238		
Large Demolished Vessel	41-28-41.28	70-32-58.25		
Lieut. Sam Mengel	42-19.560	70-39.354		
Llewellyn Howland	41-26.197	71-20.852	14402.0	43977.5
Long Skinny	41-31.655	69-59.051		
Louise B. Crary	42-29.030	70-16.000		
Map	41-30.695	69-59.252		
Marcie's Dragger	42-28.553	70-40.610		
Marcie's Wreck	42-31.392	70-41.812		
Mars	41-56.795	70-29.356	13956.8	44093.5
Mary E. Olys	43-21-20	70-25-36		
Mary F. Barrett	43-50.664	69-43.951		
Michael David (tug)	44-07-36.77	68-52-52.80		
Millicent Ann	42-01.996	70-10.621		
Mini Opus	41-13.731	71-06.897		
Mohave	42-18.308	70-50.784		
Mount Hope	41-35.601	71-22.735		
Mystery Collier (Stellwagen)	42-34.722	70-15.672		
Neptune II	41-23.161	71-11.135	14353.4	43941.6
New Hampshire	42-34.228	70-44.783		
Nina T	42-34.133	70-40.550		
No Name	41-07.377	70-57.240		
No. 703 (Perth Amboy barge)	41-47.447	69-52.532		
No. 740 (Perth Amboy barge bow)	41-47.606	69-52.552		
No. 740 (Perth Amboy barge stern)	41-47.627	69.52.588		
No. 766 (Perth Amboy barge bow)	41-47.555	69-52.615		
No. 766 (Perth Amboy barge stern)	41-47.539	69-52.632		
Northern Voyager	42-34.451	70-36.295		
Number 3666 (Train)	43-05.160	70-45.748		
O-9	42-59-48	70-27-27		
Oakey L. Alexander (bow)	43-31.823	70-10.312		
P. T. Teti	41-20.912	71-14.572	14382.5	43930.8
Paul Palmer	42-11.668	70-16.311		
Pemberton	41-31.257	70-37.982		
Pendleton (stern)	41-35.137	69-37.738	13867.7	43914.0
Pentagoet (false)	42-13.840	70-09.067		
Perkiomen	41-34.934	69-53.309	13843.5	43906.8
Perth Amboy barge No. 703	41-47.447	69-52.532		
Perth Amboy barge No. 740 (bow)	41-47.606	69-52.552		
Perth Amboy barge No. 740 (stern)	41-47.627	69-52.588		
Perth Amboy barge No. 766 (bow)	41-47.555	69-52.615		
Perth Amboy barge No. 766 (stern)	41-47.539	69-52.632		
Pete's Wreck	41-43.153	69-50.832		
Pevere (false)	41-43.153	69-50.832		
Pick Up Sticks	42-26.009	70-47.957		
Pinthis	42-09.362	70-33.660	13924.4	44175.3
Polias	43-53-16	69-15-24		
Poling (bow)	42-33.899	70-36.955		
Poling (stern)	42-34.342	70-40.280	13840.9	44327.8
Pollock Rip Lighthouse	41-32.910	69-55.746	13867.6	25123.3
Port Hunter	41-29.808	70-33.213	14907.0	43930.7
Portland	42-28.348	70-17.238		
Post Office	41-32.758	69-56.766		
Post Office Piece #1	41-32.678	69-56.596		
Post Office Piece #2	41-33.711	69-56.884		
Pottstown (coal barge)	41-47.177	70-28.999	13997.8	44033.7
Pug Wreck	42-24.733	70-48.746		
Regal Sword	41-28.111	69-30.922		

Name	Lat	Lon	Loran 1	Loran 2
Reliance	42-22.212	70-45.950	13982.2	43484.1
Republic	40-28.827	69-37.986	14073.1	43453.4
Romance (boilers)	42-23.712	70-51.829	13969.4	44290.6
Romance (bow)	42-23.727	70-51.851		
Royal Tar (AWOIS poor)	44-12-00.28	68-47-58.10		
Rudder Post Wreck	41-31.370	69-59.558		
Sagamore	41-28.701	70-32.981		
Samuel J. Goucher	43-00-50	70-36-00		
Schooner Barge	42-20.423	70-40.990		
Scribbe	42-20-12.35	70-57-33.17		
Scusset Barge	41-46.698	70-29.566		
Seaconnet	41-22.135	71-00.377	14290.9	43918.8
Sebastian	40-28.718	70-03.381	14154.6	43484.8
Sebastian	40-28.718	70-03.381	25199.6	43484.8
Seneca (barge and crane)	41-27.136	70-18.083	14019.6	43891.9
Ship Outline	41-21-34.26	71-21-06.62		
Shore Barge	42-20.567	70-53.713		
Sleeper	41-34.529	71-19.017		
Smoke Stack Wreck	41-31.421	70-00.126		
Snetind	42-20.890	70-40.990		
Somes Sound Wreck (target #1)	44-19.825	68-18.709		
Somes Sound Wreck (target #2)	44-19.718	68-18.682		
Southland	42-16.219	70-36.569		
Spar Grounds	41-38.720	69-49.501		
Starfish	42-20-14.35	70-58-36.67		
Stella-Marion	43-39.740	71-44.602		
St. Francis	41-27.606	71-06.251	14307.0	43964.6
St. Francis	41-27.596	71-06.243		
Steel-hulled Fishing Vessel	41-24-38.91	71-14-07.48		
Stellwagen Coal Barge	42-13.840	70-09.067		
Stockless Anchor	41-29-40.61	70-34-16.89		
Strathdene	40-24.287	69-28.388	25094.0	43428.9
Suffolk	40-52.622	71-13.138	25644.7	43726.0
Sunapee Two Boats	43-22.368	72-04.205		
Taber	41-28.550	70-42.750		
Talisman (SC-196)	42-27.403	70-47.209		
Texas Tower #3	41-00-869	69-29-523		
Toilet Bowl	42-01.529	70-12.605		
Topless Barge	42-31.276	70-53.748		
Train (Number 3666)	43-05.160	70-45.748		
Trojan	41-22.489	71-00.638	14291.4	43921.4
Tugboat (60 feet long)	41-20-54.57	71-14-33.92	14382.5	43931.2
Turtle Barge	42-21.251	70-53.883		
Twilight	45-28-09	69-37-15		
Twin Barges	42-20.271	70-54.093		
Two Anchor Wreck	42-22.573	70-42.742		
Two Boats (Sunapee)	43-220368	72-04.205		
U-853	41-13.594	71-25.126	14472.9	43894.9
Unidentified (Stellwagen)	42-22.340	70-22.220		
Unidentified (Stellwagen)	42-11.119	70-12.062		
Unknown Dragger	41-49.489	70-08.550		
Unknown X1	42-17.842	70-56.951		
Unknown X2	42-20.209	70-54.568		
Unknown X3	42-20.436	70-54.186		
Unknown X4	42-21.254	70-53.884		
Unknown X5	42-21.277	70-53.749		
Van	42-26.778	70-38.988		
Vineyard Sound lightship	41-23.830	71-01.176	14289.6	43931.3

GPS / LORAN NUMBERS - ALPHABETICAL

W.A. Marshall	42-22.870	70-22.718		
Washington B. Thomas	43-30-12.30	70-18-22.17		
Wathen (near)	41-46.220	70-29.073		
Weetamoo	43-20.094	72-02.520		
Wenonah (Edmund Burke)	43-22.317	72-02.520		
West Virginia	41-35.139	69-52.675	13838.7	25131.4
Weybosset	41-33.698	69-54.159		
Wild Cat	43-07.704	70-51.429		
Winifred Martin	41-31.940	69-59.867		
Wooden Sailing Vessel	41-15-23.78	71-05-58.73	25607.8	43880.6
Wooden Schooner Barge	41-35-18.00	69-52-27.00	13838.7	25131.5
Wooden Trawler	41-30-05.91	70-37-29.71		
Wooden Wreck	41-32.671	69-55.744		
Wooden Wreck	41-31.421	70-00.126		
Wooden Wreck	41-31.057	70-00.304		
Wooden Wreck	41-29.633	70-01.816		
Woods Hole Barges	41-31.415	70-40.654		
Wreck	41-33-41.79	69-54-09.23		
Wreck	41-32-45.58	69-56-45.84		
Wreck	41-31-39.26	69-59-04.22		
Wreck	41-31-25.28	70-00-07.60		
Wreck	41-31-22.20	69-59-33.48		
Wreck	41-31-03.58	70-00-18.45		
Wreck #1	41-31.057	70-00.304		
Wreck #2	41-29.633	70-01.816		
Wreck #4	41-32.671	69-55.744		
Yankee	41-32.514	70-52.747	14205.6	43975.9
YF-415	42-24.287	70-40.415		
YMS-14 (gun)	42-22.091	70-54.829		
YMS-14 (rudder)	42-22.060	70-54.831		
YSD-56	41-16.378	70-49.086		

Name	Lat	Lon	Lat (alt)	Lon (alt)
Twilight	45-28-09	69-37-15		
AWOIS 10041 (wooden ribs)	44-53-59.47	67-00-16.20		
Hada County	44-36.378	66-41.261		
AWOIS 2957 (wooden barge)	44-35-21.46	68-51-52.12		
AWOIS 2959 (wreck)	44-33-59.76	68-47-42.21		
Gypsum King	44-28-48	66-49-54		
AWOIS 2963 (wreck)	44-27-52.77	68-52-35.71		
AWOIS 7175 (wreck)	44-27-31.00	68-53-51.00		
AWOIS 7176 (110-foot wreck)	44-27-29.00	68-53-50.00		
AWOIS 7178 (140-foot steel hull)	44-27-13.97	68-46-59.10		
AWOIS 10726 (wreck)	44-26-17.91	68-54-03.08		
Gardiner G. Deering	44-22.916	68-46.476		
AWOIS 3010 (wreck debris)	44-21-00.47	68-51-25.59		
Alice E. Clark	44-21.022	68-51.299		
Somes Sound Wreck (target #1)	44-19.825	68-18.709		
Somes Sound Wreck (target #2)	44-19.718	68-18.682		
F.C. Pendleton	44-19.630	68-54.498		
AWOIS 3029 (wooden deck/beams)	44-16-40.28	68-54-58.00		
AWOIS 7191 (beams/cross pieces)	44-15-17.00	68-55-07.00		
AWOIS 3015 (wood ribs)	44-15-04.18	68-55-15.61		
Royal Tar (AWOIS poor)	44-12-00.28	68-47-58.10		
AWOIS 8896 (wooden wreck)	44-11-28.52	68-26-33.55		
Michael David (tug)	44-07-36.77	68-52-52.80		
Amaretto	44-05.590	68-59.881		
Castine	44-04-42	68-57-31		
City of Portland (AWOIS poor)	44-02.932	69-02.998	44-02-27.29	69-02-25.14
Cornwallis (AWOIS poor)	44-01-00.30	68-19-58.05		
Cumberland	44-01.697	68-50.941		
Irvington	44-00.799	69-02.135		
Cora F. Cressy	43-59.066	69-24.862		
Georgia	43-55-39	69-01-40		
Albany	43-55-39	69-01-40		
Polias	43-53-16	69-15-24		
Joseph S. Zeman	43-53.640	69-06.971		
Edna M. McKnight	43-51.112	69-37.911		
Cambridge	43-50.683	69-18.934		
Mary F. Barrett	43-50.664	69-43.951		
D.T. Sheridan	43-45.369	69-19.308		
AWOIS 11122 (wooden barge)	43-44-12.46	70-08-18.00		
Hartwelson (AWOIS low)	43-43-47	69-37-26	43-43-45.30	69-37-28.16
AWOIS 11127 (wreck with 2 masts)	43-43-29.29	70-11-39.08		
AWOIS 11129 (100-foot wood wr.)	43-43-22.26	70-11-08.31		
AWOIS 11130 (small wreck)	43-42-58.11	70-08-05.74		
AWOIS 10561 (wreck)	43-40-08.62	70-13-08.20		
AWOIS 11126 (wooden barge)	43-40-07.22	70-13-14.87		
Edward J. Lawrence	43-40.132	70-13.134		
Stella-Marion	43-39.740	71-44.602		
AWOIS 10426 (wreck)	43-38-38.06	70-09-48.90		
AWOIS 7391 (hulk)	43-37-45.70	70-54-15.70		
Lady of the Lake	43-35.285	71-23.238		
Bohemian	43-34-28	70-11-53		
Bay State	43-34-28	70-11-53		
Howard W. Middleton	43-33.679	70-16.361		
Gov. Endicott	43-33.202	71-27.672		
Charles	43-32-31	70-13-14		
Jessica Ann	43-32.113	70-12.235		
AWOIS 11619 (wreck)	43-31-49.40	70-10-18.76		
Oakey L. Alexander (bow)	43-31.823	70-10.312		

GPS / Loran Numbers - Descending 4 Line

Name				
Washington B. Thomas	43-30-12.30	70-18-22.17		
Two Boats (Sunapee)	43-220368	72-04.205		
Sunapee Two Boats	43-22.368	72-04.205		
Wenonah (Edmund Burke)	43-22.317	72-02.520		
Edmund Burke (Wenonah)	43-22.317	72-02.520		
Mary E. Olys	43-21-20	70-25-36		
Charles H. Trickey	43-21-20	70-25-36		
Weetamoo	43-20.094	72-02.520		
Wild Cat	43-07.704	70-51.429		
Empire Knight (bow)	43-07.640	70-24.900	Joe Cushing	
Empire Knight (bow)	43-07.601	70-24.898	Don Stevens	
Empire Knight (stern)	43-06.239	70-26.966	Joe Cushing	
Empire Knight (stern)	43-06.200	70-27.100	Don Stevens	
Anne El (fishing vessel)	43-05-10	70-45-44		
Train (Number 3666)	43-05.160	70-45.748		
Number 3666 (Train)	43-05.160	70-45.748		
AWOIS 10753 (wreck in ruins)	43-04-54.32	70-43-07.19		
AWOIS 10754 (schooner keel)	43-04-53-12	70-43-07.19		
Samuel J. Goucher	43-00-50	70-36-00		
O-9	42-59-48	70-27-27		
Charles S. Haight (engine)	42-40.685	70-34.985	13773.2	25813.7
Charles S. Haight (hawsepipe)	42-40.613	70-35.125		
Chelsea	42-38.892	70-34.211	13777.6	44319.8
Crane Wreck	42-37.152	70-33.559		
Crane and Barge	42-37.152	70-33.559		
Mystery Collier (Stellwagen)	42-34.722	70-15.672		
Northern Voyager	42-34.451	70-36.295		
Poling (stern)	42-34.342	70-40.280	13840.9	44327.8
Chester A. Poling (stern)	42-34.342	70-40.280	13840.9	44327.8
New Hampshire	42-34.228	70-44.783		
Granite State	42-34.228	70-44.783		
Nina T	42-34.133	70-40.550		
Poling (bow)	42-33.899	70-36.955		
Chester A. Poling (bow)	42-33.899	70-36.955		
Gallatin	42-33.897	70-44.865		
Albert Gallatin	42-33.897	70-44.865		
Colburn	42-33.884	70-44.267		
Alice M. Colburn	42-33.884	70-44.267		
Alice M. Colburn	42-33.819	70-44.186		
AWOIS 11615 (wreck)	42-32-14.06	70-49-37.47		
City of Rockland	42-32.743	70-47.854		
Fishing Vessel 2 (Stellwagen)	42-31.679	70-14.780		
Marcie's Wreck	42-31.392	70-41.812		
Topless Barge	42-31.276	70-53.748		
Brenton Reef Lightship	42-29.740	70-43.625		
Granite Wreck (Stellwagen)	42-29.140	70-16.260		
Louise B. Crary	42-29.030	70-16.000		
Frank A. Palmer (bow)	42-29.030	70-16.000		
Frank A. Palmer (stern)	42-28.942	70-16.146		
Marcie's Dragger	42-28.553	70-40.610		
Portland	42-28.348	70-17.238		
Augusta W. Snow	42-27-42.35	70-34-46.14		
Holmes	42-27.509	70-45.718		
Alma E.A. Holmes	42-27.509	70-45.718		
Talisman (SC-196)	42-27.403	70-47.209		
Van	42-26.778	70-38.988		
Pick Up Sticks	42-26.009	70-47.957		
Herbert	42-24.910	70-51.470	13961.2	44297.1

Name	Lat	Lon		
Pug Wreck	42-24.733	70-48.746		
YF-415	42-24.287	70-40.415		
AWOIS 10238 (barge)	42-23-39.20	71-00-56.20		
AWOIS 10237 (barge)	42-23-37.60	71-00-57.50		
AWOIS 10224 (wreck)	42-23-03.60	71-02-19.80		
Romance (bow)	42-23.727	70-51.851		
Romance (boilers)	42-23.712	70-51.829	13969.4	44290.6
Baleen	42-23.478	70-44.302		
Eagle 42	42-23.133	70-39.750		
AWOIS 10243 (wreck)	42-22-50.00	70-59-35.00		
AWOIS 10216 (wreck)	42-22-29.50	71-02-32.50		
W.A. Marshall	42-22.870	70-22.718		
Two Anchor Wreck	42-22.573	70-42.742		
James M. Hudson	42-22.573	70-42.742		
City of Salisbury (bow)	42-22.419	70-51.604	13974.1	44283.3
City of Salisbury (stern)	42-22.367	70-51.605		
Unidentified (Stellwagen)	42-22.340	70-22.220		
Coyote	42-22.221	70-43.061	13920.8	44266.2
Reliance	42-22.212	70-45.950	13982.2	43484.1
YMS-14 (gun)	42-22.091	70-54.829		
YMS-14 (rudder)	42-22.060	70-54.831		
AWOIS 10372 (100-foot barge)	42-21-08.85	70-53-33.67		
AWOIS 10364 (barge)	42-21-07.31	70-54-38.54		
Unknown X5	42-21.277	70-53.749		
Unknown X4	42-21.254	70-53.884		
Turtle Barge	42-21.251	70-53.883		
AWOIS 10369 (steel barge)	42-20-24.35	70-53-56.17		
AWOIS 10371 (270-foot barge)	42-20-19.36	70-53-09.17		
Starfish	42-20-14.35	70-58-36.67		
Scribbe	42-20-12.35	70-57-33.17		
AWOIS 10366 (giant barge)	42-20-06.36	70-53-44.17		
Snetind	42-20.890	70-40.990		
Jeff's Barge	42-20.890	70-40.990		
Shore Barge	42-20.567	70-53.713		
Unknown X3	42-20.436	70-54.186		
Schooner Barge	42-20.423	70-40.990		
50/50 Barge	42-20.408	70-53.748		
Twin Barges	42-20.271	70-54.093		
Unknown X2	42-20.209	70-54.568		
Lieut. Sam Mengel	42-19.560	70-39.354		
Bone Wreck	42-19.560	70-39.354		
Kiowa (cargo area)	42-19.246	70-51.683	13991.6	44265.5
AWOIS 2047 (wreck)	42-18-57.35	70-51-34.06		
AWOIS 10348 (wreck)	42-18-54.15	71-00-52.38		
Fishing Vessel 1 (Stellwagen)	42-18.737	70-17.824		
Mohave	42-18.308	70-50.784		
AWOIS 10338 (wooden wreck)	42-17-56.36	71-00-10.18		
AWOIS 10342 (wreck)	42-17-54.76	70-56-07.97		
AWOIS 10383 (wreck)	42-17-14.56	71-02-01.78		
AWOIS 10380 (barge)	42-17-10.60	71-02-17.40		
AWOIS 10382 (wreck)	42-17-08.76	71-02-08.18		
AWOIS 10381 (wreck)	42-17-07.76	71-02-15.18		
Unknown X1	42-17.842	70-56.951		
Southland	42-16.219	70-36.569		
AWOIS 10334 (wreck)	42-15-23.36	70-58-46.17		
AWOIS 10333 (100-foot wreck)	42-15-23.36	70-58-48.17		
AWOIS 10332 (110-foot wreck)	42-15-22.76	70-58-50.57		
AWOIS 10337 (barge)	42-15-15.36	70-55-32.97		

Name	Lat	Lon	Loran 1	Loran 2
AWOIS 10331 (125-foot wreckage)	42-14-55.86	70-58-21.17		
Delaware	42-14.969	70-44.531	13965.5	25714.4
Stellwagen Coal Barge	42-13.840	70-09.067		
Pentagoet (false)	42-13.840	70-09.067		
Kenwood (near)	42-13.258	70-42.207		
Paul Palmer	42-11.668	70-16.311		
Unidentified (Stellwagen)	42-11.119	70-12.062		
Josephine Marie	42-10.925	70-13.466		
Pinthis	42-09.362	70-33.660	13924.4	44175.3
Bump	42-03.166	70-32.820		
Colbrook	42-02.314	70-30.030		
Keith's Wreck	42-02.103	70-10.158		
Cormorant (FV)	42-02.010	70-10.266		
Millicent Ann	42-01.996	70-10.621		
Flyer (FV)	42-01.858	70-10.432		
Toilet Bowl	42-01.529	70-12.605		
Coal Barge	42.22.571	70-42.699		
Mars	41-56.795	70-29.356	13956.8	44093.5
Henry Endicott (barge)	41-54.747	70-29.624	13967.7	44081.1
Endicott (barge)	41-54.747	70-29.624	13967.7	44081.1
James Longstreet	41-49.887	70-02.548		
Dragger	41-49.811	70-08.550		
GKB Dragger	41-49.630	70-22.283		
Unknown Dragger	41-49.489	70-08.550		
Catherine Marie (FV)	41-49.327	70-23.403		
Helldiver	41-47.943	70-05.980		
Perth Amboy barge No. 740 (stern)	41-47.627	69-52.588		
No. 740 (Perth Amboy barge stern)	41-47.627	69.52.588		
Perth Amboy barge No. 740 (bow)	41-47.606	69-52.552		
No. 740 (Perth Amboy barge bow)	41-47.606	69-52.552		
Perth Amboy barge No. 766 (bow)	41-47.555	69-52.615		
No. 766 (Perth Amboy barge bow)	41-47.555	69-52.615		
Perth Amboy barge No. 766 (stern)	41-47.539	69-52.632		
No. 766 (Perth Amboy barge stern)	41-47.539	69-52.632		
Perth Amboy barge No. 703	41-47.447	69-52.532		
No. 703 (Perth Amboy barge)	41-47.447	69-52.532		
Pottstown (coal barge)	41-47.177	70-28.999	13997.8	44033.7
Scusset Barge	41-46.698	70-29.566		
Barge (empty)	41-46.698	70-29.566		
Wathen (near)	41-46.220	70-29.073		
Pevere (false)	41-43.153	69-50.832		
Pete's Wreck	41-43.153	69-50.832		
Asa H. Purvere (false)	41-43.153	69-50.832		
Spar Grounds	41-38.720	69-49.501		
George Hudson	41-38.004	69-46.030		
Wooden Schooner Barge	41-35-18.00	69-52-27.00	13838.7	25131.5
Mount Hope	41-35.601	71-22.735		
Cannon Wreck	41-35.487	69-59.050		
Aransas	41-35.440	69-52.543	13837.0	43909.1
West Virginia	41-35.139	69-52.675	13838.7	25131.4
Pendleton (stern)	41-35.137	69-37.738	13867.7	43914.0
Perkiomen	41-34.934	69-53.309	13843.5	43906.8
Coke Bottle Wreck	41-34.888	69-57.964	13870	43913
Sleeper	41-34.529	71-19.017		
Wreck	41-33-41.79	69-54-09.23		
Post Office Piece #2	41-33.711	69-56.884		
Weybosset	41-33.698	69-54.159		
Alva (bow)	41-33.332	69-54.268		

Name	Lat	Lon		
Alva (stern)	41-33.315	69-54.248		
Horatio Hall	41-33.158	69-54.159	13856.2	43897.0
Wreck	41-32-45.58	69-56-45.84		
Dixie Sword	41-32.956	69-58.854		
Pollock Rip Lighthouse	41-32.910	69-55.746	13867.6	25123.3
Post Office	41-32.758	69-56.766		
Post Office Piece #1	41-32.678	69-56.596		
Wreck #4	41-32.671	69-55.744		
Wooden Wreck	41-32.671	69-55.744		
Yankee	41-32.514	70-52.747	14205.6	43975.9
Wreck	41-31-39.26	69-59-04.22		
Wreck	41-31-25.28	70-00-07.60		
Wreck	41-31-22.20	69-59-33.48		
Wreck	41-31-03.58	70-00-18.45		
Winifred Martin	41-31.940	69-59.867		
Long Skinny	41-31.655	69-59.051		
Florence Nowell	41-31.542	69-55.886		
Wooden Wreck	41-31.421	70-00.126		
Smoke Stack Wreck	41-31.421	70-00.126		
Woods Hole Barges	41-31.415	70-40.654		
Rudder Post Wreck	41-31.370	69-59.558		
Pemberton	41-31.257	70-37.982		
Wreck #1	41-31.057	70-00.304		
Wooden Wreck	41-31.057	70-00.304		
Wooden Trawler	41-30-05.91	70-37-29.71		
Map	41-30.695	69-59.252		
Stockless Anchor	41-29-40.61	70-34-16.89		
Formless Wreck	41-29-09.35	70-34-16.48		
Port Hunter	41-29.808	70-33.213	14907.7	43930.7
Wreck #2	41-29.633	70-01.816		
Wooden Wreck	41-29.633	70-01.816		
Crane Barge	41-29.241	71-24.293		
Edward E. Briry	41-29.236	69-55.941	13883.6	43875.5
Briry	41-29.236	69-55.941	13883.6	43875.5
Large Demolished Vessel	41-28-41.28	70-32-58.25		
Kershaw	41-28.756	70-32.977	14094.6	43922.1
Sagamore	41-28.701	70-32.981		
Taber	41-28.550	70-42.750		
Cape Fear	41-28.512	71-21.032	14394.7	43993.5
Lackawanna (tug)	41-28.302	70-07.315	13952.5	43884.7
Cowen	41-28.258	70-58.336		
Corvin	41-28.258	70-58.336		
Corvan	41-28.258	70-58.336		
Corbin	41-28.258	70-58.336		
Colonel William B. Cowin	41-28.258	70-58.336		
Angela	41-28.233	71-01.635		
Regal Sword	41-28.111	69-30.922		
St. Francis	41-27.606	71-06.251	14307.0	43964.6
St. Francis	41-27.596	71-06.243		
Seneca (barge and crane)	41-27.136	70-18.083	14019.6	43891.9
Addie M. Anderson	41-27.104	71-24.923	14424.0	43989.9
Arches	41-27.072	71-19.676	14291.4	43981.5
John Paul (Schooner)	41-26-51.83	70-23-10.07	14050.3	43897.0
Barge	41-26-06.20	71-04-45.53		
Hilda Garston	41-26.892	71-02.124	14284.0	43983.4
Belleville	41-26.618	71-21.046	14401.7	43980.5
Llewellyn Howland	41-26.197	71-20.852	14402.0	43977.5
Explorer	41-25.908	71-18.102	14386.0	43970.8

GPS / LORAN NUMBERS - DESCENDING 4 LINE

Name				
Ardandhu (AWOIS #)	41-25.066	70-49.968	14201.9	43929.1
Steel-hulled Fishing Vessel	41-24-38.91	71-14-07.48		
Alice Lawrence (bow)	41-24.334	70-13.004		
Alice Lawrence (stern)	41-24.309	70-12.991		
John Dwight	41-24.270	70-52.978	14238.0	43922.3
Dwight	41-24.270	70-52.978	25514.5	43922.3
Fishing Boat (possible)	41-23.983	70-01.154		
Vineyard Sound lightship	41-23.830	71-01.176	14289.6	43931.3
L-8	41-23.196	71-22.501	14423.2	43959.2
Neptune II	41-23.161	71-11.135	14353.4	43941.6
Trojan	41-22.489	71-00.638	14291.4	43921.4
Seaconnet	41-22.135	71-00.377	14290.9	43918.8
Ship Outline	41-21-34.26	71-21-06.62		
Herman Winter	41-21.118	70-50.380		
Tugboat (60 feet long)	41-20-54.57	71-14-33.92	14382.5	43931.2
P. T. Teti	41-20.912	71-14.572	14382.5	43930.8
YSD-56	41-16.378	70-49.086		
Wooden Sailing Vessel	41-15-23.78	71-05-58.73	25607.8	43880.6
Mini Opus	41-13.731	71-06.897		
U-853	41-13.594	71-25.126	14472.9	43894.9
No Name	41-07.377	70-57.240		
Argo Merchant (stern)	41-02.200	69-27.500		
Texas Tower #3	41-00-869	69-29-523		
Argo Merchant (bow)	41-00.700	69-27.200		
Suffolk	40-52.622	71-13.138	25644.7	43726.0
Andrea Doria (stern)	40-29.345	69-52.041	25148.5	43481.0
Republic	40-28.827	69-37.986	14073.1	43453.4
Sebastian	40-28.718	70-03.381	25199.6	43484.8
Sebastian	40-28.718	70-03.381	14154.6	43484.8
Strathdene	40-24.287	69-28.388	25094.0	43428.9
Jason	40-00.51'	70-01.23'	13772.1	44071.2

The Popular Dive Guide Series

Shipwrecks of Maine and New Hampshire
Shipwrecks of Massachusetts: North
Shipwrecks of Massachusetts: South
Shipwrecks of Rhode Island and Connecticut
Shipwrecks of New York
Shipwrecks of New Jersey (1988)
Shipwrecks of New Jersey: North
Shipwrecks of New Jersey: Central
Shipwrecks of New Jersey: South
Shipwrecks of Delaware and Maryland (1990 Edition)
Shipwrecks of Delaware and Maryland (2002 Edition)
Shipwrecks of the Chesapeake Bay in Maryland Waters
Shipwrecks of the Chesapeake Bay in Virginia Waters
Shipwrecks of Virginia
Shipwrecks of North Carolina: from the Diamond Shoals North
Shipwrecks of North Carolina: from Hatteras Inlet South
Shipwrecks of South Carolina and Georgia

Shipwreck and Nautical History

Andrea Doria: Dive to an Era
Deep, Dark, and Dangerous: Adventures and Reflections on the Andrea Doria
Great Lakes Shipwrecks: a Photographic Odyssey
The Great Navy Wreck Scam
The Fuhrer's U-boats in American Waters
Ironclad Legacy: Battles of the USS Monitor
The Kaiser's U-boats in American Waters
The Lusitania Controversies: Atrocity of War and a Wreck-Diving History (Book One)
The Lusitania Controversies: Dangerous Descents into Shipwrecks and Law (Book Two)
The Nautical Cyclopedia
NOAA's Ark: the Rise of the Fourth Reich
Shadow Divers Exposed: the Real Saga of the U-869
Shipwreck Heresies
The Shipwreck Research Handbook
Shipwreck Sagas
Stolen Heritage: the Grand Theft of the Hamilton and Scourge
Track of the Gray Wolf
Underwater Reflections
USS San Diego: the Last Armored Cruiser
Wreck Diving Adventures

Books by the Author

Dive Training
Primary Wreck Diving Guide
Advanced Wreck Diving Guide
The Advanced Wreck Diving Handbook
Ultimate Wreck Diving Guide
The Technical Diving Handbook

Nonfiction
The Absurdity Principle
Lehigh Gorge Trail Guide
Lehigh River Paddling Guide
Wilderness Canoeing

Science Fiction
A Different Universe
A Different Dimension
A Different Continuum
Entropy (a novel of conceptual breakthrough)
A Journey to the Center of the Earth
The Mold
Return to Mars
Second Coming
Silent Autumn
Subaqueous
Tesla and the Lemurian Gate
The Time Dragons Trilogy
  A Time for Dragons
  Dragons Past
  No Future for Dragons

Sci-Fi Action/Adventure Novels
Memory Lane
Mind Set
The Peking Papers

Supernatural Horror Novel
The Lurking: Curse of the Jersey Devil

Vietnam Novel
Lonely Conflict

Videotape or DVD
The Battle for the USS Monitor

Visit the GGP website for availability of titles:
http://www.ggentile.com

www.ingramcontent.com/pod-product-compliance
Lightning Source LLC
Chambersburg PA
CBHW051050160426
43193CB00010B/1137